Designing Sustainable Communities

Bloomsbury Visual Arts
An imprint of Bloomsbury Publishing Plc

Imprint previously known as AVA Publishing

50 Bedford Square
London
WC1B 3DP
UK

1385 Broadway
New York
NY 10018
USA

www.bloomsbury.com

British Library Cataloguing-in-Publication Data

A catalogue record for this book is available from the British Library.

ISBN: PB: 978-1-4725-7290-5
          ePDF: 978-1-4725-7291-2

Library of Congress Cataloging-in-Publication Data
Library of Congress Cataloging-in-Publication Data

Names: Friedman, Avi, 1952- author.
Title: Designing sustainable communities / by Avi Friedman.
Description: New York : Bloomsbury Visual Arts, 2017. |
Includes bibliographical references and index.
Identifiers: LCCN 2016011172| ISBN 9781472572905 (pbk.) | ISBN 9781472572912 (epdf)

Subjects: LCSH: Planned communities. | Real estate development--Environmental aspects. | Land use--Planning. | Sustainable development.

Classification: LCC HT169.55 .F75 2017 | DDC 307.76/8--dc23 LC record available at https://lccn.loc.gov/2016011172

Series: Required Reading Range
Cover design: Louise Dugdale
Cover image © Vince Cavataio/Getty Images
Designed and typeset by Marcus Duck Design
Printed and bound in China

To find out more about our authors and books visit www.bloomsbury.com. Here you will find extracts, author interviews, details of forthcoming events and the option to sign up for our newsletters.

Designing Sustainable Communities

Avi Friedman

Bloomsbury Visual Arts
An imprint of Bloomsbury Publishing Plc

BLOOMSBURY
LONDON · OXFORD · NEW YORK · NEW DELHI · SYDNEY

Contents

Preface

The social challenges we face in the first chapter of the twenty-first century demand innovation in planning theory and practice. Demographic transformations are redefining our families as populations age and the average household size shrinks in the developed world. On the economic front, the transfer of employment to low-wage nations—and as a result, the disappearance of job security—has made it harder for first-time buyers to have a house of their own. Climate change and global warming have brought drought to some regions and raised sea levels in others. The need to curb urban sprawl and the rapid growth of cities has led to a drastic rethinking of density. It is evident: Innovation in planning has taken on a fresh urgency.

This book focuses on this innovation in planning at the neighborhood level. I here offer both original approaches to neighborhood planning and reintroduce older strategies that have fallen out of favor. While it is neglected, I believe that the work in this latter group is highly relevant to our current context and is of great merit. Further, I aim to provide insight to both planners of new neighborhoods and those involved in rehabilitating old ones.

Chapter topics have been selected in support of this basic premise: Low-density, car-dependent neighborhoods composed of single-family homes are simply not sustainable. In their construction and occupancy, vast tracts of land have been swallowed and natural resources depleted, burdening future generations. It is evident that in order to meet the aforementioned social challenges—sorely neglected in this paradigm—practices must change. The need to chart a new course for the field is clear.

To clarify the structure of the book, it is important to first define the neighborhood itself. As an academic unit of analysis and practical delineation alike, the term's usage has varied widely. That said, there are identifiable parameters. A neighborhood is almost always considered in a geographic context, as a sub-element of a larger urban whole, be it a city or a small town. Neighborhood populations vary from as low as 5,000 to approximately 20,000. In terms of land size, they have been said to have stretched over several city blocks in high-density areas; while in places with lower density, such as suburban locations, they have been considered as occupying far larger areas of land. Some have their own governance structure, while others are run by a central municipal government.

Yet, regardless of such factors, researchers agree that it is common to expect higher personal familiarity and social interaction within a neighborhood's population as compared to larger planning units. Indeed, some neighborhoods may have a unique ethnic composition and tradition. Their urban scale, layout, and inherent cultural attributes make such encounters more likely.

The make-up of a neighborhood can be understood as the overlap of several layers. These include—but are not limited to—land use, roads, parking, and open spaces. This book was written to address each of these layers separately. Each chapter begins by establishing a context and rationale for the recommended practices that follow; these practices are then illustrated with case studies from around the world, complete with plans and photos. The communities explored herein have been selected as examples for their unique approach to the overall design of that sub-component.

The first chapter provides a background for the book: It aims to contextualize the rest of the text by giving the reader a basic grasp of neighborhood planning, sustainability issues, and their interactions. It begins with a historical account tracing the evolution of neighborhood design. A review of the social challenges faced by today's neighborhoods, further, the impact of these realities on planning, follow. A basic framework of sustainable planning practices—the core theory behind the methods found in the rest of the book—rounds out the discussion.

The second chapter focuses on designing neighborhoods along public transit corridors. Efficient means of transportation that do not rely on the private vehicle are discussed and illustrated here. It is also demonstrated that mixing land uses, amenities, dwelling types, and socio-demographic groups is a valued strategy for the creation of walkable and "complete" communities. Chapter 3 articulates and illustrates methods for planning such places.

The fourth chapter discusses active mobility. Opportunity for this mode of transport is an important feature of the well-planned neighborhood. Reducing vehicular traffic, integrating walking and cycling paths, designing shared streets, and introducing public transit are discussed therein.

Chapter 5 elaborates on the ecological, psychological, and economic values of common open spaces in neighborhoods. This exploration demonstrates that while an imperative increase in building density implies a decrease in the land allocated to private yards, this does not necessarily function as a loss to a neighborhood. Instead, it is a ripe opportunity for the resourceful and forward-thinking designer.

Planning neighborhoods for growth and change is the topic of Chapter 6. Resilience is an important mark of a healthy community—and the key to this, in turn, is adaptation to emerging circumstances and new realities. Methods for building neighborhoods and homes with said flexibility are considered closely.

In Chapter 7, focus is shifted to affordability. Buying a home has become a challenge in many of the world's urban centers and critical to sustainable living. The factors that govern the cost of neighborhoods and individual dwellings are detailed, as are the means to reduce these costs through design.

Homes and communities that sustainably consume and generate energy are reviewed in Chapter 8. The goal of net-zero design, wherein buildings produce their own power and/or consume very little energy, is brought into focus. Also explored are the exciting possibilities presented by district heating innovations, a design that relies on planning in the form of a network.

Chapter 9 discusses physical health in the neighborhood context. Rates of obesity and inactivity are still on the rise in many countries, but planners have the means to work against this ongoing shift. The opportunity for physical activity can be far more effectively built into neighborhood life than as is the current standard.

Neighborhood as "bread basket" is the topic of Chapter 10. Using open spaces for urban agriculture has become a vibrant component of local community in many cities across the world. The practice not only produces plenty of nutritious food but also engages dwellers in physical activity and social interaction.

Whereas Chapters 1 through 10 focus on subjects vital to the building of sustainable communities, as a conclusion Chapter 11 offers practical aspects for the building of these communities. It describes basic steps that planners can follow at the outset of their design, offers an outlook on home building and buying, and outlines common environmental certification methods.

Each chapter ends with a Summary and Key Considerations segment where the principal issues that were discussed in that chapter and ways to implement them are outlined. An Exercises segment at the end of each chapter is offered for the convenience of instructors and students.

Many subjects are critical to the creation of sustainable developments. The topics that were selected for this book promise to contribute both to the environment and the people who use it and live in it. As for planning, increasing density rationally—also referred to as "smart growth"—stands in my view to have the greatest impact on creating sustainable communities. In contrast to suburban communities where people drive often and walk less to amenities, compact places have a greater chance to yield better outcome. In this regard, the book builds on the ideas put forward by theorists such as Charles Kibert, Stephen Wheeler, and E. F. Schumacher among others whose work serves as an underling base for mine. I also closely looked at ideas and examples put forward by writers such as Douglas Farr, Jan Gehl, Sim Van der Ryn, and Peter Calthorpe, who examined and demonstrated various practical aspects associated with applying sustainability.

One also needs to be aware that implementing the ideas and concepts that are advocated in this book is not simple. Municipal regulations and the development industry may not be open to them all. Yet, the structure of the book (i.e., offering principles illustrated by case studies) is a demonstration that sustainable ideas can successfully be implemented.

No exploration of neighborhood sustainability can be exhaustive, given that this field is highly varied and ever-evolving—as are communities, as is design. That said, the topics and planning methods that are assembled here have proven to ground the creation and maintenance of such places in practice. It is hoped that this work will best serve in the planning of neighborhoods, so that these neighborhoods might best serve their people.

Chapter 1
The Broad View

Contemporary social, economic, and environmental challenges that affect the built environment require an innovative approach to the planning of neighborhoods. This of course means that current practices must change; yet, it is vital that these changes be understood as an evolution—a transition with direct connection to the past. This chapter clarifies this connection. First, a short history of neighborhood design will be given. This is followed by an exploration of social issues that are imperative considerations for the field today. In closing, a framework of sustainable design principles to propose a way forward will be outlined.

Forms of Communities

A variety of research has attempted to explain the origin of the human community, and of these investigations, the work of Jane Jacobs is an excellent starting point. In the *Economy of Cities* (1969), she suggests that the origin of human settlement is rooted in agriculture and trade. This explanation references a time when most societies were predominantly nomadic. People lived in bands of hunter-gatherers, surviving on what nature could provide. In these groups, population size and ecological footprint were determined by food supply (Schoenauer 2000). This way of life was transformed with the invention of agriculture into one of permanent settlement. Gathered or hunted food no longer dictated a group's size.

Historian Spiro Kostof (1991) argues that the interest of the authority, rather than any particular form of activity, led to the establishment of many towns. Governments—both centrally organized and distant seats of power—settled and populated early communities of loyal subjects for political gain, as a means to establish and expand their power. For example, many European cities grew from their Roman origins.

Kostof also suggests that communities, be they cities or neighborhoods, follow two distinct patterns of urban form. The first are *planned* or *created* cities; these are places whose form follows a charted plan much like post–Second World War suburban towns. The second kind is that of *spontaneous* settlements, communities that grow by a less regulated process.

Kostof goes on to identify four urban planning typologies that cities and neighborhoods are likely to follow, each with a different appearance and function (Figure 1.1). A layout that developed by way of uncontrolled growth is categorized *organic*. Many Mid-East communities, as well as some medieval cities, fit this pattern. Kostof's second type, a *grid* layout, is based on geometrical or orthogonal principles that are thought to have been developed by the Greeks and spread far afield by the Romans. Rooted in the *Milesian*, named after the town of Miletus form of town planning, neighborhoods of this form are divided into relatively autonomous areas. Further, there is the *diagram* pattern based on formal geometry. Kostof dictated that cities of this type are designed by an individual in accordance with their ideals—manifestations of a vision as to how a community should function and how its inhabitants should live. Ben-Joseph and Gordon (2000) suggest that such geometrical schemes were rarely built, condemned to a life only on paper. The final category of Kostof's typology is that of the *grand manner*. In these designs, buildings, streets, and public spaces are arranged to convey visual effect of grandeur and coherence. Such patterns are typical of the Renaissance.

The Origins of Contemporary Neighborhood Planning

Contemporary planning practices can in good part be traced back to the thinking of Ebenezer Howard. In 1870s England, Howard was exposed to the ongoing debates surrounding the squalid conditions suffered by urban residents. In response, he conceived of a new type of community—one that attempted to draw upon the best that both city and country living could offer. This led to his seminal work *To-Morrow: A Peaceful Path to Real Reform* (1898) (three years later renamed *Garden Cities of Tomorrow*). In summary, he argued for the population's withdrawal from overcrowded industrialized cities to their outskirts, thus creating communities that would combine the social conveniences of towns with the healthier, more peaceful aspects of rural life.

Howard's *Garden City* deserves close consideration. His original proposal included a city population cap of 32,000, to his mind ensuring that the aforementioned benefits of rural life were protected. The design itself is composed of layered circles, but it does not specify a particular architectural style for the buildings involved. Industry is centrally located, surrounded by a ring of parkland. Around this park is a *crystal palace*: a glass arcade that houses a shopping area. The next layers were to be houses with attached gardens (Howard 1902; Macfadyen 1933). Howard divided his diagram city into six identical wards, each housing 5,000 people; in the heart of each ward, in an open space designated Grand Avenue, he proposed a school.

Figure 1.1:

A variety of urban planning typologies for cities and neighborhoods: grid layout in the ancient Greek city of Miletus (top left); Howard's diagram of Garden City (top right); grand manner used in the planning of Washington, DC (bottom left); and New Urbanism in Seaside, Florida (bottom right).

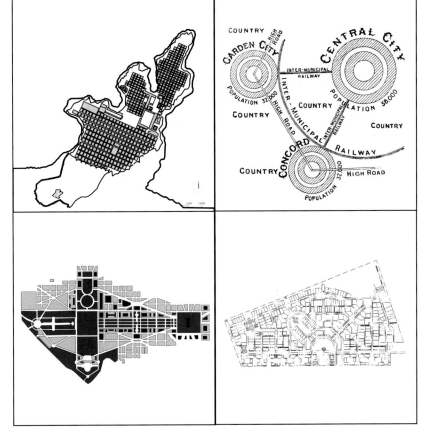

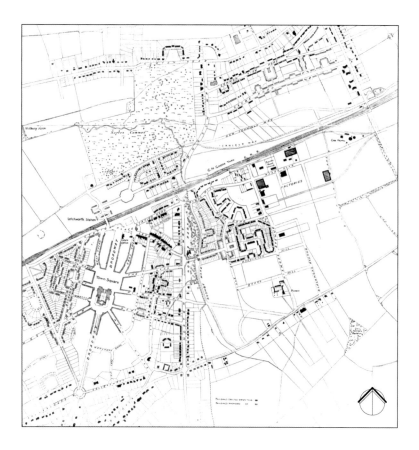

Figure 1.2:

The planners of the City of Letchworth attempted to implement Howard's Garden City concept.

It was the first time that the ideal population for a neighborhood had been precisely delineated in modern times. This was not the only standard that Howard set. Many of the more original components of the work became dominant elements in designing contemporary communities: defined population size; hierarchical order; inclusion of green spaces; a public transit link to the big city; land-use distribution among industry, agriculture, and housing—and the list goes on.

Howard's plans were realized, an obvious further measure of influence. Most notably, they were followed quite closely in the design of the town of Letchworth. In 1903, the Garden City Pioneer Company bought 1,529 hectares (3,822 acres) of land north of London. Raymond Unwin and Barry Parker were hired to translate Howard's diagram for the site. A centralized civic area in Letchworth was enclosed by a park,

and housing radiates from this center (Figure 1.2). Years later, the town of Hampstead Garden Suburb was planned and built. Designed as well by Unwin and Parker, it included some of Howard's principles (Unwin 1909, Miller 1992). The next stage in the evolution of the Garden City schema was to cross the Atlantic, where it was to take on a new life in the American context.

In 1922, two American planners Clarence Stein and Henry Wright traveled to England to meet Howard and visit Letchworth. Upon returning to the US, they informed a small group of colleagues of what they had learned. The group, which came to be known as the *Regional Planning Association*, and included architect and sociologist Lewis Mumford, discussed and incorporated many avant-garde planning and social ideas of the time. Their goal was to rethink the planning of America's large, industrial cities—then beset with destitute living conditions—and replace them with more humane environments. They sought to reach these goals primarily by following the innovations in Garden City. Stein and Wright realized this dictate, going on to design communities that would embody that vision. Radburn, New Jersey, is the most renowned product of their partnership. Houses were sold in Radburn as opposed to being rented in garden cities and new towns in the UK. Though elements were sacrificed in this implementation (for example, the greenbelt surrounding the towns was never purchased because of the Great Depression), the overall result was a safe, healthy community for young families. Radburn also included a variety of housing types, and neighborhoods were serviced by small retail centers. Their forms followed those of cul-de-sacs and scenic, curving streets (Figure 1.3).

Figure 1.3:
The plan of the community in Radburn, New Jersey, USA, acknowledged the growing importance of the automobile in twentieth-century living.

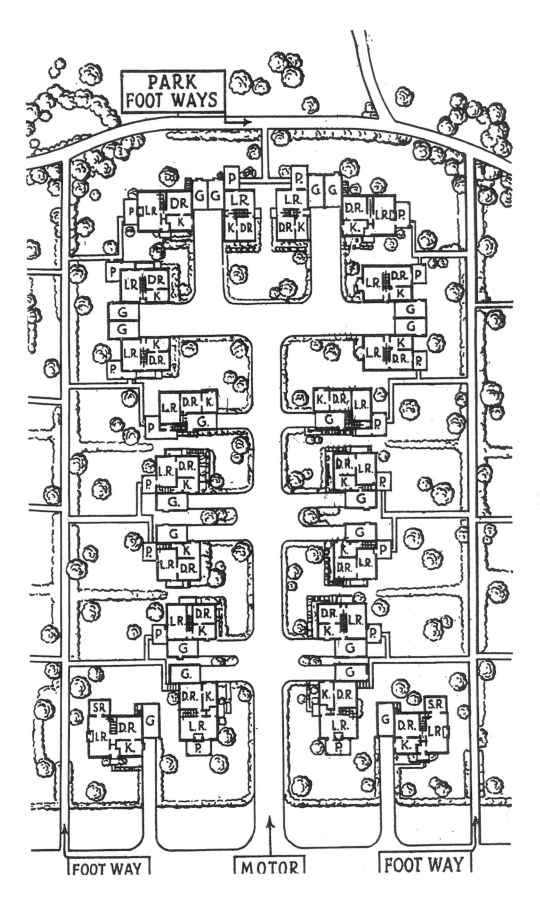

Part of Radburn's success was due to its accommodation of the automobile, whereby the pedestrian and the automobile were completely separated. This new phenomenon stimulated many novel development patterns. Circulation designs were used to separate pedestrian and vehicular traffic via interior paths and overpasses. Although most dwellings in Radburn were single-family, some rental units existed in garden apartments (Schoenauer 2000). Individual unit planning was oriented toward the internal open areas rather than to the streets. These design articulations made Radburn a model of planning in suburbia for the following decades, notably the suburbs built post–Second World War. But perhaps the greatest impact on suburban planning that emerged was that of segregated land-use planning.

Euclidean zoning, which separated large swathes of uniquely residential areas from all other occupancies, emerged in 1926. It was created to simplify the speculative development process and also resulted in geographical segregation by income (Logan 1976). Members of the Regional Planning Association drew inspiration from the most influential intellectuals of their day, not least American Clarence Arthur Perry, a planner, sociologist, author, and educator.

Similar to Howard, the driving forces behind Perry's pivotal ideas were social needs. In 1907, he went on to work for the Russell Sage Foundation, which was established to improve living conditions in cities. He resided in Forest Hills Gardens, a Sage Foundation development, in Queens, New York. Living in a community planned by Frederick Law Olmsted Jr., this experience helped him define his *neighborhood unit* concept.

When observing Forest Hill, Perry noted five aspects that contributed to its successes: clear boundaries, an internal street system of superior design, a variety of well-chosen land uses, the provision of open spaces, and, vitally, the presence of a central area. Based on his observations, he went on to conceive of his own innovative planning principles. First, Perry designated that the unit needed to have a shape wherein all sides were of equal distance from the center. He suggested an ideal 0.4-kilometer (0.25 miles) radius and a size of 65 hectares (160 acres). The neighborhood center was to have communal amenities including a school grouped among a central green space, while shops, or shops under apartments, were to be located in outer corners. Small parks and open spaces were to be scattered in each quadrant, and account for 10 percent of the neighborhood area. Arterial roads were to be bound to the unit's sides. Finally, Perry dictated that streets were to be both curvilinear and straight to reduce traffic.

Perry's contribution to modern planning was not only in the simplicity and logic of the plans themselves. Like Howard, his utilization of dimensions and figures that planners could easily grasp set an important precedent. Another aspect of his influence, not to be underestimated, was that his plan ushered neighborhood planning out of the carriage era and into the automobile age.

It is arguably true that Howard, Perry, Stein, and Wright improved the standard of living of many. Their ideas went on to offer dwellers of crowded cities an alternative by inventing a new form of communal living; each family enjoyed a house and a yard of their own. Yet, these benefits were not to be without cost. As hindsight can attest, by way of rampant consumerism, long commutes, social segregation, social isolation, high pollution, and the exhaustion of natural resources, this new all-American lifestyle came at a dear price.

On a more contemporary note, planning concepts such as *New Urbanism* and *Smart Growth* attempted to offer an alternative to suburban sprawl. Put forward by Andres Duany, *Transect*, for example, defines zones that range from rural areas to urban centers with each having scales which make development linked to one another with a mix of residential and commercial land uses.

New Times, New Challenges

The twenty-first century has proven a perfect storm of social change. Our communities, in turn, are transforming. These transformations require rethinking of old planning policies and strategies. We must introduce innovative design to our communities and homes.

The following is an examination of three domains wherein fundamental changes have taken place and affected urban systems: the social domain to include population aging and the emergence of the nontraditional small household; the environmental domain, which includes the negative effect of low-density developments and as a result the excessive use of motor vehicles; and lastly, the economic domain, which covers aspects related to the inability of many first-time buyers to afford homes.

However, it should be considered that variations exist in the manifestation of these trends between continents, nations, and cities alike; the information included here cannot be taken as exhaustive. That said, these phenomena are relevant in a general sense and are certainly applicable to the majority of Western nations.

The Social Domain

First, in the social domain, drastic demographic change is on the horizon. Known as the "graying" of society, the proportion of the population composed of seniors (defined as those aged 65 and older) is rising rapidly (Figure 1.4). This can in large part be attributed to the disproportionate numbers of "baby boomers" (those born between 1946 and 1964) that make up Western populations as compared to subsequent generations. As this group reaches retirement age in the coming decades, the significant number of seniors is expected to put a strain on public services. Yet, it can also offer an opportunity to some communities to put in place a much needed sustainable health and social infrastructure for future generations.

Residential mobility is highly characteristic of aging—thus, this demographic transition is a vital consideration for today's planner. Some retirees are projected to trade a large, hard-to-maintain home with a smaller unit. Those who can afford it will move to regions with comfortable weather year-round and proximity to basic amenities. Those who stay will look for an apartment adjacent to or above shopping hubs or transportation routes. Demand for nontraditional dwelling types and intense remodeling activities will inevitably rise. There will be a growing interest in arrangements that accommodate aging in place, multi-generational homes, and assisted living.

Figure 1.4:

Canadian seniors by age groups as percentage of the total population 1921–2041.

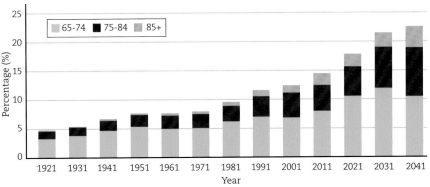

Canadian seniors by age groups (1921–2041)

The rise in the number of seniors can offset the demographic continuum of some communities. Communal activities in many places, primarily small towns, are based on the contributions and participation of volunteers. These groups often meet in evening hours—a time when older participants, particularly those living in cold climates, have difficulty making such trips. Planning neighborhoods that are walkable or well-served by public transit and, in cold regions, have sheltered micro-climate areas, is of paramount importance. Another notable demographic trend is a decline in the size of an average household. Coupled with housing affordability challenges, this may entail an increased demand for neighborhoods with below-average-sized homes and apartments.

The Environmental Domain

Next, the environmental domain demands consideration. In recent decades, society has become aware and has acted to counter its toll on the environment. A link has been made between economic development, urban forms, and their environmental implications. Chief among the indexes used to evaluate environmental performance are the measures of carbon and ecological footprints. These can be applied to both dwellings and communities. Policy will doubtless adapt to these considerations, and this will have significant consequences for urban planning and the economy of neighborhood construction.

The negative environmental impacts of urban sprawl and single-family home development within have given rise to a call for densification. The residential construction sector is the third largest contributor to greenhouse gas emissions in developed nations, exceeded only by the industrial and transportation sectors (International Energy Agency 2008). That sector also consumes vast amounts of natural resources. The construction of a new single 153 square meter (1,700 square foot) family home consumes

0.4 hectares (1 acre) of forest and produces several tons of waste (Nebraska Energy Office 2006). In the US, residents living in communities with higher densities tend to drive three times less than those who live in neighborhoods with single-family homes. The driving forces behind these intentions are to reduce various forms of consumption and justify investments in public transit and other amenities (Center for Transit-Oriented Design 2011). Increasing densities is seen as a common-sense approach to urban planning. The need to curb urban sprawl has also brought to the forefront a call for mixed-use developments. Considered together with the trends in density, planners are now looking to design denser communities with a wider range of land uses; they hope to create what have been coined "complete communities." In sum, this means, in many ways, a return to traditional practices, with many living above or next to a store.

The negative effects of driving are another aspect with direct environmental ramifications. Residents of low-density areas commonly rely on distant urban centers for their upper-level services, necessitating the extensive use of private vehicles. In 2005, the transportation sector in Organization for Economic Co-operation and Development (OECD) countries consumed 26 percent of the total energy demand and produced 25 percent of the direct and indirect carbon dioxide emissions. A large portion of this can be attributed to the extensive use of private cars. The United States Census Bureau found that the common daily commute to work in 2009 was 25.1 minutes (McKenzie and Rapino 2011). Locating employment hubs next to residential developments is seen as a strategic response to the need to reduce reliance on private vehicles in small towns.

The individual home is yet another environmental concern unto itself. Some organizations have established standards that set strict building codes and efficiency criteria, acting essentially as an accreditation system by which projects are distinguished. LEED and BREEAM are two organizations on the forefront of this practice. As such practices proliferate, the design of energy-efficient buildings is itself gradually becoming more popular.

The Economic Domain

The contemporary economic landscape requires our consideration as well. Global economic transformations have taken their toll on wealth generation, labor markets, and on the lives of citizens. Governmental budgeting for deficit reduction has led to cutbacks in social services; international trade agreements have created employment in some countries and eradicated many jobs in others; and recessions and sluggish economic growth have weakened the confidence of investors, employers, and everyday consumers. In addition, persistent high unemployment also suggests that other sectors of the economy, including manufacturing, are not generating wealth and thus are struggling to position themselves in a highly competitive world. These macro trends will affect the economies of even the smallest of communities. These changes may demand great adaptation for the planner.

For one, the rise of "homegrown" initiatives seems to be a natural outcome of said transformations. Establishing an economy somewhat independent of global and national trends has always been an aim of many communities, but recent crises may increase interest in this goal considerably. Cities may soon take greater measures to encourage people to use local products and services.

New economic realities also put the single-family detached home beyond the reach of a growing number of first-time home buyers in many nations, increasing the demand for less expensive, smaller units. An affordability gap has emerged, where the rate of increase of house prices has far surpassed the growth of family incomes. This widening gulf in affordability in some regions can be explained by higher land and infrastructure costs, offering another argument for densification and the building of affordable neighborhoods.

The need to foresee the evolution of commerce and the effect of a hyper-connected world is necessary to the understanding of local economies. The line between global and local has become blurred in recent years. Companies no longer need to be tied to a particular location and can run their affairs from afar using digital communication. As a result, the nature of commerce has also changed. It is hard to tell whether large-format stores will be as trendy in the years to come or whether there will be a surge in a desire to shop in more local, intimate, and personal settings. What has become apparent is that in recent years online shopping has expanded to rival in-person purchases. These trends are likely to affect the shape of consumption in many communities and as a result their needs in relation to their immediate built environment.

Planning for Sustainability

A review of the social transformations above begs the question: How should the needed changes be ushered in? How should communities be planned anew or retooled? Sustainability, as a philosophy and organizing principle, has been put forward as an answer to these questions.

The origin of the term *sustainable development* can be traced back several decades. In 1992, the United Nations Conference on the Human Environment in Stockholm dealt with concerns that humanity is stretching the carrying capacity of the earth to its limits (Canada Mortgage and Housing Corporation 2000). The meeting served as a forum for the first international discussion on the relationship between ongoing environmental damage and the future of humanity. It was recognized then that population growth in some nations and overconsumption in others left ecological footprints in the forms of land degradation, deforestation, air pollution, and water scarcity.

Years later, this reflection has led to the establishment of the international initiative World Commission on Environment and Development (WCED). In a 1987 report, *Our Common Future*, the authors regarded sustainable development as one that meets present needs without compromising the ability of future generations to meet their own needs. This definition established a conceptual approach to development, whereby any action taken must be pursued with its future effects in mind. The commission also created a paradigm for development whose main

anchors are a need for social equity, incorporation of fair distribution of resources within and among nations, and the need to resolve the conflict caused by development pressures and the environment. Over time, these underpinning issues—and their influence on and relations to one another—have become the standard through which the success of all development activities is judged.

The three original pillars of sustainable development emerging from this document were *social, economic*, and *environmental* sustainability; however, it soon became abundantly clear that *culture* and *governance* must be part of any sustainability initiative if it is to succeed. A sustainable approach to culture and governance dictates that practices must reflect and respond to the values and traditions of the *particular sociopolitical context* in which they are implemented. While these factors have not always been considered by international efforts in the past, they have proven essential to their success (or failure).

These five pillars of sustainable development provide essential guidance for today's planners—so let us consider each in turn, beginning with social sustainability. The phrase *social needs* implies a broad, all-compassing concept that can be explained and interpreted in a multitude of ways. It might be best understood by way of example. For instance, when the creation of a sustainable healthcare system is an objective, ensuring that sufficient funds will be continually available is essential. A contribution to public health can be achieved by encouraging fitness. It has been shown that people with an active lifestyle are less likely to suffer from cardiovascular- and diabetes-related illnesses. It is, therefore, in the best interest of municipalities that their neighborhoods are designed with bicycle and pedestrian pathways, integrating both residential and nonresidential functions.

Cultural sustainability is equally vital. Promoting vernacular culture and preserving local traditions contributes to society in both direct and indirect ways. Most obviously, old buildings are visible reminders of human history, giving us a direct connection to the past. More indirectly, heritage inspires young architects and planners, thus improving the quality of future buildings and designs. Conserving and converting old buildings also avoids demolition, helping to reduce the consumption of natural resources that may otherwise be used in new construction.

We cannot, of course, afford to ignore economic sustainability. Bad planning decisions today burden the generations of tomorrow. Building excessively wide roads, for example, will have long-term economic effects. Such streets will need to be resurfaced periodically, and in cold climates, more snow will accumulate, requiring more funding for its removal. When a development is privately initiated, the cost of wider roads will raise the price of each house. This forces buyers to borrow more money that they will then be forced to repay over a longer period of time, thereby putting at risk their own financial sustainability.

Environmental sustainability is concerned with ecological attributes created by the construction and upkeep of a development, including its roads, open spaces, and homes. A "cradle-to-cradle" cycle assessment is necessary when planning a development. This is in regard not only to the initial effect of choice of materials, for example, but also their long-term performance and recyclability. Asphalt-covered roads will make rainwater runoff stream to manholes. Creating bio swells at the sides of roads will promote the growth of rainwater flora when it is planted, thereby saving runoff.

Lastly, we must consider sustainable governance. Planning strategies and concepts, innovative as they may be, will not be implemented unless a municipal leadership establishes appropriate policies. Our political leaders are also responsible for communicating visions of long-term planning to citizens. Further, an effective political system will draw new, younger participants to public service, creating a continuity of ideas and actions.

These five pillars critical to sustainable development can be viewed independently. Yet, when one closely examines the inner workings of neighborhoods that are designed and built on sound sustainable principles, it is evident that the confluence of these aspects is absolutely critical. All integrate to affect the built environment; they operate in an elaborate balance. It is this complex nexus that this book intends to clarify for the reader. While these five overlapping issues are presented separately as a way by which to organize concepts and illustrations, it is no less than essential to recognize the interrelationships that connect them. General principles are, therefore, articulated in the following section to aid the recognition of these relationships in the neighborhood context.

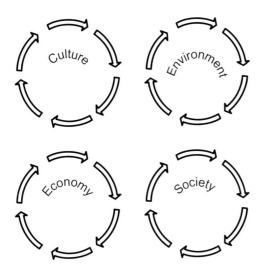

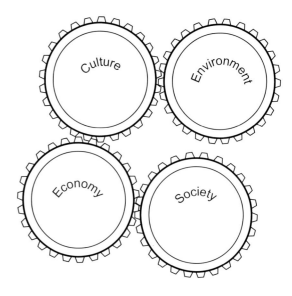

Self-sustaining generators   Supporting relation

Principles of Sustainable Systems

When a development strategy for a community is crafted by a planner these four principles can act as a guide (Figure 1.5). When exercised jointly, these ideas can help articulate a vision and an action plan for a sustainable community.

The first principle can be referred to as the *path of least negative impact*. It dictates that decision-makers must minimize any negative impact their work might have on social, cultural, economic, or governmental practices, and of course, on the environment. In short, at the outset of any planning process, impact assessments should ensure limited short-term or long-term disruptive and costly ramifications.

An application of this principle is to establish an economic base that will not hinder future initiatives. Having a heavy polluting industry, for example, may not render a good image for a community that may want to develop tourism. Another example would be locating a school away from a residential area, which will limit the walking or cycling opportunities of students.

Establishing a *self-sustaining system* is the second principle at hand. In a fluctuating economy, reliance on a single source of municipal revenue or energy is not sustainable. It places a community in a "survival mode," making long-term planning vulnerable. Another manifestation of self-sufficiency is patronizing local businesses. When this occurs, energy is not spent on transporting goods from faraway places, the cost of these goods is reduced, and local jobs are created. This requires, in part, micro-level behavioral change, and thus a public consciousness concerning issues of sustainability.

Figure 1.5:

Diagrammatic representation of sustainable systems.

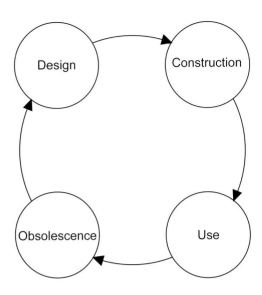

Cradle-to-cradle

The final principle to keep in mind is that of a *life cycle approach*. This simply means taking a long-term view of processes. It advocates that while following the course of their chosen path, a planner's overall strategy must remain flexible to accommodate ongoing change as the need may arise. Any planning process's elasticity and ability to adapt to various emerging circumstance are among its key attributes.

Consider that when public institutions are designed for adaptability and can be easily modified to accommodate newer needs, investment in their future alteration will be smaller. A similar view should prevail, for example, when codes and bylaws are created. They ought to provide a framework for action, yet not restrict the introduction of amendments and changes when times and circumstances require them. It is also essential to respect past decisions and have continuity of governance. Too often when municipal governments change and newly elected officials are appointed, a fresh set of objectives are set and many older but completely sound ones ignored. Incredible tenacity is essential in following a strategy with long-term implications.

Another related concept is *resiliency*, which is the capacity of a system from individual people to a whole community to hold together and function in the face of outside change and pressure. It is very likely that events will take place in the life of a neighborhood that will demand response and adjustment for which advance planning will be needed.

Recognition of the *supporting relationships* between the five pillars noted above is another vital principle. For example, it is highly unlikely that enterprises will be drawn to a place with a municipal government that appears to be overly bureaucratic. Another example: Building smaller homes in a denser configuration will result in a reduction of urban sprawl. It will also save on cost of land and infrastructure that, when transferred to the eventual occupants, will result in the production of affordable housing. Municipalities will benefit by attracting and keeping young, first-time home buyers in the community and ensure a much-desired demographic continuum.

The various frameworks—the aforementioned social changes of the twenty-first century, pillars of sustainable development, and not least, principles of sustainable systems— together form a prism through which to view neighborhoods that reveals incredible insight. Taking this perspective, the following chapters cover a range of exciting theory and practice.

Summary and Key Considerations

- When discussing the origin of cities, historian Spiro Kostof suggests that governments—both centrally organized and distant seats of power—settled and populated early communities of loyal subjects for political gain as a means to establish and expand their authority.

- Kostof also identified four urban planning typologies that cities and neighborhoods are likely to follow, each with a different appearance and function. They are organic, grid, diagram, and grand manner.

- In the book *Garden Cities of Tomorrow* Ebenezer Howard (1902) argued for population withdrawal from the overcrowded industrialized cities to communities that would combine the social and public conveniences of towns with the healthy and serene aspects of rural life. He proposed a city with a 32,000-resident limit, where the countryside and its benefits would be accessible to all.

- In Stein and Wright's design of Radburn, New Jersey (a community inspired by Howard's Garden City), concept houses were sold as opposed to being rented. The overall result was a safe, healthy community for young families. They contained a variety of housing types and were defined by cul-de-sacs and scenic, curving streets.

- In 1907, American planner Clarence Arthur Perry drew a neighborhood unit concept, the main elements of which were clear boundaries, a well-planned internal street system, a variety of land uses, a central area, and open spaces. Perry's concept established general physical and numerical principles for the design of neighborhoods. Some of these ideas were also critical to the creation of contemporary sustainable communities as illustrated by Douglas Farr in his book *Sustainable Urbanism: Urban Design with Nature*.

- The twenty-first century has proven a "perfect storm" of social change. These include social, environmental, and economic transformations, all of which, in turn, are impacting our communities and require reconsideration of our planning practices.

- The "graying" of society will require the planning of walkable communities with adaptable dwelling types. Smaller households may look for smaller, affordable dwelling units.

- Designing neighborhoods and dwellings while considering their environmental implication mandates better use of natural resources before and after occupancy. It should include significant reduction in the use of nonrenewable materials, proper building, and community orientation to take advantage of passive solar gain, minimization of the area devoted to roads, and avoiding damage and alteration of existing flora and fauna.

- New economic realities make homes unaffordable to first-time home buyers and necessitate design of smaller-sized affordable housing. For many, the home may be a workplace and must be designed accordingly.

- In the World Commission on Environment and Development report, *Our Common Future* (1987), the authors defined *sustainable development* as "development that meets present needs without compromising the ability of future generations to meet their own needs." The five pillars of sustainable development are social, economic, environmental, cultural, and governmental sustainability. These aspects must also be considered in parallel when planning new communities. Leaving any of these aspects out may run the risk of having "unbalanced" places.

- In the context of this book crafting a development strategy for a community, four guiding principles are vital. The four guiding principles are following a path of least negative impact; creating a self-sustaining system; fostering supporting relationships; and a life cycle approach. When exercised jointly, they can help articulate a vision and an action plan for designing sustainable place.

- The planners and builders of a new development should not by their actions damage existing natural, social, or economic structures.

- When designing, effort should be made to create self-sustaining systems or those that tax the environment the least, such as having net-zero homes and edible landscapes.

- Communities should be designed with supporting relations between their parts. For example, excess energy from self-powered homes can light the community's public areas.

- Designers should look into the distant future while conceiving a community. For example, the use of products made up of materials that can be recycled should be considered.

Exercises

1. Describe the contribution that Ebenezer Howard's ideas made to the development of modern residential communities and their form.

2. What were the key principles of Clarence Perry's neighborhood unit concept, and how is it different from earlier development patterns?

3. What contemporary social changes are, in your view, going to have a lasting effect on community design, and why?

4. What are the key pillars of sustainable developments? Give examples for their application in everyday life.

5. What are the key principles of a sustainable system? Give examples for their application in your community or design.

Chapter 2
Transit-Oriented Development

Transit-oriented development (TOD) is an approach to regional planning that integrates public transit and urban concepts. It promotes environmental sustainability, walkability, cycling culture, and urban growth—all while retaining the flexibility to accommodate changing lifestyles and market demands. In the context of the four sustainability principles that were outlined in Chapter 1, TOD can be considered as part of reducing the negative impact of single-driver motor vehicles. This chapter explains and illustrates the planning principles behind successful TOD and considers them in the larger context of contemporary sustainability issues.

Adjusting to New Realities

The term *transit-oriented development* was coined in the early 1990s by planner Peter Calthorpe. His proposal mainly delineated improved land-use policies for areas adjacent to transit systems as a way to manage metropolitan growth and attendant heavy migration between urban centers and outlying communities (Calthorpe 1993). Calthorpe's ingenuity was in using transportation itself as a primary design tool.

Though the term is relatively new, many of TOD's fundamental principles are not. In fact, before the urban sprawl of the post–Second World War era and the building of highways to link cities and their peripheries—a form of TOD was the norm in planning. In fact, towns like Letchworth in the UK were linked by rail lines to major hubs. Today, as property prices in urban centers rise faster than incomes and travel by private car becomes steadily more unaffordable, it is little wonder that the method is experiencing resurgence. Indeed, today's planners are highly cognizant of the darker side of the automobile: More people driving means greater health risks, greenhouse gas (GHG) emissions, and global warming. Although the particular composition of motor vehicle exhaust varies according to fuel type, the primary constituents that pose health risks are present throughout. Carbon monoxide (CO), nitrogen dioxide (NO_2), ozone photochemical oxidants, and suspended particulate matter all contribute to the deterioration of air quality (Schwela and Zali 1999).

Meanwhile, a 2010 US Department of Transportation meta-analysis recommended that public transportation can effectively cut GHGs. The study details three principal processes of GHG reduction. The first, and most obvious, is that public transport provides low-emission alternatives to driving. Second, it facilitates compact land use, thus reducing the need for longer trips. Lastly, the carbon footprint produced by both the construction and operations of transit is on the whole minimized (Figure 2.1).

Motor vehicles also emit heat, and, further, new roads contribute to the *urban heat island* effect (a phenomenon that occurs because urban lands are warmer than surrounding rural areas due to the distribution of absorbing heat surfaces, like concrete and asphalt). In TOD planning, fewer people will own private vehicles, mitigating these effects directly. Further, parking lots can be made smaller and green areas can be increased (CMHC 2009). The abundance of greenery will also help decrease heat absorption (Health Canada 2011).

This greenery encouraged by TOD—along with the method's discouragement of auto use and emphasis on higher-density building—promotes environmental sustainability in yet another way. In effect, TODs are more energy-efficient on both the macro and micro levels when compared to a conventional low-density suburb (Hodges 2010). Therefore, add energy efficiency to GHG and urban heat island effect reduction, and it is clear that this planning scheme boasts an impressive power to create a greener future.

If the environmental benefits of investing in public transport are insufficiently compelling, consider that developing new roads is actually proven to increase congestion (Gehl 2010). This is despite the common misconception that auto infrastructure alleviates traffic pressure. In fact, 60 to 90 percent of new road capacity is consumed by new driving within five years of their construction (Litman 2004).

Importantly, the parks, pedestrian walkways, and bicycles intrinsic to the TOD formula aid physical health. A 2005 Canadian Heart and Stroke Foundation Survey has found that those living in suburbs, smaller towns, and rural areas—essentially places heavily reliant on the automobile—are often at a higher risk of heart disease and stroke than their city-dwelling counterparts. Meanwhile, recent transit integration in Charlotte, North Carolina, was projected to save US $12.6 million in health care expenditures over nine years as a result of residents walking to and from their newly available transit station (Stokes, MacDonald, and Ridgeway 2008).

As to economic sustainability, consider a recent study by The Canadian Mortgage and Housing Corporation examining ten Canadian communities planned in a TOD orientation (CMHC 2009). In all ten, developers perceived the community's proximity to transit as being a boon to the marketing of the project. Nine of the ten TOD projects met their economic goal, and the tenth had unrelated and unpredictable delays in construction and assembly (CMHC 2009).

Figure 2.1:

Tailpipe emissions of common transport modes per passenger mile.

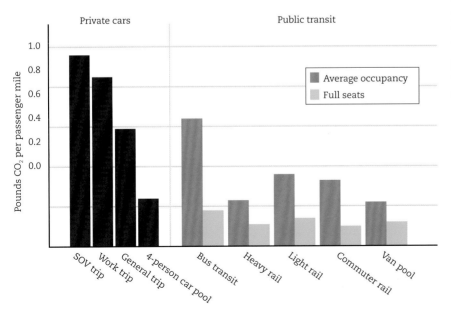

TOD's mixed land-use methods also increase employment opportunities in the town's center (Calthorpe 1993), and pedestrian-friendly environments help support local retail (Litman 2004). A study of consumer expenditures in UK towns found that those who walk to and from downtown shopping districts spend about 50 percent more per week supporting local retail establishments (Litman 2009). Meanwhile, the study suggests that spending on fuel and vehicles tends to contribute relatively little to the support of local employment or business activity. Moreover, transit access helps market-driven projects and has a track record of delivering financial success for developers. In short, TOD generally improves the economic viability of the neighborhood (Calthorpe 1993).

TOD neighborhoods benefit from more than just the zoning front; a mixture of housing types allows for the construction of affordable housing, which contributes to the viability of the transit hub by increasing the number of users. Mixed incomes mean a mix of work schedules, therefore making transit sustainable at off-peak hours, which allows residents to use the public transit system for more than their daily commute to work. A TOD neighborhood would also have a more resilient housing market, as its mix of housing types could respond to fluctuations in housing demand.

For very low-income families who spend almost two-thirds of their earnings on housing and transportation, access to good transit service can reduce commuting costs by 50 percent. Such savings offer the possibility of genuine affordability. In the US, for example, two-thirds of all transit users live in households with an annual income of US $37,000 (Poticha and Wood 2009). Many of these people cannot afford to own a vehicle. By offering housing near transit points, a larger, stable ridership is ensured, and, in a sense, development is democratized in the process.

Figure 2.2:
Movement of people and vehicles should be regarded as an interconnected system.

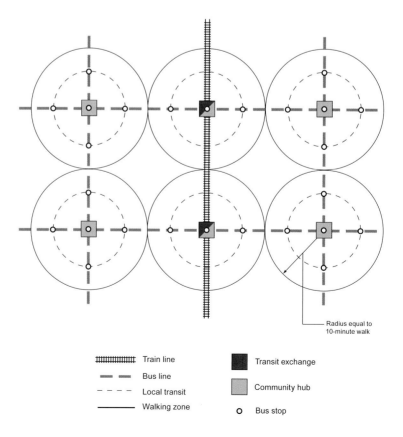

Radius equal to
10-minute walk

⊞⊞⊞⊞ Train line		■ Transit exchange	
— — Bus line		▨ Community hub	
– – – Local transit		o Bus stop	
—— Walking zone			

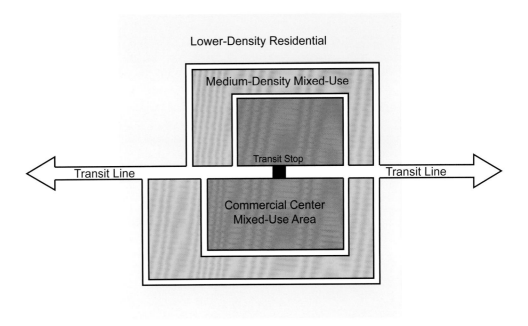

Lower-Density Residential

Medium-Density Mixed-Use

Transit Stop

Transit Line

Transit Line

Commercial Center
Mixed-Use Area

Lastly, high-speed innovations designed in line with TODs confer unique and complex sustainability benefits. Among new mass-transit methods, Bus Rapid Transit (BRT) is notable—a design utilizing longer buses for which a special traffic lane is dedicated. Another exciting trend: Conventional and high-speed trains that run more frequently during rush hours (Deng and Nelson 2011). The effects of these transit methods on outlying areas are significant; according to Garmendia et al. (2008), residents enabled by this transit who would otherwise move to big cities choose to remain in less urbanized areas. In fact, the authors found that many who are working in the city are choosing to move to these smaller, transit-enabled communities and commuting to work, given the more affordable housing options this arrangement presents. This, in turn, benefits the economies of these outlying regions—not only supporting local housing markets but further fostering overall economic growth.

Transit-Oriented Neighborhoods

TOD neighborhoods are built within 800 meters (2,625 feet)—or a ten-minute walk—from a main transit hub that links to other urban centers. The transit hub can have express buses, at grade, underground, above-ground rail transits, or even ferries as illustrated in Figure 2.2 (CMHC 2009). Near the hub, the neighborhood will commonly be composed of moderate- to high-density housing in a mixed-use development.

Planning principles of TOD neighborhoods suggest that dwellings, basic amenities, employment, and entertainment hubs should be within a walkable distance from a transit stop. A diagrammatic layout of a TOD neighborhood is illustrated in Figure 2.3. Public buildings and spaces should be located near the core area, since it helps to create a strong sense of community, comfort, and safety within the neighborhood. Each neighborhood might be composed of pedestrian walkways, bicycle lanes, high-quality public spaces (including green patches), and a core commercial area near the transit hub (CMHC 2009).

Figure 2.3:

In a TOD neighborhood, public buildings and open spaces should be located near the core area to help create a strong sense of community and foster safety.

A chosen transit technology commonly defines the TOD corridors, yet they also depend on the system's design and quality. Properly designed stations, high-frequency service, and proximate residential developments provide certainty to investors and users that the project will not lose money or be suddenly abolished (Center for Transit-Oriented Design 2010, Center for Transit-Oriented Design 2011).

The planning of TOD at the corridor level benefits not only the region as a whole but, specifically, the communities adjacent to transit routes. There are essentially three transit corridor types: *destination connector, commuter*, and *district circulator*. While in practice corridors tend to have a more complex structure and are usually composed of a mix of types, these are still useful abstractions. Destination connectors accommodate ridership in both directions throughout the day because they serve employment centers and other public or residential destinations. Commuter-link major hubs within a wider region and district circulators run public transit loops within districts.

Building advanced transit systems using the latest methods and technologies requires large investment. Such costs can only be justified when those systems are well used. Further, a large number of paying users will render these systems economically sustainable. Indeed, popularity is the metric commonly used when studying the issue academically; in considering the successes and failures of public transit system projects, economists emphasize what they term *accessibility*, arguing that a system is as good as its number of users (Hall 2008). This is intuitive—investing in an unused network does not make economic sense. In addition, when a new transit system can have subsidiary advantages, such as job creation or expanding the stock of affordable housing, investments are further justified.

In planning a neighborhood, high-density housing should be located near the transit hub while the surrounding areas should be of mixed density so as to provide a population large enough to support a light rail or express bus service. Here are more precise standards: According to Calthorpe (1993) an average of 44.5 dwellings per hectare (18 dwellings per acre) is necessary for a successful TOD neighborhood. Again, areas located nearest the hub require a higher concentration of dwellings—64.3 dwellings per hectare (26 dwellings per acre). Small-lot family homes, which run at a density of 24.7 dwellings per hectare (10 dwellings per acre), should occupy the perimeter of the development.

The needs of the population mentioned above, can be addressed in these medium- to high-density taller buildings. Such buildings would be "active street walls" with a potential for economic activity on ground floors. The units in such buildings will include a range of innovative dwellings such as multi-generational, live–work, and micro units for singles and childless young couples.

TODs can be built in existing sites, such as redevelopments, or in new urban growth areas, so long as the essential features outlined above are accommodated (again, a core transit hub linked to a commercial area, public buildings, and spaces). Undeveloped sites, also known as infill sites, are surrounded by other urban developments, while new-growth areas lie at the edges of existing communities. Indeed, these infill sites offer developers and municipal planners a great opportunity to transform heavily auto-dependent regions into TODs (Calthorpe 1993).

TODs can be categorized into two types: urban and neighborhood. Urban TODs lie on the main trunk line of a transit, and residents of these areas have direct access to the transit system. These TODs have a large commercial potential and moderate-to-high residential density. Each urban TOD is located 0.8 to 1.6 kilometers (0.5 to 1 mile) apart. Neighborhood TODs lie further off the main trunk line, within ten minutes of the transit stop by bus. Neighborhood TODs are located close together along a corridor of TOD nodes (Calthorpe 1993). Neighborhood TODs are more than capable of replacing the traditional suburban model. They are walkable and provide an abundance of public facilities and parks—this reduces traffic, creates affordable alternatives for families without cars, and fosters an overall community feel.

Both the neighborhood and the urban TODs expand radially, with parks, plazas, green spaces, public buildings, and services located near the core transit hub. That core area transitions into a secondary area near the ten-minute perimeter of the TOD. This is composed of lower-density housing for more auto-oriented residents. That said, there must be sufficient bike and sidewalk connections to the transit hub. Schools also occupy this perimeter area, along with retail—though these retail areas should not compete with the main commercial center. For example, if a supermarket is located in the center, preferably there should not be another supermarket at the outskirts of the neighborhood. Heavily car-dependent businesses, such as car dealerships and motels, should be located outside both the TOD and the second perimeter (Calthorpe 1993).

Learning from Others

A community's success can be quantified. For example, reduction of car use can be measured in the attendant decrease of pollution and emissions. The accessibility to parks and pedestrian pathways can be measured by their conferred health benefits. However, qualitative considerations are also vital in assessing community life. For example, in the documentary film *Cities for People* (2010) Danish architect Jan Gehl argues that a busy city district can be "warmed by [the] intimate social activity" of dynamic street life. TOD provides developments with a social character that supports work, life, and play—it excels in creating qualitatively distinct success stories. The best way to access both this quantitative aspect of success, along with the qualitative, is to consider these achievements on a case-by-case basis. This is a particularly exciting endeavor today with regard to TOD given that recent years have seen a significant resurgence in advanced public transit systems in many countries (Kuby et al. 2004, Cervero 2008).

2A

Project:
Ørestad

Location:
Copenhagen, Denmark

Design Firm:
APRT and KHR Arkitekter

Copenhagen's "Finger Plan," as shown in Figure 2.4, was conceived in 1947 (demonstrating that, incredibly, TOD has a more than sixty-year history in the city). The plan designated five corridors of urban development along rail transit services, existing or new, creating a hand-like form. At each transit hub, high-density housing was placed alongside shopping areas. It was successfully implemented in twenty-nine municipalities, and legally encored in the 1973 regional plan of the city.

By the 1990s, Copenhagen was experiencing economic decline and required new development. Four large-scale projects were established, two of which were investments in public transit. These were supported by research suggesting that the creation of integrated public transport systems enhances a city's international competitiveness (Docherty et al. 2009). One of the major projects was an added corridor—or finger—along the western side of the Island of Amager to the south of Copenhagen (Knowles 2012).

Ørestad is Copenhagen's most recent expansion. Plans were developed in 1997 and building began in 2001. A linear-development plan was utilized, with focus placed on a central transport artery. This main artery consists of a light rail system, bicycle lanes, and a motorway. The light rail system has intentionally been raised above ground level. This prevents the system from acting as a barrier to pedestrians and cyclists, while also firmly asserting its presence in the community.

Cycling is one of the most popular modes of transport in Denmark; therefore bicycle lanes play an important role in the daily lives of its residents. Bike lanes are offered along Ørestad's main roadway, as well as behind the Western line of buildings. The latter offers the bicyclist a picturesque ride with plenty of natural scenery. Both trails offer direct access to the central business district and run to the end of the development.

Though a main motorway runs along the main artery of Ørestad district, only one automobile lane is offered in each direction. As an extra incentive to limit car use, residents must pay a large fee each month in order to use a parking space. The vast majority of parking is in large garages, ensuring that the district's landscape is not crowded with parked vehicles. Many offices and residences, such as Bjarke Ingels' Mountain Residence, have tactfully incorporated these parking garages into their structure.

Ørestad is strategically placed on Amager Island and serves as a link between Copenhagen Airport, the Swedish city of Malmö, and Copenhagen's central business district. The completion of the Øresund Bridge in 2000 created a link between Copenhagen and Malmö. Car travel between Denmark and Sweden is discouraged by a heavy toll for vehicles wishing to cross the bridge, to say nothing of the competition provided by a significantly cheaper train system running the same route.

Figure 2.4:
The regional plan of Copenhagen designated five corridors of urban development along rail transit service.

■ Historic Areas

■ Newer Industrial Areas

— Transit Connections

2.5

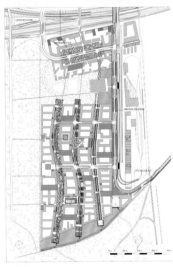

2.6

2.7

Figure 2.5:
Regional plan.

Figure 2.6:
Community plan.

Figure 2.7:
Aerial photo.

Figure 2.8:
An elevated train line.

Figure 2.9:
Arne Jacobsens Alley.

2.8

2.9

Figure 2.10:
Night view of a station.

Figure 2.11:
8 house.

Figure 2.12:
Canal between buildings.

Figure 2.13:
Housing complex.

Figure 2.14:
Bicycle cellar under the water basin.

Several companies have moved their main offices into Ørestad following its development. In 2002, Ferring, the Swedish pharmaceutical company, moved its various units in Malmö, Copenhagen, and Kiel to an Ørestad twenty-story head-office building located immediately beside a metro stop. Today, one-third of its employees make a daily commute from Sweden: 75 percent of which travel by train, and only 25 percent by car. Of its Danish employees, over 50 percent travel by train or metro, 10 percent by bike, and 37 percent by car. Rambøll is another example of such a relocation. Despite a mean travel distance increase from 17 kilometers (10.6 miles) to 23 kilometers (14.3 miles) following the move, 93 percent of employees now live within 3 kilometers (1.9 miles) of a train or metro station that can quickly and efficiently get them to work. The number of car commuters within the company fell by 49 percent, and 27 percent now commute by public transit, as opposed to a previous 9 percent.

In sum, Ørestad has successfully made public transit and cycling primary methods of transportation. Companies have flocked to the area and their employees are reaping the benefits of minimized car travel and convenient transport alternatives. The project serves as an excellent example of how TODs can benefit both the residential and commercial sectors of a community.

2.10

2.11

2.13

2.12

2.14

2B

Project:
Contra Costa Centre Transit Village

Location:
Contra Costa Centre, California, USA

Design Firm:
McLarand Vesquez Emsiek and Partners and Sasaki Associates

The Contra Costa Centre Transit Village illustrates how transit systems can be used to spawn sustainable and diverse communities in the US. Located 48 kilometers (30 miles) northeast of San Francisco, it serves as a connection point between three cities: Walnut Creek, Pleasant Hill, and Concord. Prior to the TOD effort, this area was semi-rural, and comprised mainly of single-family, low-density housing.

TOD came to Contra Costa by way of the Bay Area Rapid Transit (BART) system—a 167 kilometer (104 mile) light-rail track that serves forty-four stations. Contra Costa station is currently one of the area's most important commuter-hubs; it consistently has the greatest number of morning passengers and serves 350,000 annually. Developers recognized the importance of this station early on—in fact, in the 1970s—and attempted to create a transit village on the surrounding land. However, due to various complications, the project was only recently realized.

By way of a design charrette, Sasaki Associates and McLarand Vasquez Emsiek & Partners were chosen to draw the final plans. They were given an interesting set of advantages and disadvantages to work with. One problem: A huge surface-level parking lot previously surrounded the Contra Costa station, creating a physical and visual barrier between pedestrians and the station and wasting copious amounts of space. This was taken down and the transit village was developed in its stead. As to advantages—the spot was already extremely well connected with the BART station, Iron Horse Regional Trail, and a massive six-lane automobile roadway.

Developers wished to deprioritize car commuters and place greater emphasis on pedestrian and cycle traffic. Pedestrian comfort was of utmost importance in the design process. The main street, Treat Boulevard, was built in such a way that it encourages pedestrian activity and has evolved into an established social center: The wide walkways are separated from vehicle traffic by a row of car parking, and a 3.7 meter (12 foot) buffer zone divides parking and vehicle lanes. These measures increase pedestrian safety and reduce the noise of vehicles heard by pedestrians, creating an ideal environment for outdoor dining and socializing.

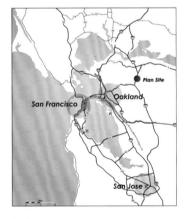

2.15

2.16

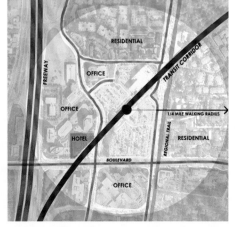

2.17

Figure 2.15:
Regional plan.

Figure 2.16:
Site context.

Figure 2.17:
Street-level plan.

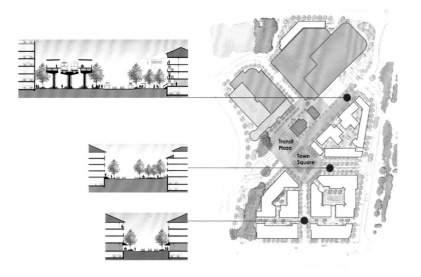

2.19

2.20

2.18

Figure 2.18:
Urban fabric—streets and blocks.

Figure 2.19:
Treat boulevard.

Figure 2.20:
Building and block sections.

Figure 2.21:
Transit view.

As per the developer's goals, Contra Costa is not only a walkable environment but a cycle-friendly village as well. Two bike lanes, the Iron Horse Regional Trail and another newly constructed path, run vertically along the edges of the development. These two bike paths are connected horizontally by yet another lane that runs through the center of the village. This lane intersects the BART station, the village square, and the bus-transit station. The BART station has been equipped with infrastructure to lock and store bicycles, and a proposal has been made to build a bike station.

The mixed-use, high-density nature of the development—there are 522 residential units, ten live-work units, and several shops and restaurants on the pedestrian level—has stimulated the local economy and incentivized those in the surrounding area to visit for purposes outside of their daily commute. Further, it is easy for such visitors to reach the development using the BART or bus system, or by way of the comprehensive network of pedestrian and cycle routes connecting the community with the surrounding area. Indeed, the local economy thrives: There are currently 6,000 residents and 7,000 jobs in Contra Costa Village. Further, the development has not decreased the value of dwellings in the surrounding area, despite the influx of more desirable property.

As to the aforementioned goal of limiting auto dependency: By 2008, the development had achieved a 30 percent reduction of individual vehicle use by daily commuters. This is in good part the work of a comprehensive transit network. It is no less than an incredible achievement.

2.21

Figure 2.22:
Elevation—Avalon Walnut Creek.

Figure 2.23:
Plaza view at dusk.

Figure 2.24:
Leasing building.

Figure 2.25:
Transit oriented development—
evening view.

Figure 2.26:
Plaza fountains.

BLOCK A OAK ROAD ELEVATION

BLOCK A COGGINS STREET ELEVATION

2.22

2.23

2.25

2.24

2.26

2C

Project:
Greenwich Millennium Village

Location:
London, UK

Design Firm:
Ralph Erskine and EPR
Architects Ltd.

Figure 2.27:
Site plan.

Figure 2.28 (right):
A passageway in front of the project.

The Greenwich Millennium Village (GMV) is a unique TOD in outer London, UK. It is situated on the southern banks of the River Thames, 9 kilometers (5.6 miles) away from the city center. All of its 1,095 units are currently occupied, 20 percent of which qualify as affordable housing. Its developers aimed to produce viable transport solutions for residents living on the city's outskirts while limiting car travel, and to create, on the whole, a sustainable community.

London is facing a major congestion issue, made worse by an overall rise in personal vehicle ownership. The developers of GMV are attempting to fight this by placing an emphasis on public transit, cycle paths, and pedestrian routes. Although car ownership rates are about the same as the rest of London, car usage rates are significantly lower. This shows that although many of GMV's residents may own a car, it is not necessary for travel within the community.

In GMV, public transit is the center of community life; this is perhaps best demonstrated in the two bus-exclusive laneways running through the center of the village on main streets. These lanes have been funded by English Partnerships, a public development corporation, as part of their contribution to the community. They have a considerable aesthetic presence: Each is painted a vibrant brick red and separated from normal automobile paths by distinct green medians. Car access within these parameters is prohibited. The buses offer service to grocery stores, entertainment, shops, and other amenities frequented by locals. They also serve as an important connection to London's extensive Underground network. Residents can even take the bus directly from their homes to the North Greenwich Underground station, and from there, connect to virtually anywhere in the city.

This station serves eight bus routes and the Underground, acting as a major transit hub for the area. It is accessible by foot or bike as it is located just one kilometer outside the village. For commuters in a rush, however, the aforementioned bus service is the fastest and most convenient means of access. The Underground service is the most popular transportation service amongst residents compared with train or bus; it allows workers to access the central business district quickly without car travel. Seventy-three percent of workers use the Underground for their daily commute, as opposed to 51 percent in inner London, and 38 percent in outer London.

Figure 2.29:
A view of the public space.

Figure 2.30:
The water-facing façade.

Figure 2.31:
The building along Main Street.

Figure 2.32:
A view of the project from afar.

Figure 2.33:
Elevation.

As aforementioned, priority has been placed on pedestrian and bicycle travel: There are dedicated active-transportation paths throughout the community. A walkway connects the community to the popular O2 arena, a large sports and music venue. Bicycle storage units are provided with space for two to three bicycles per residence, and further, there are weather-protected bike shelters throughout the community. These considerations are especially important to students, one-third of whom commute daily by bicycle and either cycle or walk to purchase groceries.

Car parking is extremely expensive, and individual parking spots cannot be purchased; instead, residents pay for a spot in the local parking garage. Visitors may not use this facility. They must either park illegally on the streets or in the lot beside the North Greenwich underground station.

GMV is yet another exemplary modern TOD. In particular, its centrally located transit stops bring various amenities and longer-distance transport to the residents' front door. The village proves that car travel is not a necessity for those living on the outskirts of the city—so long as a community is thoughtfully designed.

2.29

2.30

2.31

2.33

2.32

Summary and Key Considerations

- Transit-oriented developments (TODs) are higher-density communities that are located near transit corridors where walkability, bicycle culture, and mixed land use form a key planning principle.

- Having TOD is instrumental in reducing the negative impact of a single-person-driven motor vehicle.

- It is imperative that TOD neighborhoods be built within 800 meters (2,625 feet) or a ten-minute walk of a main transit hub. This hub will be linked to other urban centers via an efficient mode of affordable transit.

- The common modes of transit are express buses, at-grade rail, underground rail, above-ground rail transits, and/or ferries.

- Neighborhoods near TOD corridors need to be composed of moderate- to high-density housing in a mixed-use development and include innovative dwelling units such as multi-generational, micro, and live-work units.

- A great advantage of TOD communities lay in their overall energy efficiency. Energy is saved in the macro level (reducing consumption of fusil fuel) and micro levels (higher-density communities) when compared to a conventional single-story suburb.

- To be economically resilient, TOD neighborhoods need to have a range of dwelling types to better respond to fluctuations in housing demand.

- TOD neighborhoods should be designed to limit excessive road and parking lot construction, which would curb the urban heat island effect.

- On a macro level, by living in TOD developments, residents have important health benefits and therefore individual and communal healthcare-expenditure savings.

Exercises

1. Describe the environmental, economic, and social benefits of transit-oriented developments. Illustrate the contribution of using such a transit system in your area.

2. List the different types of transit corridors, their advantages and disadvantages, and find examples for each in your region.

3. What are the chief characteristics of transit-oriented neighborhoods? Draw a conceptual diagram of one.

4. What is the uniqueness of Copenhagen's transit-oriented system? Pay particular attention to the neighborhoods that are located around the transit corridors.

5. What are the main characteristics of the mobility strategy of Friedberg, Germany?

Chapter 3
Mixing Dwellings and Amenities

The segregation of land by use into residential, commercial, and industrial zones was introduced in the 1920s. These practices encouraged automobile dependency and limited sustainable features like diversity and density.

Neighborhoods composed of various dwelling types and mixed-land uses help curb urban sprawl. This is to say nothing of the fact that they offer richer built environments and social opportunities to their residents. This chapter illustrates the merits and modes of mixing a variety of housing types and amenities in neighborhoods.

The Merit of Mixing

Urban sprawl poses a significant challenge to regions dealing with the complexities of metropolitan growth. Peripheral developments force residents to commute long distances in their everyday lives—hours merely to work, shop, or study—and create a burdensome demand for highway infrastructure. Suburban development also contributes to the decline of the urban core, as sprawl creates an arrangement wherein residents have less motivation and money to visit city centers (Brueckner 2000, Tombari 2005). Studies show that those who live in low-density settings lead less healthy lifestyles and weigh up to an average of 2.7 kilograms (6 pounds) more than their city counterparts (Badland and Schofield 2006, David Suzuki Foundation 2014).

These challenges can be mitigated by *mixed developments* given that they attract diverse populations and businesses. Notably, mixed developments open communities to a wider range of socio-economic groups, and these groups, in turn, require diverse housing types—everything from single-family dwellings to townhouses and apartments. This ability to encourage social and built diversity contributes to the viability of a community in that it can foster inclusion, equity, and security (Feehan and Feit 2006). Also, in providing affordable housing, which crosses all income groups, age ranges, and races, this practice may encourage greater social cohesion (Andrews and Townsend 2000, Thibert 2007).

Mixed dwellings also support those who work from home, a population comprising a substantial sector of today's workforce given the power of digital communication. Mixed communities can in themselves offer these residents varied and stimulating lives, reducing their commutes to city centers. As well, growing demographic contingents including singles, childless couples, seniors, and young, career-oriented professionals are creating demand for nontraditional housing and have lifestyles suitable to mixed developments (AIA Economics 2006, Kim et al. 2005).

This form of planning offers other less obvious advantages, too. It cuts infrastructure and maintenance costs and leaves more open spaces (the topic of Chapter 5) (Friedman 2005). A mix of household types can even enhance public safety by ensuring that activities in public spaces are spread over day and night.

Planning Methods of Mixed Neighborhoods

The merits of mixed neighborhoods now well established, let us now turn to the planning strategies used to implement and maintain them. The methods can be organized into categories based on *neighborhood configuration* (this refers to the way commercial and residential zones are integrated), *spatial organization, transit nodes*, and *retail hubs*.

The first method at hand is a type of neighborhood configuration: the conversion of large-scale retail centers, like shopping malls or big-box retailers, into what are called *transition nodes* (Llewelyn 2000). Within this scheme, smaller buildings are planned to encircle larger stores, fostering a sense of community and introducing human scale to a retail sector, as illustrated in Figure 3.1. Organizing commerce in this way reduces traffic congestion and creates an aesthetically pleasing, diverse environment. Taller buildings help create a pleasing microclimate that blocks wind, sheltering pedestrians in cold regions. Further, residences located near or within transition nodes benefit from the nearby amenities. Another advantage: They are not subject to the unattractive street façades common to large, isolated shopping malls or big-box retail establishments.

Another practice of neighborhood configuration is the introduction of light industry to residential areas. Technological advances have alleviated the environmental concerns associated with the integration of industry and agriculture into urban regions, including issues of pollution (Grant 2004). In fact, urban agriculture (further discussed in Chapter 10) is seen as a sustainable practice, as it cuts down on transportation costs and fuel consumption. As well, introducing industry to the city can generate income among households in need of work, not to mention cut travel time and expenses for those who would then live near said work.

Figure 3.1:
In a mixed-use community, a large commercial establishment can have residences along its perimeter.

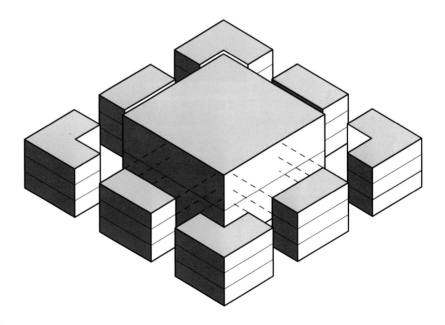

Figure 3.2:
Buildings in this Haarlem, Netherlands, neighborhood have stores on the ground floor, offices on the second, and apartments above them.

Methods related to a neighborhood's *spatial organization* focus on the horizontal and vertical separation of space and cluster organizations. Horizontal separation of space divides land into areas dedicated by use, and it places all areas within walking distance from the home. Typically, commercial space would be located along street level, with residences placed behind the stores. A method related to horizontal separation of space is to group buildings within a district, known as *cluster combination*. Streets, parks, plazas, and squares separate individual buildings, forming urban districts within a single neighborhood (Schwanke 2003). Both of these horizontal models require more land than a vertical separation of space, which entails making distinct separations within a high-rise building, segregating the various functions within. Further, the tall buildings required of this type of spatial organization function as landmarks, and so, according to Al-Kodmany (2011), reinforce the image ability of a district. Neighborhoods can also combine horizontal and vertical spaces, offering multi-use towers and complexes.

If a building is intended to contain retail, office, and residential functions, then it is advisable to arrange the work as follows: retail occupying the ground floor, offices above, and residential within the remainder. This maintains privacy for the residents, as shown in Figure 3.2. Also, it is important that each function have its own, separate entrance. As to parking, it is advisable to accommodate retail parking to an on-street location while residential and office parking is better placed behind or underneath.

The core commercial areas in a neighborhood center can also accommodate bigger retail stores along with smaller ones. Bigger stores should have two entries, one from the street and another leading from the rear parking area. Small shops can have main street entries and either on-street or rear parking lots. A main street, connected to residential areas and a transit stop, is a particularly pleasant place to walk and can attract foot traffic to local shops.

In larger neighborhoods, it is possible to have several convenience centers. However, to make each more successful, it is important that they be connected to transit stops, or are no more than five to ten minutes' walk of one, as illustrated in Figure 3.3. In fact, the promising practice of transit-oriented development (TOD), which was discussed in Chapter 2, specifically promotes the practice of building mixed developments around transit hubs. The different centers should each have distinct features—say, a sport hub or library—to draw people from other regions. Another important consideration: When planning multiple retail areas within one neighborhood, it is vital that competing areas be located at a considerable distance from each other to make them economically viable.

Mixed-use developments can also profit from concepts derived from the design of traditional towns that have a *main street* (also known as high street) (Figure 3.4). Given that they are designed with suitable human scale, they can be a key component of a town center, encouraging social interaction among residents (Robertson 2006). Further, they are pedestrian friendly and often designed such that residences are located atop stores lining the street. These factors together mean that neighborhoods with main streets and town centers feel distinctly residential, yet integrate commercial life and diverse housing styles and incomes with ease (Schwanke 2003). Main streets also offer retail niches specific to each neighborhood and so do not necessarily have to compete with big chain stores.

The concept of the mixed-income development has been introduced in public housing projects in the US. The initiatives aim to deinstitutionalize affordable housing and improve its quality without having to increase government subsidies. These projects include allocations for commercial space and higher-income residents—businesses and people capable of renting and purchasing space at their market value. Therefore, fewer superblocks of poor-quality housing are built, ending the segregation and isolation of low-income groups. The attractiveness of these developments is both in their superior design and proximity to amenities (Crowhurst and Lennard 2002). These characteristics are responsible for attracting both high-income residents and lower-income households to the neighborhood. The developments are seen as mutually beneficial to both the municipality and residents, as rental income can cover operating costs, although build costs are covered by subsidies financed by taxpayers.

Figure 3.3:
To make a retail area successful, it is important that it is located next to a transit stop or within a five- to ten-minute walk of one.

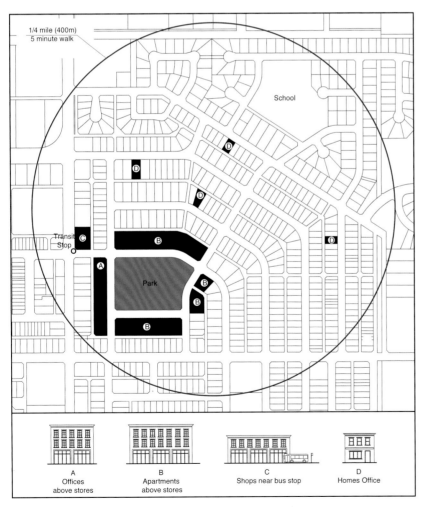

Commercial Centers and Civic Institutions

The size of a commercial center depends on population size. A regional center can serve about 20,000 people; a neighborhood center up to 8,000; and a convenience center approximately 3,000 (Van der Ryn and Calthorpe 1986). Regardless, the design approach of mixed-use development can be applied.

Civic services such as government offices, recreation centers, post offices, and daycare centers should be placed in close proximity to one another. Placing those amenities in the center will make an area walkable. At the same time, by allowing a mix of housing types in a medium- to high-density development, a number of nonresidential amenities, as well as a transit stop, can be economically sustained.

Convenience centers should generate more pedestrian traffic than public transit or car activity. Often, small local retailers cannot afford the high rent asked by developers of new buildings. Therefore, convenience centers should have a mix of amenities—for example, a daycare center, fitness club, beauty salon, and grocery store—all in proximity to a neighborhood park or open space. Indeed, a convenience center combined with thoughtfully designed space and a mix of retail services can become a node for further growth.

Neighborhood centers are bigger than convenience centers and are constituted by a mix of shops, drugstores, supermarkets, daycare centers, professional offices, and other civic amenities. According to Van der Ryn and Calthorpe (1986), at densities of around 30 units per hectare (12 units per acre), a neighborhood with a 0.4 kilometer (1/4 mile) radius can accommodate a population of around 3,800 (assuming an average of 2.5 persons per household).

Figure 3.4:
High streets, like this one in Lancaster, UK, are pedestrian friendly with residences on top of stores.

Activities that are not compatible and are auto-dependent—for instance, drive-through establishments, car washes, and car sales lots—should be discouraged. The purpose of having a cluster of services is for residents to meet their daily needs by "one-stop shopping" rather than driving to a variety of locations. Clustering these destinations will encourage transit use and reduce auto dependency.

A regional hub occupies a bigger area than a neighborhood center and houses the same facilities, not to mention a few more services. This might include, for instance, a bank, religious center, central library, bigger office buildings, a theater, and a market. A community center can be integrated with a central park or amphitheatre in order to host festivals and create a square to attract people. A community center will be successful if the surrounding residential density can be kept at medium or high—about 62 to 74 units per hectare (25 to 30 units per acre) in the 0.4 kilometer (1/4 mile) radius from the center (Van der Ryn and Calthorpe 1986). Diversity of dwellings needs to be included in residential centers. Apartments, for example, may define major squares, while townhouses are built around parks and single-family units further away.

Civic institutions function best when they are integrated with residences, commerce, and recreation, to create what is known as a *complete place*. These places foster a sense of community. Civic edifices like a city hall or library can be set near squares; they have special architectural features to differentiate them from other buildings and create activity nodes. A square that houses small civic and commercial services— like a daycare center or a post office— can form a convenience center. Another idea: When community buildings are located near parks, they can provide the social integration of elderly people.

Schools and daycares can be regarded as a focal point of a neighborhood. They can double as playgrounds, libraries, and meeting places. Elementary schools can operate at a neighborhood level while a junior high school can serve at a town level. Schools should stay connected to—or directly be designed to be a part of—residential areas and neighborhood centers, yet away from arterial roads.

Just like civic or service buildings, the architecture and location of places of worship can also lend a neighborhood identity and promote social interaction. They can be situated near public parks, or, another idea—integrated with a convenience center. It is advisable that they also be linked by public transit to all residential areas.

Mixed neighborhoods composed of a variety of dwelling types, mixed-land uses, and people offer a convenient, yet vibrant, lifestyle. By reducing traffic and the infrastructure needed to support it, supporting an extensive transit system, and encouraging walkability and further the reuse of buildings, such developments are sustainable. Mixed dwelling types also generate a socially inclusive place, creating at once both safety and diversity within a community. There are several models by which to implement mixed planning based on physical configuration, a community's retail sector, its transit hub, or even neighborhood structure. Some of these models are illustrated in the following case studies.

3A

Project:
Dockside Green

Location:
Victoria, British Columbia,
Canada

Design Firm:
Perkins + Will Architect

Dockside Green is an innovative community located on a former Brownfield site near Victoria, British Columbia, Canada. The development has been rated LEED Platinum due to the application of a "closed-loop" design process. In other words, it is a self-sufficient and extremely sustainable neighborhood.

As one would imagine, minimization of the community's environmental footprint is a result of many different efforts and processes. For one, much of the waste produced is later used to provide the development with power. Moreover, water usage is approximately 65 percent less than a typical development, with water from treatment-plant on-site recycling used in toilets, soil irrigation, and landscaping.

Another of its sustainable practices is the implementation of a mixed-use design. A variety of amenities, residential units to include apartments and townhouses, and office space join to create Dockside Green. The first phase of the project, "Synergy," is a purely residential tower; however, it has been strategically placed just west of "Inspiration"—an area functioning as both a residential and commercial space. The ground floor of Inspiration houses an organic bakery and a fair-trade coffee shop (another innovative idea of note: three propeller wind turbines on the roof help to power this bakery). Another two floors of Inspiration have been dedicated to office space, with the remainder used for residential purposes. The "Balance" buildings were the next phase realized, featuring 171 condos split between two nine- and ten-story towers, and a 165-space underground parking lot. Balance sits atop two stories of attached townhouses, each with individual entrances and semi-private terraces. The space between the two Balance towers is used as a small park and features public art. Another three-story townhouse development has been placed between Synergy and Balance; the addition of townhomes helps to moderate the density of the development while still utilizing the in-between space, and, in addition, allows sunlight to enter the two high-density phases. "Prosperity" was built next and is an exclusively commercial building—its three stories serve as offices and commercial space. It looks upon Point Hope Shipyard, an area that acts as a main retail street. Nearby, a shoreline park with a kayaking launch point has been built at Point Ellice House, offering residents the opportunity to go on a leisure paddle—or even, incredibly, to commute to work by kayak.

Figure 3.5:
Site plan.

Figure 3.6:
Aerial photo with the site plan in axonometric.

Figure 3.7:
Elevations looking west.

Figure 3.8:
Section—Synergy water recovery treatment strategy.

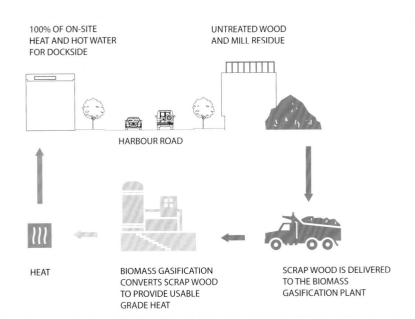

100% OF ON-SITE
HEAT AND HOT WATER
FOR DOCKSIDE

UNTREATED WOOD
AND MILL RESIDUE

HARBOUR ROAD

HEAT

BIOMASS GASIFICATION
CONVERTS SCRAP WOOD
TO PROVIDE USABLE
GRADE HEAT

SCRAP WOOD IS DELIVERED
TO THE BIOMASS
GASIFICATION PLANT

3.9

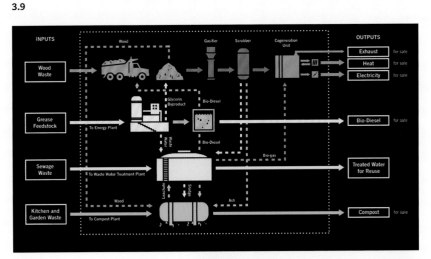

3.10

From this description, it is evident that diversity plays an important part in the developer's vision of Dockside Green. The community is meant to attract a large mix of demographics from varying income levels. The initial goal was to have 10 percent of rental units affordable for low-income households. Within Synergy and Balance, twenty-six units have been priced under market value by way of government subsidy. In addition, a three-story with below-market value housing that has been recently approved for construction is underway—the work of the firm Number 10 Architects. It will feature two levels of micro-condos atop a single level of commercial space.

By placing the need for sustainability above the desire to maximize profit, the developer has created a healthy, well-balanced community in Dockland Green. This has allowed for a greater mix of amenities and businesses in addition to an increased housing density. Perhaps most impressively, this development proves that sustainable living is not a lifestyle exclusive to the wealthy.

Figure 3.9:
Biomass district heating system.

Figure 3.10:
Biomass synergies.

Figure 3.11:
Waterway near the Synergy building.

Figure 3.12:
Night view of the Balance building.

3.11

3.12

Figure 3.13:
Front view of the townhomes.

Figure 3.14:
View of the Inspiration and Balance buildings.

Figure 3.15:
Green wall on the façade of the Balance building.

Figure 3.16:
View of the Inspiration building.

Figure 3.17:
View of Balance townhome.

Figure 3.18:
Detail of Synergy wastewater.

3.13

3.14

3.15

3.16

3.17

3.18

3B

Project:
87 Chapel Street

Location:
St. Kilda, Victoria, Australia

Design Firm:
MGS Architects

Figure 3.19:
Site plan showing lower-level units.

Figure 3.20:
Side elevation.

Figure 3.21:
Rear elevation.

87 Chapel Street serves as a residential project in St. Kilda, Australia. A fascinating variety of forms, colors, and materials make the property an immediately appealing place. Further, the self-conscious design scheme implemented herein ensures that the development does not interfere with the eclectic nature of the adjacent Chapel Street. In fact, the project, in many ways, improves it.

The primary concerns of the client, Port Phillip Housing Association, were to secure long-term financial benefits and security, create low-cost rental accommodation for locals, and integrate with and support the rich character of the neighborhood. The first two goals may seem contradictory but today both have been harmoniously realized: The

rental units of 87 Chapel Street serve to benefit the community in that they provide low-income housing while still producing a regular source of income to the association. The last of the aforementioned goals has arguably been achieved, too—more on that later.

First, to explore its achievement of affordability: There are a total of eighty-one units, with twenty of these units being set aside for private sale to the market, and the remainder offered as affordable rental units. In other words, the development offers affordable rentals in addition to the future option to provide more permanent market-rate private-ownership residences. The design of the complex removes any stigma associated with low-rental housing. It is responsive and unique—giving the impression of a sought-after private condo complex. It is created in the spirit that affordable housing should not be uncomfortable nor be of low-quality design.

Given this approach, the development has attracted a diverse mix of people. The design not only accommodates various income levels but also the elderly and those with special needs. Set-down terrace entrances and bathrooms allow for easy accessibility. Street-level access to the building eliminates the need to climb stairs or ramps. The courtyard surrounded by the two apartment buildings gives residents a nearby leisure space and allows them to leave the house without having to travel far. The development's location on the highly commercial Chapel Street also provides close proximity to groceries and other amenities.

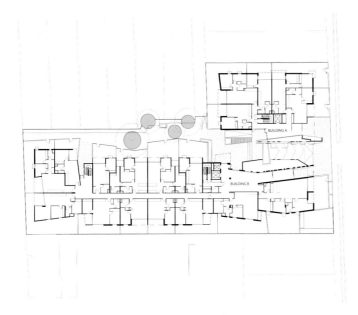

3.19

3.20

3.21

The aforementioned open space formed in the center of the two buildings serves as a wonderful meeting place for residents and is intended to operate as a welcoming environment for the surrounding community as further development on the adjacent city blocks occurs. Indeed, the space is intended to be open to pedestrians walking along Chapel Street and the neighboring Inkerman Estate, increasing the permeability of the site. Openness to the surrounding community was an important feature for the developer, as it ensures that the housing development and tenants remain strongly connected to the local neighborhood.

Though the development supports car use—what with seventy parking spaces—car ownership and the attendant parking-spot rental cost are options, not necessities. Aside from the various environmental benefits, this opens the development to individuals who cannot afford a private automobile. Bike racks are placed both outside the residences and inside of the parking garage. The racks inside the garage provide increased bicycle security and create extra space in the apartments (given that residents do not have to store their bikes in their own units as a result). The racks out front are for quicker visits or daytime parking. Ample access to public transport connects the development with the surrounding city: Tram routes run along Chapel Street and the nearby Barkly Street providing links to Melbourne's extensive public transport system.

Figure 3.22:
Main street view.

Figure 3.23:
Side view.

Figure 3.24:
Street view of Building B.

3.22

3.23   3.24 (right)

3.25

3.26

3.27

3.28

Figure 3.25:
Street view of Building A.

Figure 3.26:
Side view of Building B.

Figure 3.27:
View of lobby.

Figure 3.28:
View of typical corridor.

The mix of affordable rental units with private residences has served to benefit both the developer and community. With this design, the developer is provided with a stable income through rentals in addition to a substantial financial benefit by way of private owners. This, in turn, enables the developer to undertake further low-cost and affordable-housing development. In this way, the community is provided with low-cost housing that does not carry a stigma and offers comfortable, luxurious living. In short, the development of 87 Chapel Street demonstrates that it is possible to create a residence that equally profits both the public and private realm.

3C

Project:
Stadstuinen Rotterdam

Location:
Rotterdam, the Netherlands

Design Firm:
KCAP Architects & Planners

Figure 3.29:
Site plan.

Figure 3.30:
Side elevation and section of a typical block.

Stadstuinen Rotterdam is part of the Kop van Zuid housing development. Formerly the southern docklands of the city, a major regeneration project in the early 2000s turned the area into a residential and commercial hub. The gardens act as a transition between the large towers surrounding Wilhelmina Square, Headland and Peperklip, and the social housing neighborhoods of Vuurplaat. The area has been designed to reap the benefits of both suburban and urban lifestyles, creating a wonderful environment for both residents and workers.

Four separate architectural firms took part in creating the development. This allowed for a diverse environment, where one mindset does not dominate the design process. Each of the firms consulted one another throughout and agreed beforehand on which materials to use. This rendered a clean and cohesive product.

A large rectangle is enclosed by a perimeter of seven- to nine-story buildings. This outer portion functions as both a residential and commercial space. The ten tower blocks, along with the interior residences, house approximately 570 units. Underneath the towers is a parking garage. The ground floor serves as retail space, while the remaining layers are purely residential. Placing businesses on the ground floor of the residential towers ensures easy pedestrian access and eliminates the need for extra exclusively commercial buildings. Incorporating businesses into the community framework allows residents to work close to their homes, stimulates the local economy, and ensures that residents do not have to travel far to gain access to urban amenities. The residential units in this part of the development have large bay windows and balconies. Apartments on the top floor also have rooftop access.

Modern furnishings create a beautiful living environment and form an attractive community. Residents are drawn by both the practicality of the neighborhood and the aesthetically pleasing surroundings. The variety in styles of the four participating firms establishes a greater variety of form and peaks aesthetic interest.

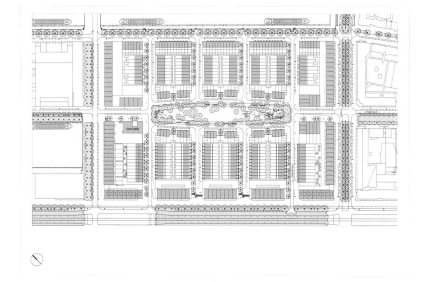

3.29

3.30

Figure 3.31:
Green balconies of elderly complex.

Figure 3.32:
A block facing Main Street.

Figure 3.33:
Green front yard serves as a buffer between the street and townhouses.

Figure 3.34:
Lower floor of townhouses and businesses.

Figure 3.35:
View of elderly complex to block and school across.

3.32

3.33

3.34

3.31

3.35

Figure 3.36:
Sidewalk along one of the blocks.

Figure 3.37:
Street-level store.

Figure 3.38:
Green park makes the heart of the project.

Figure 3.39:
Direct-entry street to lower-level units.

Figure 3.40:
Lower-level units and businesses.

Figure 3.41:
Stores under apartments.

In the center of this massive rectangle are communal gardens with a more open and welcoming atmosphere than the outer area. Smaller-scale residences occupy the rectangular space, and individual units are generally accessible from the ground level. Villas have been placed at the corners of the space. A primary school has made use of one of these buildings, and the rest are residential. The presence of a neighborhood school, partnered with the car-free interior, makes the development an excellent space for young families.

The wonderful central space in Stadstuinen also helps to attract visitors to the area. People enjoy touring the gardens, which helps to provide business to the retail spaces on the ground floor of the exterior rectangle. It also promotes the liveliness of the area and establishes its relevance to the city as a whole.

Rotterdam's Stadstuinen is quickly becoming a pertinent and exciting district of the city. The various shops, businesses, and residences have formed a true urban center where residents, workers, and visitors alike can enjoy their surroundings. An efficient use of space coupled with a welcoming public area has placed Stadstuinen back on Rotterdam's urban scene.

3.38

3.39

3.40   3.41 (below)

3.36

3.37

3D

Project:
1221 Broadway

Location:
San Antonio, Texas, USA

Design Firm:
Lake|Flato Architects & OCO Architects

1221 Broadway is a successful refurbishment project at the convergence of Interstates 35 and 37 in San Antonio, Texas. When purchased by the developer, it was merely an abandoned industrial and residential building in an opportune location. The building was then in a decrepit state and had been occupied by the city's homeless population. Today, it has been transformed into prime residential and commercial units.

The architects chose to reuse the building's existing superstructure, saving on costs and resources. That said, its former skin was stripped, allowing them freedom in the façade design. In the process, many of the balconies had to be punched into the façade, rather than protrude out, in order to accommodate the limitations of the structure.

The decision to recycle the structure rendered a unique mix of housing types. There are a total of forty different floor plans for the 300 residential units. These range from studio lofts to two-bedroom, two-bath apartments. As a result, the community attracts people from several different demographics and income levels, creating great social diversity among residents. Some of these layouts resemble a typical loft floor plan. For these, the architect chose to leave certain surfaces as exposed concrete. This smart choice both took advantage of trendy exposure techniques and further cut expenditure.

Its interior courtyards create beautiful public spaces and allow residents to relax outdoors. In one, a partially constructed pool from the pre-existing site was finished and turned into a central community feature. There are also several retail spaces in these outdoor areas, encouraging use by residents and the general public alike. The shops serve to open the space to a broader community and help to distinguish between public and private zones. These courtyards play an important part in communal life and add to the pedestrian-oriented nature of the development.

The site's Broadway Street façade was utilized as retail and business space. This creates further amenities for residents and brings the outside public into the community. Prior to the renovation, this was an area that people would avoid walking through for fear of safety—the addition of shops on the street level establishes the development as a secure environment. Broadway Street is a popular pedestrian route, and today, the community has helped render it a continuous, uninterrupted stretch, optimizing its walkability. Further, pedestrian bridges help to connect the residences with public and commercial spaces around the site, creating circulation and increasing pedestrian accessibility.

Figure 3.42:
Site plan.

Figure 3.43:
View of the community's public space.

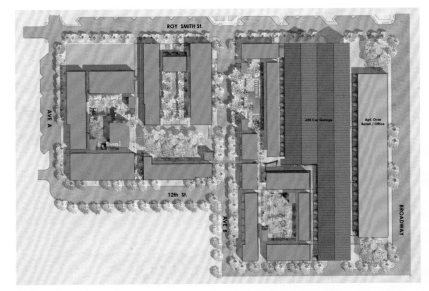

3.42

3.43

Figure 3.44:

Bridge connecting two apartment buildings over a street.

Figure 3.45:

Some of the buildings have been built with open lower floors for seating.

Figure 3.46:

Public passage near buildings.

Figure 3.47:

View of one of the apartment blocks.

Figure 3.48:

Balconies are featured on many of the apartment buildings.

Figure 3.49:

Kitchen and living space in an apartment building.

Figure 3.50:

A night view of a bridge connecting two apartment buildings.

The 1221 Broadway development is a unique example of economically feasible social and environmental responsibility in the realm of private development. Rather than build a new building atop the site, the architects went to great lengths to preserve what already existed. As a result, they saved both money and resources—all while impressively mixing the project's typologies. Through meticulous floor-plan design, the architects managed to work around the existing structure, creating an environment that is truly welcoming to people from all walks of life.

3.47

3.48

3.49

3.45

3.46 (below)

3.44

3.50

Summary and Key Considerations

- A mixed development is made up of residential, retail, and office spaces.

- By having residences and businesses, a well-designed neighborhood with mixed-land uses contributes to the reduction of commute times and use of motor vehicles, and results in lower emissions.

- Mixed neighborhoods should be designed to foster walkability, which helps make a community become more vibrant.

- Residents with varied incomes are known to have different work schedules, which helps sustain a frequent and therefore more appealing transit schedule to reduce the use of private motor vehicles.

- Van der Ryn and Calthorpe (1986) suggest that with densities of around 30 units per hectare (12 units per acre), a mixed-use neighborhood with a 0.4 kilometer (1/4 mile) radius can accommodate a population of around 3,800 (assuming an average of 2.5 persons per household).

- Mixed-use and mixed-income neighborhoods can respond to the need for community cohesion by providing affordable and inclusive housing that crosses all age ranges and income levels.

- The diversity of residents' age groups ensures that activities in public spaces are spread over day and night to distribute demand and support variety.

- Several strategies can be used to implement mixed neighborhoods. These methods can be organized into categories based on *neighborhood configuration, spatial organization, transit nodes*, and *retail hubs*. Each has its own unique attributes that result in a different physical environment.

- The concept of mixed-income development has been introduced in designing public housing projects in several nations. These initiatives support the goal of deinstitutionalizing affordable housing, and, further, increasing its quality without increasing government subsidies.

- Income generated by developers in mixed-use developments supports the introduction of affordable designs. As a result, more people are capable of renting and purchasing space at a lower cost.

Exercises

1. What are the advantages of having communities with mixed dwellings and amenities? Demonstrate these advantages using a case study in your region.

2. Draw diagrams illustrating the various types of neighborhoods with mixed dwellings and amenities, and analyze the uniqueness of each.

3. What are the social and economic advantages of having a variety of dwelling types in a community?

4. Draw a diagrammatic illustration of a neighborhood center. What amenities will you include in it, and how should they be linked to the residential areas surrounding the center?

5. Using local statistical data, compare the pattern of private car use by residents in a community with a neighborhood center and one without in your area.

Chapter 4
Car-Free Neighborhoods

Auto usage and its supporting infrastructure—including parking lots, paved streets, and sidewalks—increase greenhouse gas (GHG) emissions and urban heat. Thus, walkable neighborhoods are a sustainable solution to the increasing financial and environmental costs of fuel. This is to say nothing of their power to improve the quality of life and health of residents. This chapter discusses how communities can reduce traffic and rely instead on active mobility. The methods explained below outline how to integrate streets, pedestrian paths, and parking spaces, and how public transit can create a desirable walkable environment. Together, these strategies represent an all-encompassing approach to community design.

The Effects of Driving

The environmental benefits of a car-free community are in some respects readily apparent; in others, less so. Of course, fewer cars mean decreased fuel consumption and air pollution. Yet it is also vital to consider that this amounts to less infrastructure to support automobile usage, the creation and maintenance of which is itself environmentally harmful. Moreover, less auto infrastructure leaves more space for green areas; these, in turn, help mitigate the effects of fossil fuels.

Further, a recent UN report has concluded that nearly two-thirds of global deaths are caused by three factors taken together: pollution, lack of exercise, and bad eating habits (Hood 2011). Polluted air poses a significant health risk in that it can cause inflammation of the lungs or otherwise impair their functioning. As to the other two factors, a lack of exercise and bad eating habits can together lead to obesity and thus to a host of serious attendant health issues, including diabetes and heart illnesses. It is notable that all three factors identified by the UN's study are associated with the popularity of the automobile.

Indeed, each additional kilometer (0.6 mile) walked per day reduces the likelihood of becoming obese by nearly 5 percent, while each hour spent in a car increases the likelihood by 6 percent (see Chapter 9 for further discussion of this phenomenon). This connection is alarming when one considers that the amount of time that people spend at the wheel has grown significantly across the globe. For example, in Canada, some 75 percent of the population use a car on a typical weekday and spend, on average, an hour a day commuting to work (Canadian Heart and Stroke Foundation 2005).

A 2006 study by Badland and Schofield exploring the relationship between community size and physical-activity level in New Zealand demonstrates the connection between these behaviors and the built environment. In sum, they exposed that in low-density residential areas people are less likely to utilize nonmotorized modes of travel. Further, they identified local infrastructure as the ideal mode of intervention by which to improve physical health, as opposed to traditional methods of social support.

There is a less obvious harm from the auto-oriented neighborhood: It denies the young of autonomy. According to the UN Children's Fund (UNICEF), children now account for one-third of all settlement dwellers, about one billion people, yet are generally excluded from the decisions that shape their physical environment (Torres 2009). Cities are commonly planned for adults with cars—an arrangement that deprives children of an opportunity to be independent. In rural and suburban settings, youths' mobility is especially limited until they learn to drive. In these settings, parents exercise a very high degree of control over trips and means of travel. Torres (2009) suggests that this creates a circular problem: Children are driven because it is dangerous for them to travel by other means, but it is dangerous for them to travel by other means because the world is adapted to automobiles.

In addition, it is essential to consider the cultural component of transport. Poor mobility- and connectivity-planning diminishes sense of place. When people are driving, as opposed to walking or using public transit, the likelihood that they will meet other people is reduced. As a result, the social fabric of communities can be eroded—a consequence particularly harmful in a small-town setting.

Here is another important consideration: Auto dependency can negatively impact local economies. Litman (2009) writes that creating good walking conditions tends to be financially undervalued in typical planning, the effect being a shift of resources from pedestrian and cycling to automobile-oriented land-use patterns. Yet a study of consumer expenditures in UK towns found that those who walk to and from shopping districts spend about 50 percent more per week supporting local retail establishments (Litman 2009). Meanwhile, the study suggests that spending on fuel and vehicles tends to contribute relatively little to local employment or business activity.

Creating Car-Free Environments

Many of the trips taken daily by drivers are to nonresidential destinations and could be avoided altogether if these functions were closer to home. Badland, Schofield, and Garrett (2008) found that people who reside close to their place of work or study are more likely to either perceive they can or actually engage in transport-related physical activity. These assertions are supported by Cao, Mokhtarian, and Handy (2007), who found that land-use policies designed to put residents close to destinations and provide them with alternative transportation options will lead to less driving and more walking.

There are many effective ways for planners to bring common travel destinations closer to home. Perhaps most obviously, key neighborhood amenities must be placed in strategic locations and clustered—this will make it easy to visit several destinations in a single trip. Commercial areas are especially important to make walkable. When possible, having commercial and residential uses in one building will help some citizens reduce their travel altogether. Further, the placement of schools in the community's heart can foster a culture of walking or bike riding among children. Another thought: The same school can also house a library or sport facility after hours, services not only for children but the community at large.

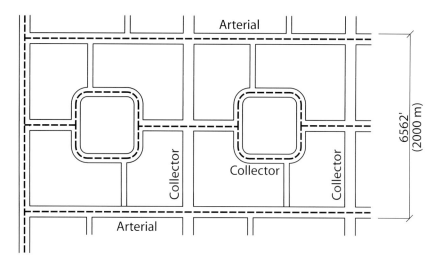

Public transit is another important element to consider in the development of local mobility networks. Most municipalities argue that such systems need to be economically self-sustaining, an objective that is hard to achieve without substantial ridership. Yet such a stance is flawed if a community values social equality: Public transit is no less than essential to sufficiently support lower-income residents. Such systems eliminate the need for the economically vulnerable to own and maintain a vehicle, an unavoidable and draining investment for the poor in nontransit-enabled communities. Buses, or at the very least partial bus service, therefore, need to be an integral part of the planning process.

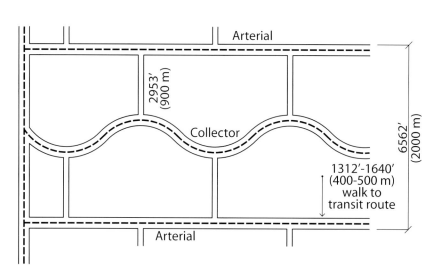

Public transit networks must be designed in conjunction with streets and paths in mind for maximum use, as illustrated in Figure 4.1. The system can be hierarchically organized, allowing residents to easily reach other buses or trains that connect with major urban centers. Other approaches to reducing the use of private cars is by initiating car pooling among residents. Also, shared auto memberships/fee programs where one vehicle can be rented and used by a number of people should encouraged.

Cost-saving measures may include smaller buses that use alternative sources of energy like those currently used in many European cities. Offering services on demand might increase convenience and efficiency. Planners must also be careful to match the frequency of service and user type—for example, in neighborhoods with younger families, more buses can travel during morning and afternoon rush hours when schools are in session. In sparsely populated areas, some services may be offered at rush hour only. Another important consideration is to provide special vehicles for seniors and others with reduced mobility.

Figure 4.1:

A recommended public transit path and walking distances to bus stops in communities.

Of course, sustainable planners cannot supplant the automobile with public transit alone —active transportation must be enabled, too. Therefore, the planners of car-free communities not only deprioritize cars, but also work to put pedestrians, cyclists, and children at play first (Tumlin 2012). For example, in the Netherlands, some streets are called *woonerf*, meaning "streets for living." These streets are shared between pedestrians, bicycles, transit vehicles, and automobiles, all with no distinction between sidewalks and car lanes. This design, which was successfully introduced in other countries as illustrated in Figure 4.2, remains safe for pedestrians given that cars traveling on these roads drive at slow speeds. The *woonerf* rely on narrow streets and gentle curves to slow traffic and create a safer environment for pedestrians and bikers. Streets with a width of 6 meters (20 feet) have been observed to accommodate both pedestrians and drivers since, again, the cars move slowly, allowing pedestrians to feel at ease.

Streets thus enabled benefit the local community beyond providing easy transport. They are narrower streets and so help to preserve existing flora and fauna. They can also support social interaction, especially if lined with street furniture like benches and planter boxes that can further slow traffic.

In speaking of active transportation, it is important to reiterate the strategic placement and clustering of amenities. Residents must have access to the services they would normally reach by car within a ten-minute walk. When people have the opportunity to live, work, and shop by foot, substantial environmental benefit and efficient connectivity result.

Figure 4.2:

Shared streets accommodate pedestrians, cyclists, and slow-moving vehicular traffic.

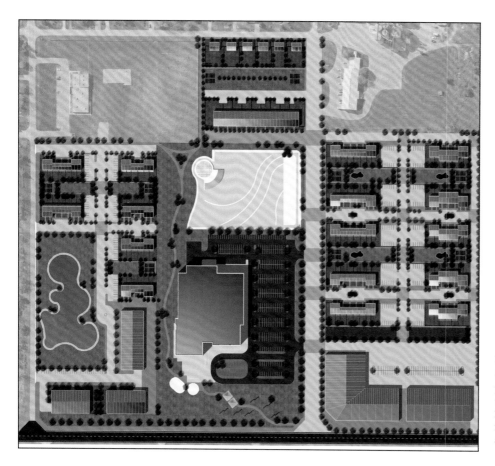

Figure 4.3:
Off-street parking made up of
permeable paving material, like
the one designed by the author in
Middlesex Center, Ontario, offers
financial savings to homeowners
and reduces the urban heat.

Another method to discourage the
use of cars is through the careful
placement of parking spaces. Parking
lots have become a dominant feature of
urban and suburban landscapes. Their
negative environmental impact has
become increasingly apparent. Parking
spaces, made of pavement, absorb heat
and collect water on their surface, not
allowing the soil below to filter the
rainwater. For this reason, parking spaces
and streets are designed to channel
water as quickly as possible to a body
of water, carrying with it the chemicals
deposited in parking spaces like
petroleum and other pollutants (Green
Parking Lot Resource Guide 2008).

Parking should be provided for those
who need it, and not as an added cost
to those who do not. One indoor parking
space per unit increases the cost of a
home by 12.5 percent and two parking
spaces increase the cost by 25 percent
(Litman 2009). Residential parking
currently dominates the main façade
of single-family homes, placing priority
on the car's role in daily life. Those
parking areas should serve more than
one function and be integrated into the
landscape. Another alternative is off-
street parking composed of permeable
paving material. It offers financial
savings to homeowners and reduces
urban heat (Figure 4.3). Parked cars
also create a physical barrier between
pedestrians and vehicles, acting as a
safety buffer. However, it is important to
consider that such a barrier also screens
activities from the driver, creating a
security risk if, for example, a child were
to run after a ball on to the street.

Grouped parking spaces also offer residents financial savings. A space that accommodates about twenty cars is recommended to maximize flexibility in arrangement of space, minimize construction and maintenance costs, and reduce negative impact on surrounding buildings. Residents in communities with shared lots regard them as vibrant social meeting places and appreciate that they protect the environmental character of the development (Environmental Protection Agency 2012).

In Downsview Park in the City of Toronto, Canada, parking lots are more like parks. Both the urban heat island effect and stormwater collection are managed to mitigate environmental damages. The large section of pavement is broken into courts and separated by pedestrian pathways with landscaping around every lot, diminishing the usual drab visual impact generated by an expanse of pavement. Said pavement is composed of a permeable material that absorbs the rainwater, which is then filtered by the soil (Downsview Park Inc. 2007).

Visual considerations in parking lots can also improve the social nature of the space, promoting community. In other words, parking lots can become public spaces resembling plazas, serving as meeting spaces or even showcasing artwork. To aid in creating such an atmosphere, trees and shrubs can provide shade in which neighbors can stop and chat. Vegetation also creates a more accommodating microclimate, especially in cold zones. In the most ambitious incarnation of this approach, careful attention to landscaping can even transform a parking lot such that it assumes the appearance and qualities of a garden.

Fostering Walking and Cycling Habits

Cycling is no longer a fringe mode of transportation. Pucher, Buehler, and Seinen (2011) noted that over the past decade, there has been a large increase in the funding of pro-bike policies and initiatives by central governments and municipalities (Figure 4.4). In this regard, the relatively limited area that neighborhoods occupy and the fewer vehicles that travel on their roads make them highly suitable for active modes of mobility.

Rohrer, Pierce, and Denison (2004) studied the associations between health and walking and found that people who perceived that they had no place to walk were significantly less healthy than those who thought they had at least one place to walk. Their studies offered two suggestions to improve public health: health education and planning walkable neighborhoods. On a related note, Besser and Dannenberg (2005) concluded that walking to and from public transportation can help physically inactive populations—especially low-income groups—attain the recommended level of daily physical exercise.

While it is evident that communities must respond to such findings, it is hard to offer a template solution for all locations—instead, the following is a selection of strategies from leading researchers to guide today's planner. Jacobsen, Racioppi, and Rutter (2009) studied methods by which to foster better coordination between motorized traffic, walking, and cycling. They recommend a number of inexpensive yet effective interventions. These include traffic calming measures, the installation of 15 km/h or 30 km/h (9.32 mph or 18.64 mph) zones, congestion charging (i.e., a daily charge for driving a vehicle within a defined zone), the placement of bicycle lanes on major streets, and giving priority to the rights and safety of vulnerable road users as opposed to vehicles. A suggestion along the same vein has been made by Dumbaugh and Li (2011). They found that factors associated with crashes in which vehicles collide with pedestrians and cyclists are largely similar to those resulting in crashes

Figure 4.4:

Various measures can be implemented by municipalities to foster convenient and safe cycling habits.

between vehicles. Therefore, increasing safety, through either design or policing, needs to be a first step in introducing modes of active transportation.

Another inexpensive measure is that of improving the built environment itself. Winters et al. (2010) suggested that well-marked paths, signage, traffic calming devices, and road markings tend to foster biking and walking. Such strategies were introduced by Dutch, Danish, and German cities to support cycling (Pucher and Buehler 2008). Those strategies included: bike-parking facilities, coordination with public transport, traffic education and training, and the enactment of supporting traffic laws. In an attempt to promote cycling, the same counties offered convenient access to bikes through sharing programs, bike-trip planning, and public awareness campaigns. Driving was discouraged by reducing automobile speed limits, increasing parking charges, automobile taxation, and strict land-use policies.

Accommodating pedestrians can also be achieved by introducing safety awareness programs. These include simple and relatively inexpensive educational interventions aimed at increasing the awareness of both walkers and motorists of one another's presence. Other measures with a higher price tag can be introduced in denser areas that are known to be more walkable (Saelens et al. 2003): Road bumps can reduce speeds or highly textured driving surfaces can also be used. The bumps can be placed at the entrance to a street to indicate an increase in residential density and the need to slow down. Stamped concrete or cobblestone segments can also be effective while adding emphasis to gateways and entrances. A technique that is particularly useful when dealing with heavily traveled streets is to raise the level of the road at intersections. As a result, the continuous and uninterrupted crosswalk ensures that pedestrians have priority.

4A

Project:
BO01

Location:
Malmö, Sweden

Design Firm:
Plan Design: Klas Tham

Figure 4.5:
A view of the water from between buildings.

Figure 4.6:
Site plan.

Figure 4.7:
Aerial view.

After a 1970s recession in shipbuilding, the Western docks of Sweden's second largest city, Malmö, were left largely abandoned. A recent project has aimed to revitalize the former shipbuilding district and establish it as a model for sustainable urban living. The community boasts 1,100 residential units. The opening of the Øresund bridge, linking Malmö with Copenhagen, and the construction of Santiago Calatrava's iconic Turning Torso, have established Västra Hamnen as an exciting new community. It has become a symbol of Malmö's economic revival.

The developers have placed an emphasis on car-free living within Västra Hamnen. In BO01, the first neighborhood to be built, most streets are shared between pedestrian cyclists and drivers; private car ownership has further been discouraged in other neighborhoods. Public transport, as well as bicycle and pedestrian infrastructure, has been of utmost importance in the planning process.

Each housing unit is within 300 meters (984 feet) of a bus stop, with elevated platforms for quick and easy access. Stops are sheltered to protect against undesirable weather. Buses run at seven-minute intervals, ensuring residents never have to wait long for public transport. Electronic timetables are provided at over 100 stops around Malmö, providing passengers with accurate and up-to-date information on arrival times. As an extra incentive for bus use, the city has given buses priority at traffic lights. Lights are equipped with radars that sense bus arrival, and in turn prompt lights to turn green.

Cycling is another important form of transportation for residents of Västra Hamnen. Malmö as a whole is considered one of the world's leading bicycle cities, with 420 kilometers (260 miles) of cycle paths. Within Västra Hamnen alone there are 8,185 meters (26,850 feet) of newly built laneways. Cyclists are given priority at traffic lights, with radar sensors detecting their approach, causing lights to change in their favor. The comfort of cyclists has also been recognized, with resting rails at all traffic lights.

4.5

4.6

4.7

A lack of private parking has been used to discourage car ownership. Parking within BO01 is limited to 0.7 spaces per unit, as opposed to the Malmö average of 1.1. This space limit was too ambitious of the developer, and a greater than expected level of car ownership has forced a new multi-level parking garage to be built. Newer additions to Västra Hamen have been allotted an increased 0.75 spaces per unit.

A green car-sharing service has also been established. One location outside of BO01 offers seven cars and another, near the university, offers one. Vehicles run on either natural gas or E85 fuel, consisting of 85 percent ethanol and 15 percent petroleum. A survey has shown that car sharing has grown from 28 percent in 2003 to nearly 47 percent in 2008.

Västra Hamnen is within close proximity to various transit hubs. It is located 1 kilometer (0.62 miles) from Malmö central station and connected to the Øresund Bridge via city tunnel. The tunnel is six kilometers (3.7 miles) long and consists of 17 kilometers (10.6 miles) of railway.

Though Västra Hamnen's planners were slightly overambitious with their goal of 0.7 vehicles per household, their efforts have still, on the whole, been quite effective in limiting car use within the community. Pedestrians, cyclists, and public transport have been given priority over private vehicles and the rate of car ownership has been lowered significantly from the Malmö average. Västra Hamnen has established Malmö as a leader in sustainable and car-free living.

Figure 4.8:
A typical shared street.

Figure 4.9:
Shared street.

Figure 4.10:
Landscaped canals run along the streets.

Figure 4.11:
Bicycle storage area.

Figure 4.12:
Many of the buildings have businesses on lower floors.

4.10

4.8

4.9

4.11

4.12

Figure 4.13:
Apartment buildings with lower level businesses.

Figure 4.14:
Shared street.

Figure 4.15:
Pedestrian passageway between apartment buildings.

Figure 4.16:
Play area in the heart of the community.

Figure 4.17:
Public art in a passageway.

Figure 4.18:
Detail of a water-harvesting canal along the pathway.

4.13

4.14

4.16

4.17

4.15

4.18

4B

Project:
Stellwerk 60

Location:
Cologne, Germany

Design Firm:
Kontrola Treuhand/BPD
Immobilienentwicklung
GmbH

Figure 4.19:
Site plan.

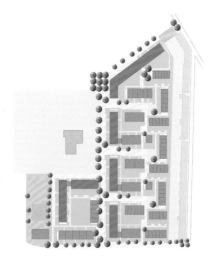

Stellwerk 60 is a car-free community within the city of Cologne, Germany. The absence of pollution and noise produced by cars, as well as the family-friendly environment, are often cited as primary reasons for moving to the area. Residents must sign a contract promising that they will not bring a car into the community, and non-car-owners must sign an additional contract ensuring that they will not attempt to park a car in the surrounding area. It is clear that living a car-free lifestyle is a choice in this community, rather than a necessity.

Retractable bollards were installed at each of the community's three entry points to restrict vehicle entry. There are very few exceptions to the rule, and the bollards are only lowered for emergency and municipal vehicles, as well as one delivery truck with weekly service.

Due to German parking regulations, the developer was asked to include a 120-space parking lot on the outer edge of the community. With 430 housing units, this is an average of about 0.3 spaces per residence; 0.2 for the residents themselves, and 0.1 designated for visitors. Sixteen spaces are offered around the community for the Cambio car-sharing program. Residents are waived of all registration fees and this service is becoming increasingly popular. Those who desire a space must purchase one for a high price and pay an additional monthly maintenance fee. These charges were deemed fit to represent the true cost of managing a parking lot on valuable urban land. All of these spaces have been sold.

Easily accessible public transit offers residents a connection to the city. Every unit is located within 500 meters (1,640 feet) of a heavy rail system, offering S-bahn (train) and Straßenbahn (metro) service, for which trains arrive every five minutes. A bus stop serving three routes is positioned at the north entrance of the community. Excluding a tram route around the periphery of the city, every transit stop offers step-free access. Monthly transit passes are cheaper than the usual costs a car-owner must pay on the running costs of a car each month.

A shared cycle and pedestrian path offers connection to the city from the southwest entrance. With the city center only ten to twelve minutes away by bicycle, cycling is a popular option amongst residents. Streets surrounding the community are designed in the favor of cyclists rather than cars. The streets are traffic calmed using humps and/or one way for automobiles. Most of the streets offer contra-flow bike lanes, allowing cyclists to take the route of least resistance, while forcing cars to take more roundabout paths. There is an average of one bicycle space provided per 30 square meters (323 sqare feet) of living space. The bulk of this space is provided by parking cellars, with an additional three racks outside each unit.

As deliveries are not permitted within Stellwerk 60 (with the exception of the weekly beverage truck), a trolley rental service is offered free to residents. Deliveries can be dropped off at the southwest entrance, from which residents can take their packages by trolley.

Though the community still allows its residents access to cars, several more appealing methods of transportation are available. As a result, car ownership in Stellwerk 60 is 20 percent of that in its district. This community serves as evidence that car-free communities are no longer a utopian vision, but a very attainable reality.

4.21

4.20 (above)

4.22 (below)

Figure 4.20:
Pedestrian passage view.

Figure 4.21:
View of a courtyard.

Figure 4.22:
Pedestrian passage view and an apartment building.

Figure 4.23:
Apartment building façade.

4.23

4.25

Figure 4.24:
Solar panels on façade.

Figure 4.25:
Solar panels also serving as a shading device.

Figure 4.26:
Façade of an apartment building A.

Figure 4.27:
Façade of an apartment building B.

4.27

4.24

4.26

4C

Project:
Grow Community

Location:
Bainbridge, Washington, USA

Design Firm:
Davis Studio Architecture and Design

Washington's Grow Community is recognized as one of the most sustainable developments in the United States. Located on Bainbridge Island, a short ferry ride from Seattle's business district, Grow Community offers its residents a small-town feel without small-town isolation (urban life being a boat trip away). The 131-unit neighborhood was planned with the intention of offering residents "one planet living," a lifestyle geared toward consuming within the bounds of our earth's resources. Currently, if every person on the planet used our planet's resources at the same rate as North Americans, 4.5 planets would be needed. An emphasis has been placed on what the developer calls "five-minute living." That is the notion that all amenities are accessible within five minutes, from any point in the community.

To reduce travel distances and to meet this five-minute requirement, the developer incorporated many urban amenities into the plan. These include grocery stores, schools, a library, restaurants, shops—even a farmer's market. The farmer's market provides residents access to locally grown food, and the grocery store is stocked with low-carbon food that requires a short travel distance. Eggs are even delivered weekly to the community center by a local farmer for pickup. Further, residents are encouraged to take part in local vegetable patches. This combination is expected to reduce consumption of high carbon foods by 70 percent.

The community is well connected by a series of bicycle and pedestrian paths. These paths are meant to provide ample transportation to residents as well as foster a sense of community. Houses, as well as public and private gardens, are placed along the paths. Residents can also use the trails to reach the main street, Madison Avenue, itself a pleasant stroll lined by shops and amenities.

Public transport and car sharing are an important part of the car-free lifestyle offered by Grow Community. Ferries connecting Bainbridge Island with the Seattle central business district leave every hour. This service makes living in Grow Community and working in downtown Seattle very achievable, even without a car. Once downtown, workers and visitors can rely on the Seattle public transport system. Grow Community aims to have many of its residents work within close proximity of their home, both stimulating the local economy and eliminating the need for lengthy commutes.

Figure 4.28:
Site plan.

4.29

4.30

4.31

4.32

Figure 4.29:

Open space in front of rowhouses.

Figure 4.30:

A pathway between homes.

Figure 4.31:

A connection between the main pathway and a home.

Figure 4.32:

Public space for community gathering.

Family living was another of the developer's primary concerns and plays a role in its encouragement of a car-free lifestyle. Children are able to play in the streets without parents having to be concerned about their being endangered by local traffic. The aforementioned "five-minute living" mode of design betters family life as well. Childcare centers are within five minutes of many businesses and homes. With such an arrangement, it is not unimaginable that parents check in on their children during their lunch breaks—such is the convenience and tight-knit nature created by clustered amenities. It is little wonder that young families are one of Grow Community's primary markets.

After moving to Grow Community, it is expected that residents will reduce their greenhouse gas emissions 76 percent by the year 2020. By 2016, it is expected that car ownership will be down to 0.6 cars per living unit, an impressive statistic when compared to the American average of 2.28.

Figure 4.33:
Community gardens

Figure 4.34:
Row of homes with solar panels.

Figure 4.35:
Homes facing the community garden.

Figure 4.36:
Homes facing additional community planting area.

Figure 4.37:
Community car share.

Figure 4.38:
Residents working in the garden.

Figure 4.39:
Dusk view of homes from the southwest.

Figure 4.40:
Rowhousing facing the park.

4.33

4.37

4.34

4.38

4.35

4.39 (above)   4.40 (below)

4.36

4D

Project:
Slateford Green

Location:
Edinburgh, Scotland, UK

Design Firm:
Hackland and Dore Architects

Figure 4.41:
Context plan.

Figure 4.42:
Detail site plan.

Figure 4.43:
Aerial view of scheme prior to completion of landscaping.

Figure 4.44:
Corner of scheme looking down street by railway.

Slateford Green was designed as a car-free community in the Gorgie district of Edinburgh, 3 kilometers (1.9 miles) from the city center. The neighborhood features 120 residential units constructed purely out of prefabricated elements. A two- to four-story housing line surrounds gardens in the center of the community, which is itself situated in a natural landscape. Sustainability and efficiency were the first principles of its creation.

A competition was held amongst Scottish and Dutch architects to design a car-free community in Edinburgh with an aim to decongest vehicle traffic in the city. The developer hoped to create a place that could illustrate the benefits of car-free living to the city as a whole. This was obviously a successful venture—today, six more communities around Edinburgh have been planned that promote a car-free lifestyle. The competition also stated that the community must be barrier free and low maintenance. Thirty-nine of the housing units are shared ownership, the other twelve are privately owned, with fourteen units designed with assisted living in mind. The site is on a former railway storage facility.

4.43

4.41

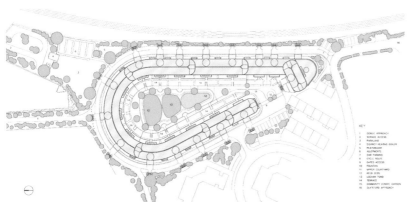

4.42

4.44

Figure 4.45:

View from second floor window to courtyard.

Figure 4.46:

View along shared surface pedestrian street looking north.

Figure 4.47:

View along shared surface pedestrian street looking north.

Figure 4.48:

View from window across courtyard.

Figure 4.49:

View along shared surface pedestrian street looking south.

4.45

4.46

Residents are highly discouraged from owning an automobile. They are allowed to purchase a car if they please, but a lack of parking and ample access to alternative transportation renders doing so impractical. If they wish to use a car, it is expected that they participate in a citywide car club. Plans for the initial car club unfortunately fell through, but efforts are being made to set up a new one. There is no on-site parking, with the exception of a few spaces for residents and visitors. This is thanks to an expansion of section 75 of the *Town and Country Planning Act 1997,* which allowed the number of parking spaces per housing limit to be minimal: 0.1. It is important to note that vehicle access to the community is granted for emergency and service vehicles. As well, a number of parking spaces are located outside of the community but are exclusively for health and maintenance workers.

Many goods and services are available within close proximity to Slateford Green. A childcare center is within the community and a primary school is 500 meters (1,640 feet) away. Recreation facilities are located nearby. These include a public park, football field, and bowling yard—all within 1 kilometer (0.62 miles). Shops, grocery stores, and a shopping center are in one of the surrounding neighborhoods. Several bus lines run along the roads bordering the community. Using the bus service, the city center can be reached within ten minutes. The main transit station is located less than 3 kilometers (1.86 miles) away.

Slateford Green has been a successful experiment in car-free living within Edinburgh. As aforementioned, an additional six communities have been planned in the same spirit. Unfortunately, however, the city of Edinburgh has lost much of its interest in car-free communities. Traffic congestion in the city remains a prevalent issue that has yet to be resolved.

4.47

4.48

4.49

Figure 4.50:
Perspective.

Figure 4.51:
View of the courtyard.

Figure 4.52:
A resident enjoying the gardens.

4.50

4.51

4.52

Summary and Key Considerations

- Car-free neighborhoods are a sustainable solution to the increasing financial and environmental costs of fuel. They also improve residents' quality of life.

- Parking lots and streets that contribute to the urban heat island effect—wherein urban areas become warmer than surrounding rural areas—can be designed to become open spaces shared between pedestrians and motorists.

- Driving can be discouraged by reducing automobile speed limits, increasing parking charges, automobile taxation, and strict land-use policies.

- The Dutch concept of *woonerf*, meaning "streets for living," allows pedestrians, bicycles, transit vehicles, and automobiles to share the street, with no distinction made between sidewalks and car lanes. They rely on narrow streets and gentle curves to slow traffic and create a safer environment for pedestrians and bicyclists.

- To create pedestrian-friendly and car-free streets, a neighborhood must be walkable. Residents should have the opportunity to live, work, play, and shop within minutes of walking from their homes.

- Walkability and the use of bicycles can be encouraged by including traffic calming measures, the installation of 15 km/h or 30 km/h (9.32 mph or 18.64 mph) zones, congestion charging, the placement of bicycle lanes on major streets, and giving priority to the rights and safety of vulnerable road users as opposed to vehicles.

- Another method to discourage the use of cars is to carefully place parking spaces. It is also notable that parking lots are a problem in and of themselves—their environmental impacts have become increasingly apparent. This is especially alarming given that they have become a dominant feature of contemporary urban and suburban landscapes.

- Parking should be located at the rear of a store in an attempt to both physically and socially place the pedestrian first. Similarly, in a residential setting, alleys or lanes built behind homes can provide homes with rear parking, thereby reducing the lot's width.

Exercises

1. List and analyze the effects of extensive use of private motor vehicles on the environment, people's health, the economy, and local sense of place. Use communities in your area and local statistics to illustrate your points.

2. Using a community in your area with poor public transit service, demonstrate how it can be reorganized for improvement. Pay special attention to routes, bus stops, and links to pedestrian paths.

3. Using a neighborhood in your area, demonstrate how it can be made car-free or have shared streets by using the various measures that were listed in the chapter.

4. In the community that you studied in question 3, demonstrate how the public parking area can be redesigned to turn it into open space used for play, for example.

5. List measures and strategies relevant to your area that can improve walkability and the safe use of bicycles.

Chapter 5
Creative Open Spaces

Open spaces are essential to the residents' quality of life. Indeed, their contribution to human physical and mental health has been considered vital for centuries: Exposure to natural areas was once used to treat diseases brought on by the poor urban hygiene of days past. Today, while cities in developed nations no longer suffer from these poor sanitary conditions, the health benefits of green space remains. Further, we now understand their ecological, social, and economic importance. Indeed, these spaces are more essential elements of the neighborhood than ever, given the present shift toward greater building density. This chapter will elaborate on the benefits of green spaces and explain the best practices with which to plan them.

Rethinking Open Spaces

Green areas improve a community's sustainability in many ways; for one, they mitigate the urban heat island effect. The annual air temperature of a city with a population of one million or more can be 1 to 3°C (1.8 to 5.4°F) warmer than surrounding areas (Peck and Kuhn 2008). Urban heat islands can also harmfully affect communities by contributing to summer peak energy demands, air conditioning costs, air pollution, greenhouse gas emissions, heat-related illness, and water quality. Strategically placed trees and shrubbery help alleviate heat peaks, as shaded surfaces are 11 to 25°C (20 to 45°F) cooler than materials exposed to direct sunlight (Bollerud 2013).

Another way in which open areas contribute to neighborhood sustainability is in their encouragement of an active lifestyle. Public health, planning, and community design are closely linked, and a sustainable community with green spaces can help tackle health inequalities, from obesity to mental health. Well-planned neighborhoods with high pedestrian activity and bike riding reduce automobile usage. Greener and accessible special environments ensure that new developments encourage physical activity and healthy living (City of Bloomington 2013).

A continuous landscape of greenery helps preserve the biodiversity of an area (Urban Design Tools 2012), allowing various species to survive and circulate much as they do in wilder spaces. Continuity of such open space can be difficult to accomplish in high-density developments, but it is achievable if corridors of greenery are combined with walkways to link urban green patches to big parks outside the community. The use of indigenous plants in landscape design helps other local flora and fauna survive.

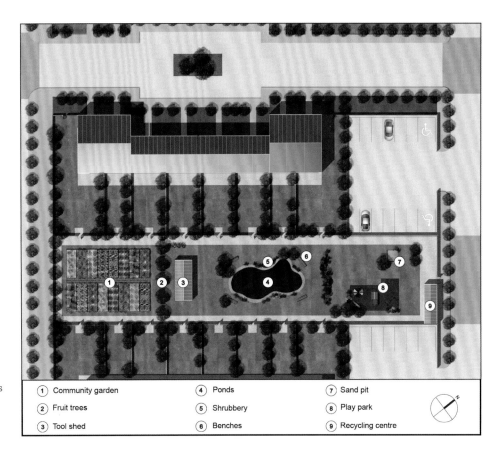

(1)	Community garden	(4)	Ponds	(7)	Sand pit
(2)	Fruit trees	(5)	Shrubbery	(8)	Play park
(3)	Tool shed	(6)	Benches	(9)	Recycling centre

Figure 5.1:

Community gardens and play areas can be shared, individual, or both, as illustrated in this project designed by the author in Middlesex Center, Ontario, Canada.

The economic advantages offered by green spaces are closely linked to their environmentally sustainable features. For instance, the incorporation of urban agriculture into designs (see Chapter 10) can save residents food costs (and reduce food transportation costs in a city's economy at large) while improving food security and lowering fuel consumption (De la Salle and Holland 2010). Green spaces can also be used to recover water runoff, in effect acting as a natural drainage system, and in doing so provide savings from reduced stormwater management (Corbett and Corbett 2000). Forward-thinking landscape design can further reduce maintenance costs; for example, planting xerophyte instead of grass reduces irrigation demands (Figure 5.2) (Gleick 2010). In circumstances wherein residents are able and willing, responsibility for the maintenance of a semi-public or public green space can be distributed among its beneficiaries, again lowering upkeep expenses.

As mentioned earlier, open spaces confer significant psychological benefits. Green areas can counter the effects of crowding in high-density housing environments. Further, Lindsay et al. (2010) identified people's ability to control their built environment as one of the most important factors to mitigate the effects of crowding. In other words, the availability of green space empowers people, ensuring they no longer feel confined in small apartments but instead have the opportunity to dramatically change their surroundings at will. Moreover, boundaries created by vegetation give residents a greater sense of control and privacy all while enhancing the sense of community and addressing security concerns (Russ 2002).

A sense of community is established from shared outdoor spaces, which encourage interaction among residents. Marcus (2003) maintains that shared green spaces beyond private backyards are a critical component of community, and they permit people to share facilities that they would not be able to afford on their own. Small children also benefit from interacting with nature and other children, an opportunity greatly beneficial to achieving healthy personal development. The benefits children experience from shared spaces also transfer to their parents. Greener neighborhoods engage their residents, propelling them to be active outdoors and engaged in socializing events and contributing to social sustainability (Piedmont-Palladino and Mennel 2009).

Planning Open Spaces

The first decision in planning open spaces involves the amount of land that will be devoted to green area. A minimum public space requirement does not imply that the land be consolidated into one large park. Often, it is better to distribute the green space throughout a development and in multiple areas creating a variety of smaller, human-scaled places that address the needs of every resident (Figure 5.3). To retain the intimacy of a neighborhood, the size of shared common space should not exceed 50 meters by 50 meters (164 feet by 164 feet). Proper scale can be ensured through the use of height-to-width ratios. A ratio of 1:3 to 1:5 for common space within a medium- to high-density development can also be considered (Russ 2002). Some municipalities also mandate that each dwelling unit have individual outdoor space. For example, the Canadian City of Vancouver's Land Use and Development Policies and Guidelines (2005) require that each unit will be provided with a minimum private area of 10 square meters (107 sqare feet).

Figure 5.2:
Landscaping of open spaces can consider future upkeep costs by planting xerophyte plant material, which reduces irrigation needs and maintenance expenses.

Figure 5.3:

An approach to planning open spaces is to distribute them throughout a development and in each create a variety of smaller, human-scaled areas that address the needs of every resident.

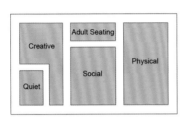

Linear space

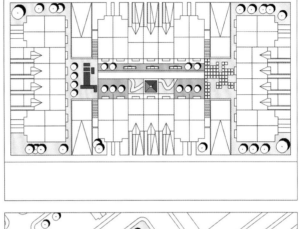

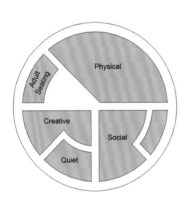

Circular space

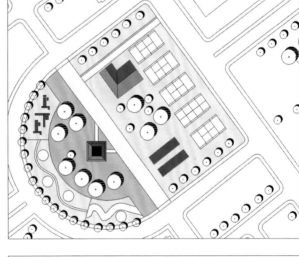

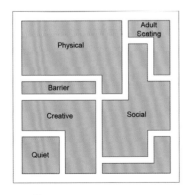

Square space

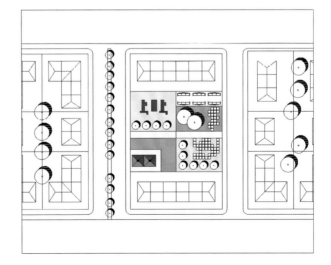

Figure 5.4:

Various approaches for the integration of open spaces in design are available to planners based on the overall concept selected for the community.

Green belt

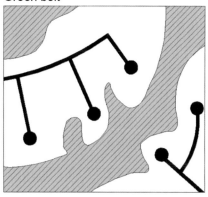
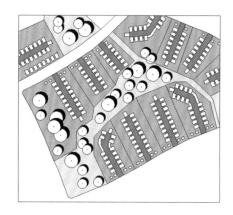

Separate patches

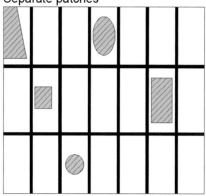
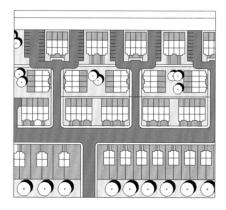

Hierarchy

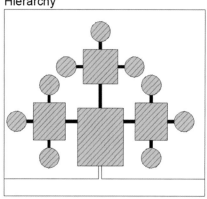
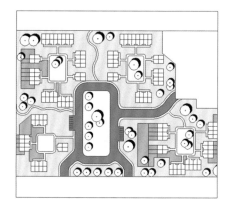

Composite urban

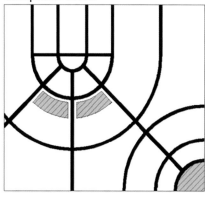
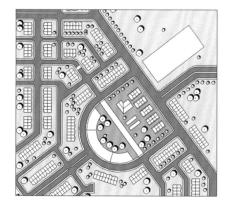

Open spaces need to be planned in accordance with residents' variable lifestyles and life stages. A divide between areas for intimate versus lively activity should be physically represented in the space. Vegetation can act as a buffer between passive sections—for leisurely picnics and reading—and active areas—for walking and biking. Passive sections are better suited to contained areas far from roads.

Just as spaces can be designed to suit activities, they might also be configured for a specific user group—especially for children of different ages, who might spend more playtime outdoors (Russ 2002). Infant play spaces require areas for adults to supervise and relax. Preschool play areas should foster physical, creative, and social play, and be located near these children's homes. School-age children require many facilities to host a range of activities, and the distribution of open space for this function will vary between neighborhoods depending on each community's actual demographic profile (and this profile's predicted variations). Weather conditions must also be considered in planning spaces for kids; it is prudent to provide areas with sunlight for sunbathing, swimming, and sports, and shadier spots for sitting and infant play (Lindsay et al. 2010). Green areas within a development can be designed so that the space and homes involved work in conjunction to provide kids with better supervision and thus safety.

Within a residential environment, the transition between private open spaces and public open spaces can be difficult to define. Clearly establishing this distinction within a design will prevent intrusions on private property and preserve both communal and individual senses of identity. Different levels of private space exist based on their physical distribution. *On-grade open space*—front, back, and side yards—in addition to courtyards and patios—help create relationships with neighboring yards. *Above-grade open space*, such as balconies and roof terraces, permit a greater level of privacy and can even offer complete seclusion (Stamm-Teske and Uhlig 2006).

When areas for community garden are provided they can be private, shared, or both (Figure 5.1). Shared garden lots should have a water supply system and a storage area for tools. Rooftop gardens can be considered when on-grade ground space is otherwise occupied (Kwok and Gronkzik 2007).

Various approaches for the integration of open spaces in design are available to planners based on the overall concept selected for the community, as illustrated in Figure 5.4. Green belts, otherwise known as corridors, maximize preservation of the indigenous plants and fauna of each area. The continuous vegetation is the most ecologically friendly configuration of an open space, but it occupies a significant amount of land and reduces the area's density. As well, the green belt tends to border a neighborhood as opposed to integrating within the area. Separate patches of greenery work well with a grid-like street pattern, as they are disconnected and can fit in used spaces. A hierarchical pattern takes advantage of the various types of public and private space and connects large public spaces to medium-sized semi-public space to small private spaces. This hierarchy offers a range of functions to a variety of users and promotes interaction. Finally, a composite urban configuration, suited to large developments, connects clusters of communal facilities and plazas but tends to ignore a site's natural characteristics.

The size of an outdoor area depends on the site's natural characteristics and the surrounding level of density. High-density developments require more open space. Similarly, if, for example, a project is located near other high-density developments, more land should be dedicated to open spaces than if the mid-density dwellings were encircled by single-family detached homes. According to Hinshaw et al. (1998), in a mid-density development, 15 to 25 percent of the site should be dedicated to open spaces, and the variance depends on surrounding density. An alternative method of calculating the green space needed is to measure by density.

Different methods of landscape design can be used to establish those ratios. Conservation design calls for the maintenance of the original landscape by designing buildings around nature, as opposed to leveling an entire site. Although initial land costs might be elevated, landscaping and design expenses are significantly reduced. An alternative method by which to create multi-function open spaces in an urban context is the use of paved areas such as parking lots and pedestrian streets (Moughtin 2003).

The residential front yard is a significant consideration in that it is a transition zone between the home's private and public realms. It links residents to the social life of the neighborhood in providing opportunity for social interaction. Yet, it also still operates as a buffer zone, giving occupants privacy. Even when the building is "pushed" forward to accommodate a larger backyard space, the identity of the front yard can be maintained with landscaping or fencing. The demarcation provided by the home's front entrance can be achieved with a step, porch, or other carefully selected detailing. When private open space in the front is highly limited, balconies can provide valuable outdoor areas.

In the backyard, the importance of visual privacy can be achieved with hedges, fences, screens, and trellises, which offer a sense of enclosure for personal activities and domestic chores. Where patios and decks are available, sliding glass doors can provide a direct link to and/or extension of the kitchen or living room. Backyards can be further enhanced by creative landscaping, covered patio space, or facility for the storage of outdoor equipment. *Microclimate* is another consideration in the design of this area: Shelter from the wind and snow, in addition to a careful balance of sun and shade, provides orientations that extend seasonal use.

It is clear that the planning and provision of open spaces in higher-density housing developments require much care and thought. Private outdoor space, whether in the forms of front or backyards, patios, decks, balconies, or roof terraces, must be provided along with public outdoor space, which can be implemented in a variety of spatial patterns. Additionally, the design of the landscape itself, including man-made features and vegetation, should be functional and aesthetically appealing to create an inviting environment.

5A

Project:
HafenCity

Location:
Hamburg, Germany

Design Firm:
KCAP/ASTOC

The HafenCity district redevelopment project in Hamburg, Germany is breathing new life into a forgotten industrial area. The site was once considered to be on the fringe of the city, but thanks to ample public transport connection it is now in proximity to the urban center. The western portion of the development is almost complete and is currently active. The eastern area poses more of a challenge, as it is not as integrated with the city but will soon be redeveloped in a similar fashion as the west.

A master plan was approved by the city council and places a focus on pedestrian experience. A network of open spaces of various sizes links pedestrians throughout the development. Many of the district's privately owned spaces serve partially public functions due to a "right of way" policy. For instance, pedestrians and cyclists are allowed to pass through private spaces between buildings, ensuring easy commutes by foot or bike. The unclear nature of private versus public space helps to open the site to a broader community.

Public spaces in the west of the development have been a huge success. The entire harbor serves as a public space, creating a pleasant environment for residents, workers, and visitors. A 340 meter (1,115 foot) long landscape has been created using pontoons, and is connected to the land by historic bridges. The two harbor terraces—named after the famous explorers Magellan and Marco Polo—function as basins and have been designed to give a sense of landscape to both land and water. The Magellan terrace fosters an urban feel, with steps descending down into the water, creating an amphitheater-like space. The Marco Polo terraces are greener and perhaps more inviting. Wooden decks and grass-covered surfaces create an oasis by the water, encouraging pedestrians to sit down and relax. A variety of plants, including willow trees, have been planted to provide shelter from both rain and intense sunlight.

Figure 5.5 (below):
Sketches articulate treatment of each area in the project.

Figure 5.6:
Context model, top view.

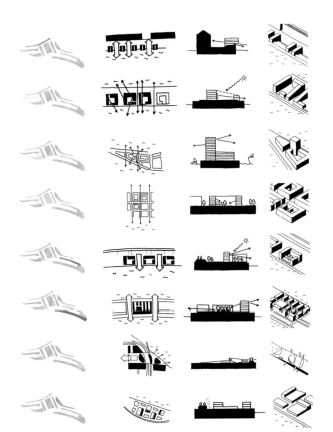

5.6

Figure 5.7:
A passageway between buildings.

Figure 5.8:
View of apartment buildings.

Figure 5.9:
Stairs have been made to act as an amphitheater.

Figure 5.10:
Masterplan.

Figure 5.11:
Public art in one of the public spaces.

Figure 5.12:
View of apartment buildings.

Figure 5.13:
Passageway under an apartment building.

The ample variety of squares and parks helps to establish the district as a cultural center within the city. Larger parks can play host to higher-profile events and concerts, while smaller squares can be utilized for events on a more local scale. The squares around the district have been designed with specific day-to-day functions in mind. For instance, Vasco da Gama Square is focused around a basketball court. Other squares and parks have been created to provide green spaces within the urban center. Sandtorpark serves as an excellent example of this effort: It boasts mounds, trees, and a grass-covered play area as its main features.

HafenCity has created a vibrant and lively district from the remnants of a once rundown and forgotten sector of the city. The development has gained the support and approval of a wider community by giving space back to the public. The bountiful abundance of public space has established HafenCity as an important player in the cultural, residential, and commercial scenes of Hamburg.

5.7

5.8

5.9

5.13

5.10

5.11

5.12

Figure 5.14:
HafenCity main square.

Figure 5.15:
Green gathering space.

5.14

5.15

5B

Project:
Superkilen

Location:
Copenhagen, Denmark

Design Firm:
BIG, Topotek 1, Superflex

Figure 5.16:
Site plan.

Figure 5.17:
Aerial photo of the site.

Superkilen is a 0.8 kilometer (0.5 mile) long park located in Nørrebro, one of the most culturally diverse neighborhoods of Copenhagen, Denmark. Its designers were tasked with improving the infrastructure of the park. In addition, their design functions to foster a sense of community and make an urban statement.

Superkilen is divided into three sections, organized by color: red, black, and green. Each section serves a different purpose, featuring fun and interesting visual cues. As a response to the neighborhood's ethnic diversity, the designers chose to include objects found from sixty different countries from which residents in the area had immigrated. In addition, trees reflecting these various geographical origins have been planted in islands throughout the park, placed closely to the aforementioned cultural artifacts.

In consultation with residents, the firms discovered that improved transportation amenities were a top priority for the population—thus, the creation of transport infrastructure has gone hand-in-hand with the park's development. The park has been used to create several new connections via various modes of transportation. The bike paths in the area have been reorganized to better suit the park and increase efficiency. The park has also created a bus connection for the citizens of Mimersgade, who were previously unserved. Importantly, these connections coordinate nicely with a larger infrastructure plan involving the district.

The first section of the park is the Red Square, which serves as a cultural, sporting, and market destination. It is in fact an outdoor extension of the pre-existing sports and cultural center. Its vast recreational area provides a place for locals to meet one another through games and activities. Its entire surface is covered in an extremely durable rubber allowing for a variety of activities including a winter skating rink. A market is held here every weekend, a popular destination for the residents of Copenhagen and those of its suburbs. It is also a popular spot for screening open-air movies and sporting events. Façades have been incorporated to fit the theme of the area and are painted red. At times, these form a curved surface with the ground to create a truly three-dimensional space. The limits of the square are marked by streets at each end and fences along the side.

5.16

5.17

Figure 5.18:

View of the site with a cycling path.

Figure 5.19:

Elements depicting aspects relevant to the community's residents have been placed on columns.

Figure 5.20:

View of the main area.

Figure 5.21:

Set swings entertain the residents.

5.18

5.19

5.20

The second section, the Black Square, is meant to function as an urban-living space. Features here are similar to the interior furnishings of a house. There are several benches, tables, and even grilling facilities. The bike lane has been shifted to the east for this section in order that it intersects conveniently with another bike lane (and to avoid the square's hills). A mound in the north serves as a popular relaxation point for residents and offers a great view overlooking the square. The designers and residents did not want this section to end in a street, and thus decided to fold the northeast corner up, thus creating a shelter.

The final section, Green Park, is a direct response to residents' wishes for more green space. The area consists of a mostly grass-covered landscape and offers access to several sports and workout facilities. Soft hills and its location adjacent to a local school make Green Park a popular place for children and families.

Superkilen shows how creative open spaces can revitalize struggling communities. The addition of a park creates a more communal feel in the neighborhood while simultaneously improving existing infrastructure. The neighborhood now has a friendly ambience and boasts better transport connections to the rest of the city.

5.21

Figure 5.22:
View of a play structure from above.

Figure 5.23:
Night view of the main area.

Figure 5.24:
A manmade rolling hill attracts
community residents.

5.22

5.23 (above)

5.24 (below)

5C

Project:
Pringle Creek Community

Location:
Salem, Oregon, USA

Design Firm:
Opsis Architecture

Figure 5.25:
Pringle Creek at the heart of the site plan.

Figure 5.26:
A plan demonstrates the potential passive solar gain of the homes.

Figure 5.27:
General view of the community's open space and Painters Hall.

Figure 5.28:
The community's natural open area.

Figure 5.29:
Bioswells on the sides of a road.

The Pringle Creek community, home to 140 units, has been designed such that sustainability fosters a sense of social cohesion and vice versa. The site, which was once the campus of the Oregon Home for Developmentally Disabled Children, has an array of open spaces and prebuilt facilities, both of which were well utilized in the developer's reimagining. A commitment to public space has created a true community in the sense that residents are brought together by their sense of environmental and social responsibility.

The neighborhood was meticulously planned, with the existing landscape thoroughly investigated beforehand. Trees, solar exposure, topography, riparian areas, existing buildings, and roadways were all taken into consideration in the planning process. Most of the pre-existing, mature trees on-site were either set aside and replanted or left in place. In the same spirit, it was important to the developer that many of the site's existing buildings be restored. A total of five were preserved, with two more recycled to build the community's parking lot. Two of these preserved buildings now serve as massive community greenhouses.

Along with the community gardens, these greenhouses provide fresh organic produce to residents. Further, over 300 fruit trees and 200 blueberry bushes have been planted in the 0.8 hectares (two acres) of community land set aside for orchards. There is also a productive relationship between residents of the community and nearby farms. The idea is to create an edible landscape, where food does not have to be sourced from faraway places, thereby lowering the community's carbon footprint. This allows residents convenient food access and decreases their reliance on cars to grocery shop.

5.27

5.28

5.29

5.25

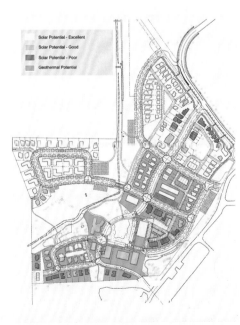

5.26

5.30

Figure 5.30:
Shared open space with
pedestrian path.

Figure 5.31:
Pringle Creek.

5.31

Figure 5.32:
A single-family home in the community.

Figure 5.33:
One of the homes' interiors.

Figure 5.34:
Shading device above windows.

Figure 5.35:
Community gathering in Painters Hall.

Figure 5.36:
Pringle Creek runs alongside Painters Hall and is a salmon-bearing urban stream.

5.32

5.33

5.34

5.35 (above)   5.36 (below)

Head architect James Meyer stated that he thought of the community's open spaces in two ways: "Passive Open Spaces" are undisturbed, naturally occurring places, like the wetlands surrounding the community's creek. "Active Open Spaces" are intentionally placed, for community gatherings and activities. An approximate 4.9 hectares (12 acres) of the community's 12.9 hectares (32 acres) have been dedicated to open space. Meyer believes that spontaneous interactions are an important part of community life and so open space fosters these types of run-ins. Gathering places, whether natural or built, allow residents to socialize with their neighbors and so create a true sense of community. Green roofing also helps contribute to the natural landscape. The community surrounding the neighborhood also benefits from the abundance of open space. People from the surrounding area often come to walk or bike through the trail system or otherwise enjoy its natural landscape.

Pringle Creek has been designed to create a sense of community and preserve the existing environment. Smaller residences help to keep open spaces from which the entire community can benefit and, moreover, are sustainable. Readily available local and organic food allows for a healthier lifestyle. This neighborhood has shown that communal open spaces render better neighborhood interactions and improve residents' quality of life.

5D

Project:
Earthsong Eco-Neighborhood

Location:
Auckland, New Zealand

Design Firm:
Algie Architects Limited

Figure 5.37:
Site plan.

Figure 5.38:
Elevations of terrace
houses—Building D.

Figure 5.39:
Elevations of fourplexes houses.

Earthsong Eco-Neighborhood is a community brought together by a shared desire for a more sustainable lifestyle. The former apple orchard was redeveloped to accommodate thirty-two residential units. A council of future residents was highly involved, advising the architects as to their specific needs. The result is a neighborhood that fosters social and environmental sustainability, creating a community both livable and environmentally conscious.

A sense of community was a driving factor behind the development. Western culture has tended to neglect the importance of neighborly living over the past century. A strong sense of community can help to build a social support system and create a sense of belonging amongst residents. In this instance, the tight-knit community network also creates a collective feeling of responsibility for the surrounding landscape.

The landscape was designed to fit a human scale, with pedestrian accessibility taking a priority. Despite a naturally hilly environment, paths have been sloped at a low gradient and most houses have level entryways, all to allow for increased accessibility. Bunches of two- and three-story houses have been placed along communal courtyards and pedestrian pathways. These shared courtyards facilitate a sense of community, creating spaces to be shared with neighbors in close proximity to the residences. The networks of paths connect residences to their neighbors and various amenities. A strategic planning method helps to distinguish and transition between public and private space.

Community facilities form the heart of the neighborhood, serving to bring the community closer together while offering services not commonly available in private houses. Here, residents can find laundry facilities, a child and teen center, as well as a community garden. One can even find neighborhood meals offered in the facilities twice a week, yet another opportunity for residents to enjoy social interaction and, further, put the beautiful community garden to use.

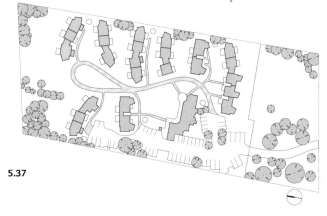

5.37

5.38

5.39

Figure 5.40:
Two rows of terrace houses, showing the gardens between them.

Figure 5.41:
Terrace houses with their gardens, on the northern sunny side.

5.40

5.41

There is no car access within the neighborhood and all car parking has been placed at the edge of the neighborhood. This creates a safer space for children to play. Public transport is in close proximity and minimizes the need for personal car use.

The community was designed to be a self-sustaining natural ecosystem. Permaculture—the creation of agriculturally active ecosystems—was at the heart of the design philosophy. This ecosystem was planned to have a diversity of plants, while maintaining a natural resilience to climate, weather, and other challenges. This allows for organic community gardens, orchards, and even an edible landscape. An organic vegetable collective has been established by a group of residents and a bee farm has also been created. This demonstrates that a diverse and innovative natural environment can create strong community ties.

As the site was previously a neglected apple orchard, efforts were made to salvage all healthy trees (as aforementioned). The presence of adult trees helped project the feeling of an established neighborhood from the start. It is expected that once new plants mature, they will produce a greater amount of food than the apple orchard. There is another improvement on its old form: Earthsong has a high diversity of plants. This is in part a product of the fact that residents can sow anything they desire on their private property so long as they adhere to the community's environmental policies.

Earthsong Eco-Neighborhood demonstrates that a strong link between community involvement and the natural environment can be created through design. One other important element of its success is that residences and infrastructure have been built around the existing landscape, a quality that not many developments can boast. It is an inspiring example of open-space planning.

Figure 5.42:

A view showing the different housing types.

Figure 5.43:

From the upper-level balcony of the Common House, the central path weaves between a fourplex (on the left) and the ends of three rows of terrace houses.

Figure 5.44:

A view of the central path from an apartment's balcony.

Figure 5.45:

Interior of a terrace house, ground floor, with doors to garden.

5.42

5.43

5.44

5.45

Summary and Key Considerations

- Cities no longer suffer from the poor sanitary conditions of the past, but open spaces remain important. Indeed, as density increases in sustainable communities, the need for green areas rises along with it.

- Outdoor areas foster informal interactions, provide space for active play, and can unite a community through a common sense of identity.

- Green areas help mitigate the urban heat island effect and contribute to keeping a neighborhood cool and shaded. Strategically placed trees and shrubbery help alleviate heat peaks, as shaded surfaces are 11 to 25°C (20 to 45°F) cooler than materials exposed to direct sunlight.

- Public health, planning, and community design are closely linked. A sustainable community with green spaces can help tackle health inequalities from obesity to mental health.

- Green spaces can also be used to recover water runoff, acting like a natural drainage system.

- A corridor of greenery allows various species to survive and circulate just as they would have in their original habitats.

- Introducing urban agriculture in open spaces is seen as a solution to improving food security within metropolitan areas and simultaneously lowers transportation costs and fuel consumption.

- A community's general impression psychologically affects its residents, potentially changing the way they feel not only about their own homes but also their own self-worth. This phenomenon is related to the increased value of homes near green areas.

- Often, it is better to distribute the green space throughout a development and in multiple areas creating a variety of smaller, human-scaled places that address the needs of every resident.

- The distribution of open space in each neighborhood will depend on the actual demographic profile and its predicted variations to come. Open spaces must also consider weather conditions—providing areas for sunbathing, swimming, and sports in addition to shadier areas for sitting and infant play.

- Proper shelter from the wind and snow, in addition to a careful balance of sun and shade, provides orientations that extend seasonal use.

- The size of an outdoor area is dependent on both the site's natural characteristics and the surrounding level of density. High-density developments require more open space, and, similarly, if a townhouse project is located near other high-density developments, more land should be dedicated to open spaces than if the townhouses were encircled by single-family detached homes.

- A ratio of 1:3 to 1:5 for common space within a medium- to high-density development can also be considered.

- When a project is located near other high-density developments, more land should be dedicated to open spaces than if the mid-density dwellings were encircled by single-family detached homes.

- Conservation design calls for the maintenance of the original landscape by designing buildings around nature, as opposed to leveling an entire site of a development.

Exercises

1. List the advantages of having green corridors and pay special attention to their contribution to an area's biodiversity. Demonstrate these attributes on an area in your region.

2. In your community, how can the outdoor areas of local schools become accessible to public use?

3. What design guidelines will you introduce to make public open spaces accessible to people of all ages? Draw a diagrammatic illustration of your ideas.

4. Using a neighborhood in your area as an example, demonstrate how several public open spaces of various sizes can be linked to become a network. How will you enhance their landscaping quality?

5. Using Copenhagen's Superkilen design principles, redesign an urban public space in your area.

Chapter 6
Neighborhoods for Change and Growth

Adaptability is a key component of sustainable design. Flexible planning practice is a way to rise to the challenges presented by the ever-changing technological, social, and economic realities of today's urban environments. An adaptable approach may also reduce energy consumption and material usage, a result of its association with long-term planning. This chapter explores design methods that embrace change and thus create resilient neighborhoods.

A Need for Change and Adaptability

Periods of modernization in building method and design are necessary upheavals in the dynamic field of architecture; the adaptability of these methods has itself changed in the course of this more general evolution. After the Second World War, housing demand increased quickly. In response, architects and developers introduced space- and cost-efficient homes that could be built rapidly. Typically, these homes have provided little opportunity for change and adaptability (Friedman 2007).

This problem has special urgency given today's demographic changes. With increasing numbers of nontraditional households—including, notably, singles and single parents—conventionally designed layouts no longer suit the population's needs. Consider also that an increased senior population has created a demand for dwellings that can be adapted to suit the lifestyle of the elderly without requiring costly and intensive alteration (Palmer and Ward 2010).

On the macro scale, neighborhoods also must be flexibly designed to prepare for the innumerable and unpredictable alterations they face over the course of their development. Today, the traditional suburban paradigm is being reconsidered, and thus the development of flexible design practice has become a necessity. Current planning methods are speculative and do not emphasize long-term considerations. Depending on the geographic, cultural, and economic realities in which they are embedded, large-scale developments can take years to build. Therefore, the design of future housing that follows a present procedure is rigid and inappropriate for an unpredictable future.

Concepts rather than concrete suggestions are more suitable guides. Municipal planning methods can be lengthy, and given the time lapse between a project's inception and its execution, the fate of a plan is subject to the whim of changing market demands. Sometimes a development project's relevancy does not even survive the time it takes to be built—this is obviously not an example of an adaptable or resilient community.

Planning Communities for Adaptability

To begin, let us explore current community-planning procedure—its advantages and disadvantages provide a source of inspiration for new, flexible residential-planning methods. Residential developments commonly undergo a time-consuming approval process at the municipal and, occasionally, provincial level. Roads, parks, subdivisions, and facilities are generally placed in this process. Further, lot and structure size must be made to follow zoning laws. Subdivisions are also required to follow a detailed plan that is established alongside the proposed generalities of the development. Following the approval process of these plans, building permits must be acquired (Friedman et al. 2002a). Several years can pass—easily—between the developer's speculations on future housing needs and the completion of a large-scale community.

This approval process is arduous and inflexible, but a new procedure has emerged that is better suited for adaptable communities. First, a broad vision of the community is defined, then key roads and infrastructure established (arterial roads are chosen at a later date). Second, general massing of housing density is laid out, in addition to civic centers and green areas. The community vision, accompanied with a descriptive code, is then presented to the municipality, reviewed, and changed. The community is composed of several subdivisions, all governed by the general code and framed by the rough guidelines of main roads and centers. Subdivisions themselves can develop later in the process, each with their own codes governing the design of individual units.

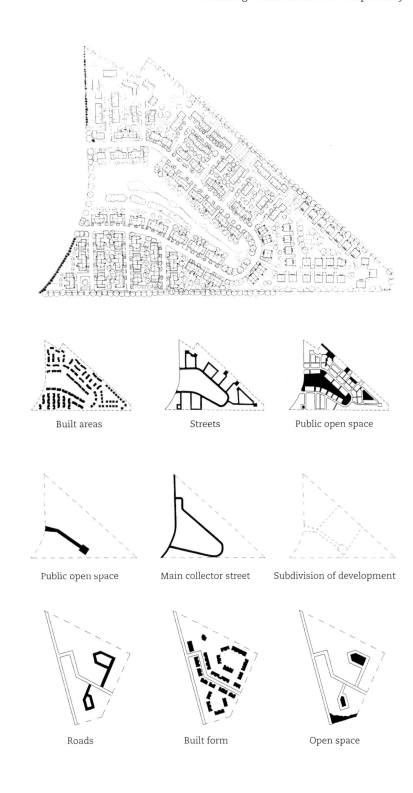

Built areas   Streets   Public open space

Public open space   Main collector street   Subdivision of development

Roads   Built form   Open space

Figure 6.1:

Conventionally detailed planned community (top and second rows), a flexible approach to planning that divides the land to smaller segments (second row from bottom) and design of segment (a) (bottom).

In tandem, verification methods by the city might also be updated. Instead of requiring constant inspection and approval by municipal officers, initiators could be held responsible to the legislation in place, and a punitive system set in place for noncompliance with attendant obligations to conform to regulation and fix any problems. This new design procedure closely resembles anterior municipal-planning methods but would save considerable time, thus making its pace more in-sync with the speed of construction and evolution of social needs. Additionally, this new method would also permit greater individual expression within architecture that is successfully built.

This strategy was implemented in the planning of a community near Montreal, Quebec, by the author, as illustrated in Figure 6.1 (Friedman 2002a). Public green space was defined, in addition to the main collector street, while the rest of the development was subdivided into neighborhoods to be developed as the population increased. As the development of a subdivision began, its secondary roads and semi-public green spaces were defined. So each subdivision was designed prior to construction, and less time passed between the design phase and the completion of the neighborhood.

In order for the neighborhoods to be built in harmony with other subdivisions, the entire development must be governed by a general code while each neighborhood is subject to a more specific code. For example, in the general code, a range of building heights is outlined; while in the neighborhood code, specific height limitations are established. The codes allow designers to respond to the particular needs of each neighborhood while keeping with the rest of the development's character.

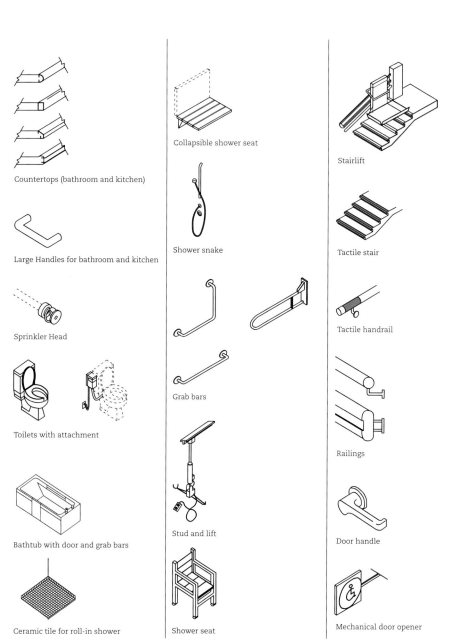

Countertops (bathroom and kitchen)

Large Handles for bathroom and kitchen

Sprinkler Head

Toilets with attachment

Bathtub with door and grab bars

Ceramic tile for roll-in shower

Collapsible shower seat

Shower snake

Grab bars

Stud and lift

Shower seat

Stairlift

Tactile stair

Tactile handrail

Railings

Door handle

Mechanical door opener

Figure 6.2:
A menu showing fixtures that an aging homeowner with reduced mobility might need to facilitate aging in place.

Designing Adaptable Homes

Another method by which to create an adaptable community is to ensure a multitude of building types. Different housing forms—from apartment buildings to row houses, detached to semi-detached housing—permit members of a community to follow the fluctuations of the housing market. Further, this variation allows a wider demographic access to a neighborhood. In turn, the more varied the population, the more economically resilient the community—consider that economic changes tend to disadvantage demographics unevenly. Through the practices outlined in the preceding paragraphs, neighborhoods will be better prepared for the inevitable shifts and growth.

Flexibility is also a desirable quality in a home. Occupants' needs evolve over time. A design that anticipates and allows for these changes reduces cost and investment (Schneider and Till 2005). For instance, an aging homeowner's mobility might be reduced and require the installation of fixtures that facilitate aging in place, as illustrated in Figure 6.2. A young family might require many bedrooms, but as children grow up, these are then transformed into rented or office space. Like in the design of a new community, key aspects of the house must be established that consider any possible future adaptations such as circulation, services, materials, light, and ventilation. For example, concrete blocks and masonry limit the changes possible to partition walls, unlike gypsum walls and prefabricated systems that are more easily disassembled (Friedman 2002).

The two common approaches to a dwelling's transformation are variations of the *add-on* and *add-in* methods, as illustrated in Figure 6.3. The add-on building method refers to the addition of rooms to an original structure. The flexibility of the home relies on provisions made for future growth in the original design, and in which direction the growth would take place. This method can be costly and requires a large-enough lot from the beginning. However, its smaller initial investment can appeal to first-time homeowners and those who do not require a large amount of space. The add-in building method refers to leaving spaces unfinished, such as attics and basements, which can later be converted into livable spaces. This method requires a larger initial investment in space and structure, but future investments are smaller (Friedman 2001). The unfinished spaces must be carefully considered so that they do no impede on the quality of life of those dwelling in finished spaces. In short, while each has its merits, both the add-in and add-on strategy can respond to the many stages of life—from the need for a home office or nursery, then a guest room, to the downsizing of one's home to rent space out.

Unlike the design of flexible communities, suggestions regarding the design of adaptable homes do not need to be limited to conceptual procedures; rather, advice can be more concrete regarding physical formats. Many different aspects of a home are affected and must be considered in order for a home to be made truly adaptable. Circulation, main utilities, condition of attachment, entries, windows, and stairs are some of the most important aspects of a structure that can be designed for flexibility—considerations we will here consider in turn.

In regard to circulation, consider the placement of new rooms in a future expansion. Rooms should be accessible through a corridor, not by another room. Circulation should also anticipate any possible accessibility needs. If owners foresee living in their home through old age, it might be prudent to widen corridors for wheelchair access. Further, stairs are expensive to install, and the structural preparation for a staircase can be constructed without the installation of the staircase.

Main services, such as bathrooms, should be centralized so that with the addition of more rooms they will still be accessible to a structure's original rooms. Using the same logic, if an expansion is planned for the rear of a home, its bathroom should be originally placed near the back, making it centralized with the addition of more rear rooms. A similar principle applies to heating and other mechanical systems, though these systems might also be placed so that they are accessed through a separate entry (in case of any future division of the home).

The condition of attachment between dwellings affects the types of expansion possible. Detached homes can expand horizontally as far as their lots and municipal regulations allow, while it is more difficult to expand a row house—unless the row house was built with a back alcove or staggered. In a truly flexible structure, units would be able to expand both vertically and horizontally. More flexible design codes would allow for vertical expansion, and small, separate units to be used as office space.

Door and window placement can also constrain the division of a home into more units and so must be considered in the original design if one hopes to expand a structure in future. For example, two small windows are preferable to one large window so that the space is not limited in regards to future subdivision (Friedman 2002)—though this is on the condition that the room is at least 5.5 meters (18 feet) wide. Windows must provide enough light for the purpose of the room; this can vary, for instance, between a bedroom and living room. Doors should anticipate divisions of property, and, further, ancillary entrances are a benefit in case of a division.

Adaptable design has historical roots in the architecture of the multi-unit plexes of the early twentieth century. During this period, a single occupant would own and manage an entire household while keeping tenants on their upper floors. Each unit of a plex had its own entrance and staircase. The front of the units were occupied by a multi-purpose living space, while main services—the kitchen, laundry, and bathrooms—were placed in the rear of the unit. The multi-purpose area allowed renters to arrange their living space to suit their individual needs. This plex design has endured a century; few changes have been necessary to this arrangement of interior space to accommodate contemporary living.

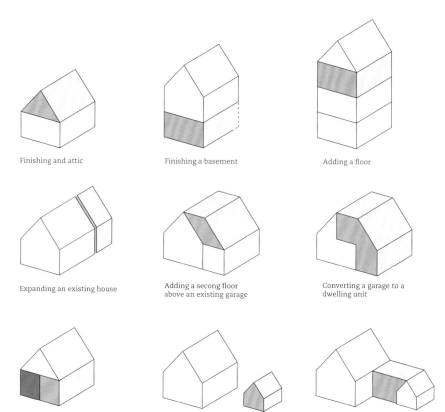

Finishing and attic

Finishing a basement

Adding a floor

Expanding an existing house

Adding a second floor above an existing garage

Converting a garage to a dwelling unit

Dividing an existing house into two dwelling units

Constructing an ancillary unit

Connecting an ancillary unit to a main house

Figure 6.3:

The two common approaches to a dwelling's transformation are variations of add-on and the add-in methods.

The interior adaptability of a room is a desirable quality even if it is not designed to withstand dramatic changes like ownership or main function. Rooms are constantly subject to smaller adaptations—their furniture rearranged to take advantage of the sun, or to better accommodate contemporary innovations and technologies. A big factor here is consumerism: This hallmark of contemporary Western life creates shifting lifestyle preferences and attitudes that can greatly affect the use and layout of rooms even over short periods of time. Prefabricated products can enable us to make these sorts of relatively quick reconfigurations and redecorations easily. Thus, rooms that are designed to the proportions of prefabricated products allow for greater interior flexibility.

The Next Home, designed and constructed on the campus of the McGill School of Architecture, in Montreal, Canada, can be subdivided and rearranged before and during occupancy, as illustrated in Figure 6.4. The structure of the building can be converted into a single-family home, a duplex, or a triplex. The flexibility of this arrangement responds to the demands of a diverse range of occupants, including single people looking to purchase a home at an affordable price. A modular size of 6.1 meters by 12.2 meters (20 feet by 40 feet) was chosen to allow for greater flexibility in the floor plan and reduce waste (Friedman 2007). The 6.1 meter (20 feet) width permits an open space free of load-bearing walls, and open-web floor joists and a horizontal chaser allow the main utilities to be located at any position on each floor. Stairs are located alongside the length of the wall, adjacent to the entrance, increasing floor space. Adding stairs is possible—even following any post-occupancy alterations to the housing arrangement—given that floor joists are doubled up in preparation for additional staircases. To respond to the range of occupants, a diverse amount of interior components is made available to residents, who choose them according to their direct needs, such as home office layouts or an extra bathroom. The façade of each row house has also been made flexible in an effort to prevent the aesthetic monotony created by repetitive structures: Occupants choose from a range of windows, add-on elements, and roof variations. The Next Home successfully integrates and illustrates the concepts described in the preceding paragraphs, demonstrating that flexibility in use, appearance, and layout is not only an attractive quality but also entirely possible.

In summary, for communities to be adaptable, they must utilize a faster development-planning procedure; for a home to be adaptable, its interior configuration must be amenable to expansion and conversion. These methods by which to achieve adaptability are, in fact, measures that achieve sustainability of all kinds. Resources—both natural and financial—are extremely effectively managed with these strategies. Wasteful home construction and renovation are avoided. Energy and material usage is decreased. Adaptable approaches to community planning create resilient spaces that rise to meet the social and economic challenges of tomorrow. We here tour some such success stories.

Single Family House · Ground level · First level · Second level · Mezannine

Duplex · Basement · Ground level · First level · Mezannine

Triplex · Basement · Ground level · First level · Mezannine

Figure 6.4:

The Next Home is a three-story structure that can be configured as a single-family, two-family, or three-family dwelling. It also permits transformation from one arrangement to another in later years.

6A

Project:
Benny Farm

Location:
Notre-Dame de Grace,
Montreal, Canada

Design Firm:
Saia and Barbarese Architects

Figure 6.5:
The Benny Farm development's
site plan.

Figure 6.6:
A building in the Benny Farm project
prior to the start of renewal.

Figure 6.7:
During the retrofitting process
the buildings in Benny Farm were
stripped of their exterior claddings.
The same bricks were reused in the
reconstruction.

The Benny Farm project was built between 1946 and 1947 to house Canadian Second World War veterans. The community functioned well and was enjoyed by many residents over the years. Over time, the buildings could no longer satisfy the needs of veterans and was unable to attract new clientele. The property owner, Canada Mortgage and Housing Corporation (CMHC), had plans to demolish the existing structures and build a luxurious complex. Following strong local opposition, the project ground to a halt. Shortly thereafter, the site was sold to the Canada Lands Company (CLC), a federal government agency, for the creation of low- to medium-income housing. Some existing structures were sold to local nonprofit organizations and the rest developed according to a comprehensive master plan. The plan served to create 535 affordable dwellings.

Intensive research of the socio-economic conditions and architectural character of the project's site—the Notre-Dame de Grace area of Montreal—was conducted prior to the design of the master plan. It was found that the majority of

patrons in the area are small, young families and seniors. The two main dwelling typologies were single family housing and duplexes. Research also revealed balconies to be an important architectural element, as they played a crucial role in the social culture of Notre-Dame de Grace.

The findings concluded that a range of dwellings was required to fit this demographic variety. Rather than create units that catered to only one type of resident, the architects realized a more efficient, cost-effective method to accommodate all demographics. Various dwelling types, each tailored to a particular lifestyle and budget, were laid out. Units were placed both on top of one another and in adjacent formations. This allowed patrons the choice of purchasing one unit (for, say, a smaller family or single resident) or multiple units. And herein lies the genius: These multiple units could then be linked together at a low cost. For instance, if a family found that their current unit size no longer suited their needs, they could purchase an extra unit at a later date.

6.6

6.5

6.7

105

Figure 6.8:

A structure made up of old retrofitted section (left) and a new one (right).

Figure 6.9:

New section (left) joins an old building section (right).

Figure 6.10:

New three-family units.

6.8

6.9

6.10

A variety of other strategies further drove down unit costs. For one, some of the apartments were left with unfinished spaces. This drove down the construction costs and allowed residents to finish the apartments when they could afford the time and money. In addition, reversibility of the design allowed even further multi-functionality. Kitchens could be placed in the front or back of the residences depending on the owner's preference. In addition, the development used back-to-back plumbing fixtures and recycled materials where possible.

Given the demographic variety within the community, the developer decided it would be best to place people with similar needs in close proximity to one another. For instance, housing best suited to veterans and seniors was grouped in one area. As a result, a quieter zone is created in the development, and, what's more, the two demographics are able to share services of mutual interest.

The Benny Farm project is easily adaptable to its residents. The community reflects the diverse demographics and pre-existing architectural nature of Notre-Dame de Grace. It is clear that this community serves the area better than any luxury condo possibly could.

6.11

6.12

6.13

6.14

Figure 6.11:
New terrace homes.

Figure 6.12:
New walk-up units.

Figure 6.13:
A community garden is located in the heart of Benny Farm.

Figure 6.14:
Pedestrian paths connect the old and the new sections of the project.

Figure 6.15:
A detail of a new apartment building.

6.15

6B

Project:
Bloembollenhof

Location:
Vijfhuizen, the Netherlands

Design Firm:
S333 Architecture & Urbanism

Figure 6.16:
Regional plan.

Figure 6.17:
Site plan.

Figure 6.18:
Dwelling typologies.

Bloembollenhof is a VINEX affordable housing development in the town of Vijfhuizen, a small suburb of Amsterdam. Its proximity to Schiphol International Airport, which offers an express train service to Amsterdam's city center, renders the town a perfect destination for commuters. Fifty-two housing units have been placed into simple yet interesting and nonrepetitive forms in the development. Houses range from large, detached forms to smaller social-housing blocks and are scattered freely, catering to several incomes and lifestyles. Additionally, it offers a cheap alternative to urban living and easy to access to amenities.

VINEX is a spatial-planning method put in place to control urban growth. This approach dictates that land be owned by the government and developed by municipal planning authorities. Strict guidelines are to regulate the community's design—the site must consist of at least 30 percent affordable housing, maintaining high unit density to address housing needs, and yet also offer ample green space. VINEX also stipulates that residences be capable of easy and affordable expansion at the discretion of their owners.

Bloembollenhof rejects the arrangement of typical VINEX communities: It at once resembles a rural village and retains dense urban characteristics. In short, the development appears more as a cluster of low-density housing typologies. It has proven that if built close to one another on small plots of land, houses can appear akin to typical suburban dwellings while in reality constituting a dense, efficient community.

The architects aimed to create a "regular irregularity" in their plan. This allows for the housing clusters to appear less formal in nature, fostering the sense of a spontaneously built community as opposed to one that is strictly regimented. Houses have been placed in ways that frame communal open spaces and play areas for children. In detail,

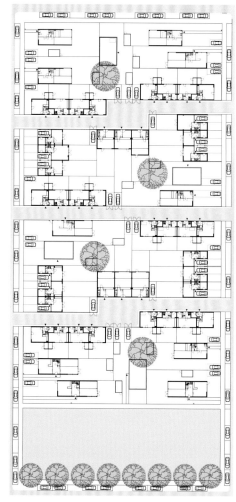

6.17

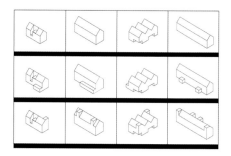

6.18

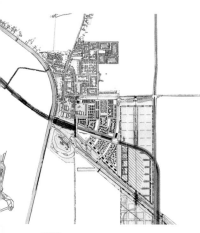

6.16

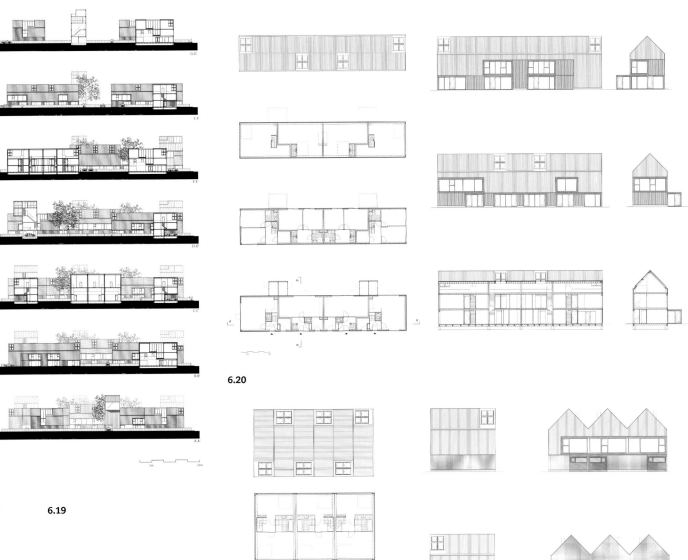

6.20

6.19

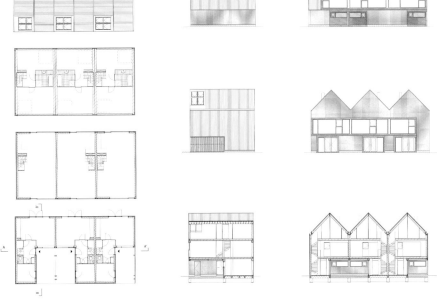

6.21

Figure 6.19:
Site sections and elevations.

Figure 6.20:
Rowhousing type 1.

Figure 6.21:
Rowhousing type 2.

6.22

6.23

Figure 6.22:
Overall site view A.

Figure 6.23:
Overall site view B.

Figure 6.24:
View of shared green space.

Figure 6.25:
Side view of a detached dwelling.

residence views often overlook these courtyards, further connecting individual units to the broader community and creating opportunities for parents to supervise their children from inside the home. Further, the placement of houses also creates shortcuts between major streets, and thus a pedestrian-oriented network of transportation routes.

Residences were designed to make their expansion easy and affordable. For one, the policy was that if a residence is purchased prior to building, future occupants are consulted to achieve the living arrangements they desire right from the start of the process. In part, as a result of this process, spaces vary, some with double-height ceilings, dormer windows, skylights, and various other additions. Generally, areas of the house are left fairly open, allowing for the later addition of dividing walls to suit changing lifestyles. Residents can also purchase units attached to theirs, make wall alterations, and increase their total living space.

Houses are made in simple geometric forms yet incorporate several amenities. Roof terraces and patios have been cut out of the main mass, making up for the small private gardening area. Some rooms have been raised to the first-floor level, improving diagonal street views. The residences also house car parking, minimizing the presence of automobiles on the street and eliminating the need for costly parking infrastructure. In order to keep costs low, houses are clad in Cimory hardwood, and an inexpensive profiled steel. Residents are encouraged to garden, be that on private property or in communal spaces. The latter provides a chance for neighbors to interact and develop social ties with those in proximity.

The Bloembollenhof community development has applied low-density housing typologies to high-density living. Through the use of small plot sizes and a scattered scheme, the development has created a dense environment that maintains many highly suburban characteristics. Perhaps its greatest strength—individuality—is strongly encouraged within the community: This is not another monotonous mass-housing development.

6.24

6.25

Figure 6.26:
View of shared path.

Figure 6.27:
Overall roofscape.

Figure 6.28:
Front elevation of rowhousing type 2.

Figure 6.29:
Detail of exterior wall.

6.28

6.26

6.27

6.29

6C

Project:
Cité-Jardin Fonteneau

Location:
Montreal, Quebec, Canada

Design Firm:
Cardinal, Hardy and
Associates Architects

Figure 6.30:
Site plan.

Figure 6.31:
Floor plans of the dwellings in
Cité-Jardin (basement, lower level,
upper level). The basements and the
attics were left partitioned for the
occupants to complete later.

Cité-Jardin de Fonteneau is a community in Montreal designed according to nineteenth-century, garden-city ideologies. The neighborhood serves as a green oasis within the urban center—this while providing residents with easy access to urban amenities including the Montreal Metro system and shopping. The community was designed with affordability in mind, catering to low- to medium-income families. The plan features residences with easy interior expandability, which makes these homes suitable for families unsure of their final family size or who lack savings but plan to accumulate them in the future.

The architects did their best to seamlessly integrate their design into the existing area. The majority of pre-existing homes were detached and built at a fairly low density. Therefore, a decision was made to place the lowest-density units—semi-detached houses—around the periphery of the development. Higher-density row houses were placed closer to the center. As a result, the community incorporates a maximal unit density yet does not seem out of place when viewed from the outside. This strategy also created a nice variety of housing types, catering to several household incomes and lifestyles.

The main collector road, Joseph A. Rodier Street, is the most public laneway in the development. This street and a parallel pedestrian path serve to connect all houses in the community with other houses, public parks, parking spaces, and other amenities. This street accommodates row houses and semi-detached homes in addition to on-street parking. Narrower roads branch off from Joseph A. Rodier Street and render a more private atmosphere. These offshoots create safe environments in which children can play given that on-street parking is not allowed therein, and, further, they help to reinforce the feeling of personal ownership.

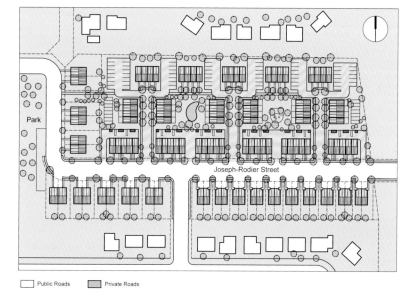

6.30

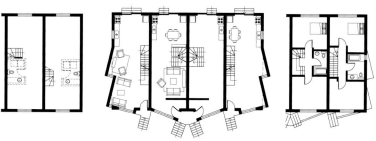

Basement   Lower level   Upper level

6.31

6.32

Figure 6.32:
A narrow private road.

6.33

Figure 6.33:
A shared yard in the rear of homes.

Figure 6.34:
A row of dwellings.

A variety of housing types are offered within the community. Model A is the cheapest typology and is designed primarily for young families, with or without children. The house is largely unfinished, with exposed concrete-block walls, unfinished flooring, and minimal partitioning. The unfinished nature of this model significantly drives down construction costs and therefore the initial cost of the home; it is easier for occupants to simply finish the unit when their budget and schedule can handle such a burden. In fact, in their housing contracts, residents take on a legal obligation to finish their unit at some point during their stay. This arrangement is optional, though; Model B is the same unit as Model A, but offers a finished interior. This caters to families who can both afford the extra cost and have no time or inclination to finish the unit themselves. Model B still utilizes an open-floor plan with minimal partitioning, allowing the space to be split up at a later date.

6.34

Figure 6.35:

The attic in this structure was left unpartitioned for the occupants to complete.

Figure 6.36:

Main floor of a terrace home.

Figure 6.37:

A community garden in Cité-Jardin.

Figure 6.38:

A close-up of a terrace home.

6.36

6.37

6.38

6.35

Model C homes feature an interior organization similar to a typical North American suburban dwelling. They feature a personal garage and a large private backyard space. The interior is partitioned, providing for a separate kitchen, living room, and dining room. Model D homes are almost the exact same as Model Cs, but feature a small modification for better garage access. Model E homes are the most expensive in the community as they accommodate highly private living.

Model Cs averaged out—on the whole—the ample public space of this community renders minimal need for private outdoor space. This both maximizes housing density and fosters a strong sense of community. Further, public gardens allow residents to grow their own produce and offer leisure gardening to those whose private outdoor spaces may be too small to allow the opportunity.

The architects of Cité-Jardin de Fonteneau have created an inclusive community catering to a diverse variety of patrons. Easily expandable and affordable housing like this creates a feeling of permanence in a community, and moreover, eliminates the need for future "step-up" housing. This creates a more affordable situation for home buyers and a housing market less consumerist in character.

Summary and Key Considerations

- The construction sector is the third-largest contributor to greenhouse gas emissions in developed countries.

- The ability to adapt is a key aspect of sustainability in construction, as it fosters long-term planning and use. Accommodation through design can be made for the ongoing changes in the needs of homeowners as life stage and demographic changes occur.

- Flexible homes and communities reduce waste and save nonrenewable resources in that they diminish the demand to build new homes.

- Current municipal planning methods are time-consuming, speculative, and do not emphasize sustainable long-term design that permits adaptability.

- A new take on the design and approval procedure is necessary: A community should be composed of several subdivisions, all governed by a general municipal code, and framed by rough guidelines of main roads and centers. Subdivisions themselves could develop at a later date with their own codes governing the design of individual units.

- By having subdivision design reflect the pace of construction and the needs of society at the time of building, the project will be less risky for the developer and result in more varied and relevant housing.

- Another aspect of sustainable design in an adaptable community is the presence of a multitude of building types.

- Different housing forms—apartment buildings, row houses, detached and semi-detached housing—allow a wider range of households access to housing in the neighborhood, thus enabling the community to endure the fluctuations of the housing market.

- Flexibility is also a desirable quality in a home. Occupants' needs change, and a design that anticipates and allows for those changes reduces costs and investment.

- Key aspects of the house that consider any possible future adaptations—such as circulation, services, materials, light, and ventilation—must be established.

- There are two common approaches to expansion, the *add-on* method and the *add-in* method. The add-on method refers to the addition of rooms to an original structure. The add-in method refers to leaving spaces unfinished, such as attics and basements, which can later be converted into livable spaces.

- The Next Home, designed and constructed at McGill School of Architecture, can be subdivided and rearranged both before and during occupancy. The structure of the building can be converted to a single-family home, duplex, or triplex.

Exercises

1. List and analyze contemporary social factors that, in your view, merit design of communities and homes for growth and change.

2. How will you restructure existing zoning bylaws or introduce new ones to permit growth and change of communities?

3. Using photographs, document a community in your area where homes have been designed to offer harmony of architectural styles and at the same time permit growth.

4. What are the design attributes that facilitate growth and adaptability of dwellings?

5. What aspects in the design of plex dwelling units make them adaptable, and how have these features been used in the Next Home?

Chapter 7
Affordable Neighborhoods

Environmentalism cannot monopolize a planner's focus to the neglect of the other aspects of sustainability. The accessibility of affordable housing is an equally vital consideration, and, further, is closely connected to other aspects of sustainability; affordability, environmental degradation, and socio-political inequality are highly integrated issues. Some of these connections are apparent in that affordable homes are smaller than average and so require fewer resources to build and maintain. This chapter explores the theory and practice behind these homes, and, of course, their neighborhoods.

Housing Affordability

Housing is considered affordable if it requires 32 percent or less of a household's income, and this expense is measured to include the attendant mortgage principal, interest, taxes, and utilities costs (Friedman 2005). The underlying rationale of this definition is that home buyers are reasonably able to respect this level of financial commitment and still have means for other of life's necessities. That said, it is important to consider that affordability requires potential homeowners not only to make payments but also to obtain financing for a home, and doing so depends on variable external factors including interest rates and down payment requirements.

Affordable housing communities can be initiated by either nonprofit or for-profit parties. Such nonprofit organizations include, in the main, government agencies and nongovernmental organizations (NGO) like Habitat for Humanity. Lines between non- and for-profit groups are in a sense blurred, though; at times, for-profit organizations like private-sector firms may be granted substantial government subsidies. Also, during an economic recession, the government may also offer first-time home buyers lower interest rates or grants, in turn making affordable housing a more attractive undertaking for buyers and developers.

Demand for affordability in building has been driven by many of the same factors creating demand for sustainable housing. For one, the home-buying population is no longer a relatively homogeneous client base, having changed significantly since the post–Second World War era. Indeed, the formerly dominant traditional-household model is giving way to a tide of mixed demographics. Many of these groups—single parents, solitary buyers, and seniors—require new models of affordable shelter. Add to this that nonrenewable energy and resources—basic materials required to build—have become scarce and expensive, and that these prices are tethered to housing markets.

Figure 7.1:

When the density increases, more land is made available for additional units and the cost of land per dwelling unit drops

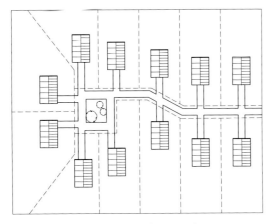

2 dwellings / acre (2 dwellings / 0.4 hectare net)
12 dwelling units
6 acres (2.4 developed hectares)

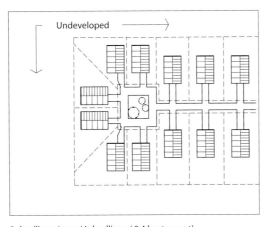

2 dwellings / acre (4 dwellings / 0.4 hectare net)
12 dwelling units
3 acres (1.2 developed hectares)

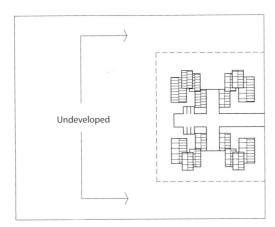

8 dwellings / acre (8 dwellings / 0.4 hectare net)
12 dwelling units
1.5 acres (0.6 developed hectares)

On a related note, global economic transformations have recently made it harder for first-time buyers to purchase a home. To borrow money, one must first secure employment; however, long-term, stable employment is a thing of the past in many sectors (Friedman 2005). Another barrier to homeownership is the widening gap between income and home price. Simply put, today's entry-level-income earners do not have the means to acquire homes in most urban centers.

Home size and shape have also transformed to become less affordable. For example, in North America the size of homes has swelled, increasing the costs of land, labor, and materials. Dwellings have also recently been price-packaged so as to include more amenities, increasing infrastructure costs associated with the linking of each home to utility lines.

In the face of today's demand, where is government action? In fact, in most nations, federal and local authorities have limited their participation in sheltering low-income households. This pushes the poor to rent accommodations instead of enabling them to achieve the stability of homeownership.

Indeed, despite the evident need for affordable homes, there are many obstacles preventing their construction, most of which are less obvious than a lack of governmental funding and support. For example, affordable housing developments are sometimes met with resistance from nearby affluent communities. Well-established neighborhoods often resist affordable projects based on fears that such buildings will bring an increase in crime and attendant decline in property value to their area. These fears are often expressed in the form of zoning ordinances, which can require low-density, wide lots, and indoor parking, making the units unaffordable (National Association of Home Builders Research Center 2005).

Planning Strategies for Housing Affordability

The cost of a home depends, obviously, on the pricing of its components; this includes the cost of land, infrastructure, material, labor, and landscaping. Of course, financing, marketing, taxes, overhead, and profit are added to the cost. The choice of site location is highly important as it can affect more than just initial costs. Additional expenses can be incurred if the homes are far from necessary amenities and if residents do not have access to public transport. Land cost itself, primarily in highly populated areas, can also easily render a project unaffordable. Intervention by local governments can vitally decrease expenses by providing infrastructure to a development, allowing use of surplus land, or reducing parking standards. Municipalities can also manipulate zoning regulation in a specific area to create high-density neighborhoods like that of Figure 7.1. This is an extremely important cost-cutting measure—the more units there are to share land and infrastructure improvement costs, the less each homeowner is required to pay. Of course, when density increases, both lot size and the area allocated to roads decrease since the homes cover much of the land. When the area allocated to residential lots decreases as such, it is

important that more land be allocated to common open green areas (Friedman 2012). Land cost can be even further decreased within these high-density areas by designing smaller lot sizes and attaching units to one another.

The grouping of units into clusters of two or more provides significant construction and energy savings, as illustrated in Figure 7.2. Grouping four detached units as semi-detached reduces the exposed-wall area by 36 percent, and grouping the four units as row houses reduces exterior-wall surfaces by a further 28 percent. Heat-loss reductions of 21 percent are achieved when two dwellings are attached. When three or more units are combined as row houses, the middle unit retains an additional 26 percent of heat (Friedman 2013). In terms of reducing energy consumption, row houses also perform well when compared to detached homes. Single-family detached housing is the least dense of housing options and the most consumptive in terms of land, energy, and water.

Figure 7.2:
By joining units, the amount of exposed wall area is reduced substantially as one or more exterior walls are eliminated, enabling construction efficiency and energy savings.

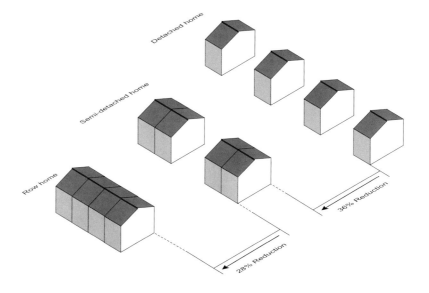

Dwelling type	1 Single detached	2 Semi-detached	3 Row house	4 Triplex	5 3-story walk-up apartment	6 Combined apartments & row houses	7 Slab block apartment	8 High rise apartment
Isometric								
Plot plan								
Dwelling units/acre (dwelling units/hectare)	8 (20)	14 (35)	19 (47)	21 (52)	65 (160)	84 (207)	90 (222)	120 (296)
Floor area ratio % open space	0.24 76%	0.38 81%	0.56 72%	0.60 80%	1.36 55%	1.92 62%	1.78 62%	2.62 87%
Unit area in square feet (unit area in square meters)	1200 (111.5)	1200 (111.5)	1200 (111.5)	1200 (111.5)	800 (74.3)	800 & 1200 (74.3 & 111.5)	800 (74.3)	800 (74.3)

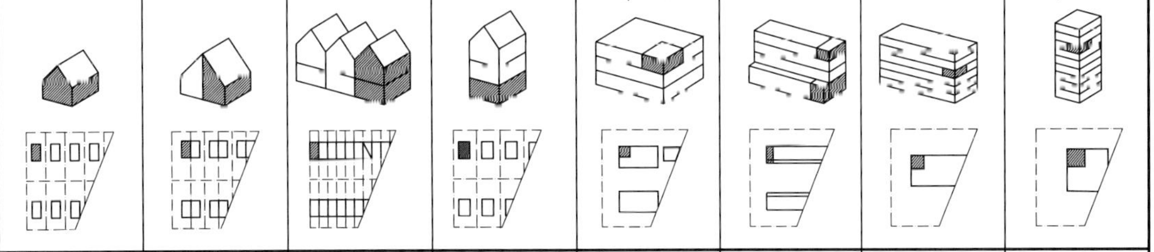

The narrow-front row house, also called a terrace or townhouse, offers prospective owners the commonly preferred characteristics of homeownership (a single-family home with a private entrance and direct access to a yard). At the same time, the density of the design confers affordability and sustainability and further benefits therein (Friedman 2012). Other housing options that are similar but that do not have private ground-level entrances or private yards—such as duplexes and triplexes—are even more affordable and sustainable (Diamond 1976) (Figure 7.3).

Narrow-front row houses are built on narrow plots, 4.3 to 6 meters (14 to 20 feet) wide, and share sidewalls with neighboring structures. The narrow width makes interior bearing partitions redundant, resulting in a greater flexibility in the arrangement of space (Friedman 2001). Large open spaces around the townhouse development may be planned to compensate for the lack of small, private spaces offered within the complex.

No matter the housing type, the choice of lot will affect affordability. Smaller lots yield significant savings. Like the townhouse itself, choosing narrow lots will significantly reduce the cost of land and infrastructure. Lots can also be angled—this may further reduce the amount of land consumed by creating shallow lots. When built on a shallower lot, a home is placed closer to the street, and this can save on the costs associated with connecting to infrastructure. Offset angled lots are yet another type of lot ideal for high-density planning. In these lots, homes sit in a tooth-saw pattern; this maximizes solar exposure and ensures that neighbors do not block one another's side-window views.

The placement of a home on a lot can also affect cost savings. Setback regulations control the distance between lot line and home. Bigger setbacks will likely require larger lots; and so, in the interest of saving on land costs, it is preferable to reduce these distances as much as possible. Narrower frontages and reduced front-yard setbacks allow for reductions in the length of road pavement per unit, shorter utility runs, along with reduced ongoing road and infrastructure maintenance costs. In urban areas, the distance between dwelling and street can even be reduced to zero, placing the home on the front-lot line, as was common practice in old towns.

Figure 7.3:

Higher-density dwelling types, such as duplexes, triplexes, and apartments, extend the affordability and sustainability further.

It is important to understand that these measures do not necessarily imply a loss of privacy. Reduced setbacks can retain a private feel if designers place an unfenestrated, north-facing wall nearest the lot line, and this also provides space and energy savings. As aforementioned, row houses can be staggered—this creates private outdoor spaces and so prevents undesirable views. Orienting the units toward common amenity spaces, such as parks or play areas, can foster a sense of distance and, again, ensure the residents' feelings of privacy.

Indeed, achieving affordable housing design in the form of high-density housing without compromising livability and comfort can seem an initially daunting task. To this end, common amenities such as parks may be integrated into the design of the affordable development. Nevertheless, in general, the planning process should avoid single-loading a road with houses in order to do so. This is because a double-loaded street shares the cost of building the road and placing the infrastructure between two rows of homes. In a single-loading development, only one side of the street carries the economic burden.

Street configuration and design can also affect the affordability of a neighborhood. In general, to avoid monotony plans should integrate lot patterns that correspond with different unit types and a variety of streets. Short blocks foster more variety but increase intersections and therefore costs. A *cul-de-sac* (dead-end street) provides space for play and lessens traffic but also results in angled lots that reduce land compactness and density. Alternatively, lot configurations around loop streets provide the privacy, safety, and economy of a dead-end street without the difficulty of turning, resulting in easier circulations to and from a collector street. With regard to land consumption, studies demonstrate that loop roads consume smaller amounts of land than a grid pattern (Tasker-Brown and Pogharian 2000).

Road and parking design is closely related to the issue of land cost, as 30 percent of a residential development can be allocated to roads and parking. In any neighborhood, and especially in an affordable housing project, the design of a circulation system should focus on reducing reliance on cars. Pedestrian and cyclist paths should take precedence, and each home should be built within walking distance of public transit. The street's width should also be considered and reflect its use. For streets with low traffic, narrow widths will slow motorists and save valuable land and construction costs. The elimination of parking space is also a great cost saver. According to Litman (2004), integrating one parking space into each unit increases the cost of a home by about 12.5 percent compared to on-street parking. Litman also suggests that in some locations underground parking can be up to ten times more expensive than surface parking. Sharing access roads with parking spots in small-lot housing and grouping parking areas as illustrated in Figure 7.4 can also be a cost-saving strategy.

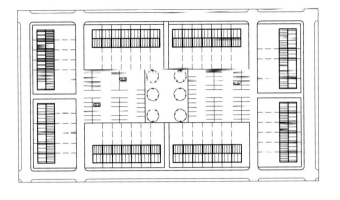
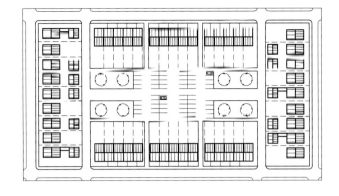
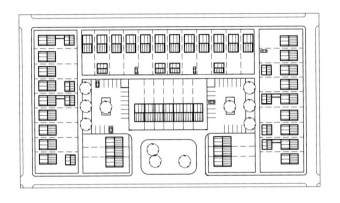
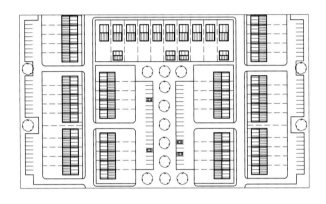

Figure 7.4:

Outdoor parking is common in high-density affordable communities and sharing access roads can be a cost-saving strategy.

Open spaces (i.e., green spaces) contribute to quality of life and are a sustainable feature in a community. As housing density increases, so does the functional and psychological importance of open space between dwelling units. Shared spaces like neighborhood greens, squares, and community gardens provide social gathering points and contribute to community identity (Evans 2003). Larger public areas can alleviate the apparent pressure caused by the concentration of taller structures. If a large open space is impossible to integrate into an affordable housing project, a series of interconnected smaller spaces of varying appearance and shape is an attractive, viable alternative. Open spaces help compensate for the high degree of repetition required for economy to be maintained at the development level. Together with some variety in the design of exterior components, landscaping can considerably alter the exterior impression of a community.

This chapter has discussed the different elements that contribute to the affordability and livability of a neighborhood, among which are open space, circulation, lot area, housing type, and housing density. The innovations highlighted therein not only cultivate a neighborhood's affordability but also its sustainability—a connection easy to perceive, as these two goals have overlapping motivations. This all comes back to the fact that homeowners no longer have the economic means to occupy large, single-family, detached homes, and neither are these houses a viable option when their expense to society as a whole is considered. Bigger is no longer better, and our homes should reflect the changing social, economic, and environmental realities.

7A

Project:
Floating Houses in IJBurg

Location:
Amsterdam, the Netherlands

Design Firm:
Marlies Rohmer Architecture
+Urban Planning

Figure 7.5:
Regional plan.

Figure 7.6:
Site plan.

Figure 7.7:
Floor plan and sections of typical
dwelling.

Affordable housing in the IJburg district of Amsterdam has taken the form of a floating community. Impressively, the project has produced homes at half the construction cost of land-based housing in the city. Further, these floating houses offer an alternative to expensive Amsterdam canal houses in that they are affordable but do not require the sacrifice of proximity to downtown. There are several forms of on-water living in Amsterdam, with many houseboats, even hotel boats, occupying the canals. This project is one of the first to apply land-built housing typologies to floating homes; the majority of pre-existing houses on the water were more like boats than typical homes. Additionally, this project aids in water treatment and frees land to be occupied by water-storage basins.

Parcels of water have been leased to the developer by the city council at an affordable rate for fifty years. The temporary nature of this contract is not an issue, as the houses are extremely mobile—they can be built at any location, then towed by tugboats to their appropriate site. The sporadic nature of this plan allows an occupant to adapt their house to their needs. It is a wonderfully flexible arrangement. For example, if a resident wished to turn their house to face the sunset or sunrise, it is, incredibly, a feasible option.

Three housing types are offered to cater to different living situations and price points. Completely private houses are available; these are detached units that rely on an individual flotation tank. Semi-detached houses combine two units on one such tank, while triplexes combine three residences that are, again, all reliant on one tank. This last selection is geared toward the rental market and understandably the most affordable.

The units are modular and easy to mass-produce, further saving on construction costs. The flotation tanks are made of double-reinforced concrete filled with polystyrene. When compared to traditional foundation types, this is a very inexpensive design. Walls are prefabricated off-site, making on-site construction extremely simple. Once individual houses are constructed using prefab parts, multi-house units can be grouped to a single flotation device. The houses are then transported and linked to the jetties (floating walkways). The materials described here are high quality and long lasting—thus the houses require minimal maintenance.

Floating houses require an average of 15 percent less energy than standard homes. Gas, water, and sewage services are supplied by insulated cables and flexible pipes. A heat pump and heat exchanger provide homes with heating and cooling. The water itself is used to control the interior temperature of the buildings.

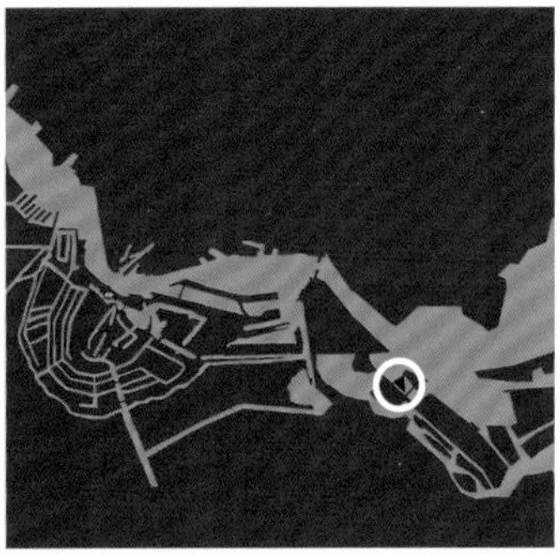

7.5

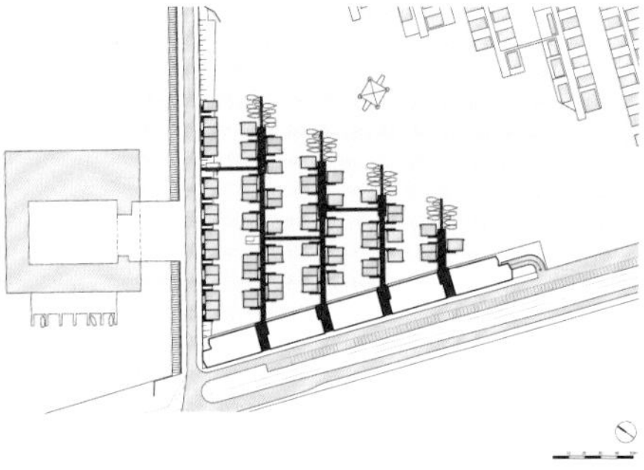

7.6

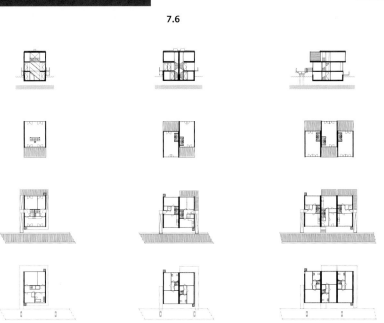

7.7

Figure 7.8:
Aerial view of development.

Figure 7.9:
Aerial view of group of homes.

Figure 7.10:
Waterside elevations.

Figure 7.11:
Waterside elevations—sunset.

Figure 7.12:
View of access path to dwellings.

While these homes are comfortable in many ways, there are of course some lifestyle changes required of occupants that may require some adjustment. Simply put, residents must be able to live their lives surrounded by water. This means that to access personal cars, residents must walk the entirety of the jetties to reach a lot outside of the community. Another important consideration: There are also some financial shortfalls, as the houses are not considered moveable property for mortgage payments and insurance premiums.

The floating development has created an alternative to expensive canal-side living in downtown Amsterdam. These homes are comfortable and accommodate various lifestyles and income levels. It has set an impressive precedent that may soon see replication—after all, there is an abundance of water space.

7.8

7.9

7.10

7.11

7.12

Figure 7.13:
Upper balcony of one of the structures.

Figure 7.14:
View of three-story house.

Figure 7.15:
Winter scene.

Figure 7.16:
Typical structure—axonometric view.

Figure 7.17:
Summer scene—water view.

Figure 7.18:
Sequence of transportation and installation of a structure.

7.13

7.15

7.14

7.16

7.17

7.18

7B

Project:
Carabanchel Housing Project

Location:
Madrid, Spain

Design Firm:
Morphosis Architects

A shortage of affordable housing in Madrid has recently sparked a series of projects involving both globally recognized firms and less widely known local talent. The goal: to create innovative housing solutions for lower-income residents. As a result, over eighteen social-housing projects were launched across the city, among them the Carabanchel Project.

The Carabanchel Project is located in a rundown suburban area of the same name in the southwest of Madrid. A large portion of its residents are new immigrants in desperate need of affordable-housing solutions. Thanks to progressive measures to increase unit density and lower overall costs, these dwellings are available for sale at an incredible one-third of average market value.

Drawing inspiration from local vernacular architecture, these iconic buildings consist of layers of small, white dwellings, densely packed beside and atop one another. This housing typology fits the low-cost residential plan well, as it encouraged a high unit density that allowed for 141 residential units.

It also allowed for the application of an interesting circulation system and vehicle-free streets. It is important to note its minimal exterior surface area—this decreases material usage and keeps the building naturally cooler.

Living spaces are small, ranging from 60 square meters (650 square feet) to 100 square meters (1080 square feet), but are comfortable by average European standards (the average house size in Spain being 90 square meters, or 970 sqare feet). The units are nicely furnished with hardwood floors, terrazzo stairs, built-in cabinets, and a large opening for natural light. In the low-rise section of the development, apartments are spread between two levels. This provides privacy for rooms on the upper floor but allows rooms on the bottom floor to participate in the community environment. Bedrooms are located on the upper level, and family living spaces are on the ground floor. There are also rooftop patios, providing private outdoor space. Unfortunately, residents living on the ground floor tend to benefit more from the public spaces than those living in the two tower complexes.

Figure 7.19:
Massing progression of the project.

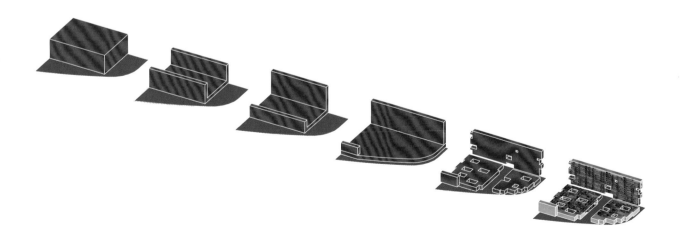

7.19

125

7.20

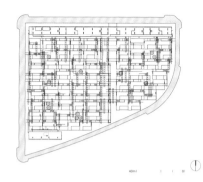

7.21

PERGOLA
+ PERGOLA COLUMN
PLANTER (TYPE X1)
PLANTER (TYPE X2)
PLANTER (TYPE X3)
PRECAST (TYPE X1)
PRECAST (TYPE X2)
COURTYARD PRIVATE UPPER
COURTYARD PRIVATE
COURTYARD PUBLIC
PUBLIC PLAZA

7.22

Figure 7.20:
First floor plan.

Figure 7.21:
Roof plan.

Figure 7.22:
Pergola diagram.

Figure 7.23:
Section.

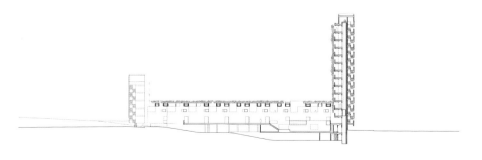

7.23

The interior streets are car-free, providing a safe atmosphere for children to play and a chance for residents to socialize. As the development is placed in a suburban context, car parking is still an important feature. The architects created a solution by placing a lot beneath the residences. This separates the parking from the homes, both physically and aesthetically. It also eliminates the need for costly parking infrastructure.

The complex has been divided into three scale typologies to create better circulation and public space. In the first type, streets are lined with small personal patios belonging to individual residences. In the next street typology, there are semi-private courtyards shared by neighbors. The third is the Paseo, a large, completely communal street spanning from the south to the north of the development. The Paseo also serves as the main entrance, with all smaller passageways leading toward it. The architects designed this space specifically to encourage public interaction and foster spontaneous moments.

Figure 7.24:
Aerial view of the project.

Figure 7.25:
Street view.

Figure 7.26:
Street view 2.

Figure 7.27:
Roofscape.

Figure 7.28:
Roofscape showing chimneys and pergolas.

7.24

7.25

7.26

7.27

7.28

Figure 7.29:
Interior street and pergolas.

Figure 7.30:
Interior open spaces.

Figure 7.31:
Interior open spaces 2.

Figure 7.32:
Stairs leading to ground level.

Figure 7.33:
Upper terraces and pergolas.

Figure 7.34:
Pergolas.

7.29

7.30

7.31

7.32

7.33

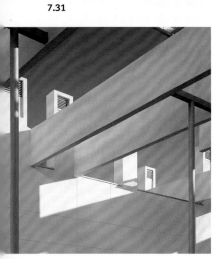

7.34

Throughout these three types of streets, there are several patches of greenery in courtyard form. Residences make use of these spaces for ventilation. The vegetation is also used to shade residences from the sun. Both processes help to lower cooling bills, though air conditioning has still been installed as a backup measure.

The development was designed specifically to counteract the urban isolation that can occur in high-density, low-income apartment blocks. Thus, the incorporation of spaces like the Paseo that create opportunities for socializing and everyday human interaction. In short, the Carabanchel Project shows that high-density, affordable communities do not have to sacrifice the spirit of community living.

7C

Project:
La Cité Manifeste

Location:
Mulhouse, France

Design Firm:
Lacaton & Vassal

Figure 7.35:
Ground and first floor plans.

Figure 7.36:
Section.

La Cité Manifeste is a social housing project designed by five teams of architects in Mulhouse, France. Each of the teams, which included Shigeru Ban and Jean Nouvel, was assigned to one section of the development. The project's design goal was to produce housing that is larger than the average apartment but offered at the same cost. Of the designs produced, the units by Lacaton & Vassal Architects are arguably the most innovative, the portion of the project we will explore here.

These designers utilized a creative mix of industrial materials and made an effort to minimize expensive detail work. The structural envelope was created first. The ground floor consists of a concrete foundation with a simple post-and-beam superstructure. The unit's supports are made of galvanized steel, its walls of translucent polycarbonate—both relatively cheap industrial materials.

The building acts as a greenhouse to provide residents with a form of climate control. Half of this greenhouse system is heated using conventional techniques, the other half can run without a heater. Instead it acts as a "winter garden": Using the natural ventilation of sliding elements on the roof and walls, residents control heat themselves. A large blind can be used to cover the front floor-to-ceiling window of each unit, shielding occupants from the sun's heat on hot days, while retaining the option of allowing light in in order to warm the building on cool ones. Indeed, the large windows provide a good source of natural lighting to the apartments; at a depth of 18 meters (59 feet), there is little need for artificial lighting, except of course at night. Using this system, residents can see a direct correlation between their habits and utility bills. This promotes environmental awareness, lowers residents' cost of living, and significantly saves energy.

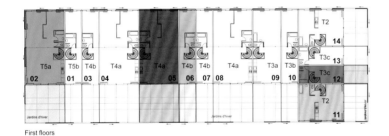

First floors

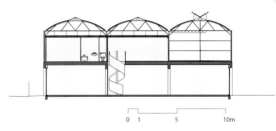

7.36

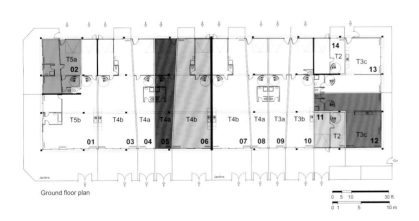

Ground floor plan

Figure 7.37:
Site plan.

Figure 7.38:
Overview of the row.

Following the creation of the envelope, the structure was split into fourteen units; these are of duplex form to maximize their interior space. The repeated use of a few inexpensive building materials within each duplex creates a consistent aesthetic while minimizing unit cost. The result is a simple, unrefined, less-is-more aesthetic. For example, exposed concrete floors work to both cultivate a trendy look and create significant savings. Further, many residents have installed self-made tables, bars, and other inexpensive furnishings composed of industrial materials and chipboard.

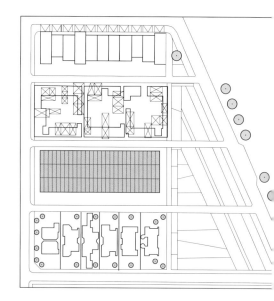

7.37

7.38

Figure 7.39:
Ground floor view.

Figure 7.40:
First floor view.

La Cité Manifeste is an important experiment in social housing for its attempt to maximize available space. The results are impressive: One of these units is priced at the same rate as an apartment in the area half its size. Indeed, given the distinctive balance of spaciousness and affordability offered therein, it is little wonder that they have proven particularly attractive to large families. The designers' savvy use of materials and thoughtful spatial arrangement are behind these successes, and hopefully set precedent for buildings to follow.

7.39

7.40

7D

Project:
2 McIntyre Drive, Altona

Location:
Altona, Melbourne, Australia

Design Firm:
MGS Architects

Figure 7.41:
Site plan.

Figure 7.42:
South and west elevations.

Figure 7.43:
South and west elevations—courtyard.

This project, composed of sixty-nine apartments in Altona, Melbourne, is notable in its attempt to integrate a higher-density housing model with that of its surrounding suburban neighborhood. It reinterprets the aforementioned suburban vernacular over multiple levels to create a connection that extends from the street to the main entrance.

This project is the only apartment complex in an area characterized by single-family dwellings. Funding for the development came via the "Social Housing Initiative" through the Commonwealth's "Nation Building" economic stimulus plan. In accordance with the objectives outlined by those funding the project, the building provides independent living accommodations for residents with disabilities and includes communal spaces, community gardens, and private open space. Parking spots, driveways, and streetscape plants, in addition to a number of existing mature trees, were retained to preserve the established character of the site (which borders a council reserve).

The design process started by establishing a U-shaped footprint to create a connection from the street to the main entrance. The center of the "U" is a gathering space—a pleasant entranceway in which to wait for a friend or while away an hour or two. It also provides a natural point of visual interest for those gazing out their windows. The architect developed this space as a large courtyard reminiscent of the perimeter block plan used in European cities (but, importantly, this design lacks the formality associated with this influence). It includes a veggie patch tended by residents, as are the front yards of the ground-floor tenants. Together, these create a pleasing, green façade.

7.42

7.43

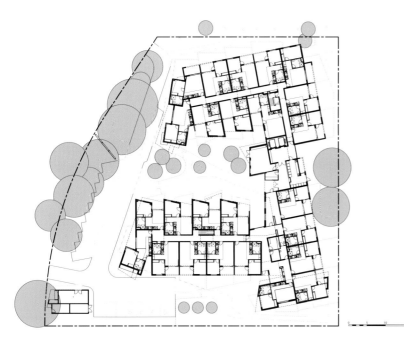

7.41

7.44

7.45

Figure 7.44:
View from driveway.

Figure 7.45:
Courtyard elevation.

Figure 7.46:
View of courtyard from resident's balcony.

7.46

Figure 7.47:

Detail of courtyard balcony.

Figure 7.48:

View from common terrace, overlooking courtyard.

Figure 7.49:

Stepping down of form toward street interface.

Figure 7.50:

Double height corridor off main entrance.

7.47

7.48

7.49

It is worth reflecting on this building as a reinterpretation of affordable housing's relationship to both physical context and social status. Identity and a sense of home were intentionally encouraged in the design; the project represents an attempt to create a communal sense of place. However, the designers were conscious of the fact that simply transplanting architectural values into a building that houses those in need, without sensitivity to context, risks a certain tackiness. It was critical to them that the design process take into account planning, scale, material, color, and form, but all in accordance with the project's all-important social dimension. An example of this approach is the nature of the design's generously landscaped courtyard, which serves as the focus of the visitor and resident experience. It offers retreat, recreation, and an opportunity for social interaction, vital to those in the community, all while consciously integrating the building into the suburbs—it maintains generous setbacks and a landscaped frontage to McIntyre Drive.

The design took into account the location and arrangement of a group of existing two-story buildings that had previously served as nursing homes. In fact, to retain a sense of established order, the designers kept the alignment of the previous building footprint to the south. They also established planting, driveways, and parking along McIntyre Drive. The generous setbacks to the street and to the boundaries with neighboring residential properties were also retained from the previous structure.

7.50

The project is respectful of the amenities of the suburb. It mediates streetscape-related concerns of scale and height by way of a mindful variation in building mass, and through experimentation in color, tone, and material texture. And, as aforementioned, parking, driveways, streetscape planting, and a number of existing mature trees were all retained in an effort to preserve the established character of the site.

In addition, the project incorporates a number of environmentally sustainable design principles, both passive and direct. These include but are not limited to: reverse precast concrete construction, providing greater thermal mass to the interior of the dwellings; hydronic heating throughout; solar hot-water systems; on-site retention of stormwater through storm gardens, and lastly water tanks for irrigation. Additionally, it is again vital to consider that the configuration of the building is fundamentally in response to the provision for community gardens. This green area allows for food and flower cultivation while at the same time minimizing stormwater wastage.

Summary and Key Considerations

- Access to affordable housing is an indicator of a society's commitment to sustainability. Indeed, they are closely tied issues—affordability is an inherent consequence of minimizing a carbon footprint, on both the individual and social level.

- Conception of affordable homes begins by having smaller units that require fewer resources to build and maintain.

- In most nations, housing is considered affordable if it requires less than 32 percent of a household's income per year.

- Today's entry-level-income earners do not have the means to acquire homes in most urban centers. Yet, in most nations, homeownership is a means to accumulate wealth, as property values increase over time.

- Homeowners have more control over a dwelling's environment than renters do, and they can even generate income by renting out unused space.

- Homeownership lowers the need for local government to support senior citizens when their incomes decline.

- The cost of a home depends, obviously, on the pricing of its components; this includes the cost of land, infrastructure, material, labor, and landscaping. In addition, financing, marketing, taxes, overhead, and profit are part of the final cost.

- Land cost has been rapidly increasing, making it an increasingly vital consideration in affordable design.

- The grouping of units into clusters of two or more provides significant construction and energy savings. For example, grouping four detached units as semi-detached reduces the exposed-wall area by 36 percent, and grouping the four units as row houses reduces exterior-wall surfaces by a further 28 percent.

- The narrow-front row house, also called a townhouse, offers prospective owners some of the most commonly preferred characteristics of homeownership—being a single-family home with a private entrance and direct access to a yard—while at the same time extending the benefits of affordability and sustainability conferred by increased density.

- The narrow width makes interior bearing partitions redundant, resulting in a greater flexibility in the arrangement of space

- As housing density increases, so does the functional and psychological importance of open space between dwelling units. These public spots—including, for example, neighborhood greens, squares, and community gardens—serve as social gathering points and create community identity.

Exercises

1. Using local census data and based on the chapter's definition of affordability, how many people in your city are facing affordable housing challenges?

2. List global and local social aspects that in recent years have made housing unaffordable for first-time home buyers. Pay particular attention to conditions in your country and city.

3. Identify urban planning aspects that are bound to have the greatest impact on affordability and elaborate how you will alter them to lower the cost of a development.

4. Identify aspects related to the design of a single unit that are bound to have the greatest impact on affordability, and elaborate how you will alter them to lower the cost of a dwelling.

5. List the strategies that contributed to cost reduction in the case studies that are described in the chapter.

Chapter 8
Net-Zero Energy Neighborhoods

As global energy consumption increases, nonrenewable resources like gas and oil are becoming more scarce and expensive. Energy demand has risen sharply with population growth, increase in the size of dwellings, and household-appliance usage in developed nations. In addition, emerging economies are steadily expanding their energy consumption, further contributing to this global surge in demand.

Many alternative clean power sources have been proposed as key tools in the struggle to meet these global energy needs. That said, thus far those innovations facilitating individual heating and cooling systems are inefficient and unsustainable— comparatively, that is. The new standard in energy efficiency is the practice of district heating: This system is up to three times more efficient in furnishing energy to individual homes than isolated heating systems (Austin 2010). A net-zero energy neighborhood, powered by a central source, offers significant financial savings and carbon footprint reduction to each household connected to its network. This chapter discusses these innovations in theory and practice.

Net-Zero Energy Systems

The term *net-zero* is commonly used to describe energy-efficient dwellings that produce and return as much energy to the grid as they use, as illustrated in Figure 8.1. The same principle applies to the *net-zero energy neighborhood* but at a larger scale. All of the dwellings in a community rely on combined heat and power systems from one shared, centralized source; this method is also known as *district heating*. The centralized energy infrastructure heats and cools the entire neighborhood using local or renewable energy sources, power from which is then distributed to individual households. Leftover energy is returned and stored in the plant's thermal storage area, redistributed later as needed.

Net-zero energy is a more feasible goal at the community level than it is at the scale of the individual dwelling. A net-zero dwelling is a costly investment and its aim would be far more easily achieved in a row of townhouses or an apartment building. Although solar heating is easier to set up in a rural or suburban home, the auto usage and attendant infrastructure in such settings counteract the project's sustainable impact (Malin 2010). All things considered, urban neighborhoods are able to most efficiently support alternative and combined power sources, in part given that the maintenance needed to support sustainable energy in many homes is limited to one plant.

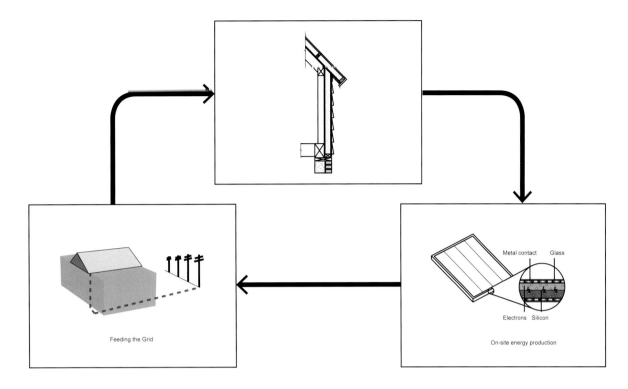

Figure 8.1:

Net-zero communities are places with energy-efficient dwellings that produce and return as much energy to the grid as they use.

However, many strategies utilized in the design of net-zero dwellings are immediately transferable to the planning of a net-zero energy neighborhood, as illustrated in Figure 8.2. Net-zero dwellings decrease energy consumption by limiting size and orienting the structure to take advantage of passive solar gain, natural daylight, and indoor airflow. Local wind patterns, sun orientation, topography, ground depth of winter frost, and shadows from other buildings and trees are other important considerations common to the design of both the net-zero energy home and community. In fact, many of these factors are more easily managed when designing at the community scale—for instance, at a district scale, one can more readily anticipate and change the topography and orientation of a street layout to take advantage of the winter sun and limit the summer heat (Malin 2010).

When houses are oriented along a north–west axis, they enjoy a maximum amount of sunlight. Units oriented along the north-westerly axis, therefore, benefit from a shorter noonday shadow than otherwise might be cast if houses

were oriented east–west. Moreover, additional units may be erected upon the cusp of neighboring house shadows if the dwelling design follows the aforementioned layout. Principles considering sunlight and shadow orientation need to avoid obstructions that will prevent the houses from maximizing sunlight.

Existing natural vegetation and new growth can also be shading devices. To minimize solar heat gain in the summer, it is beneficial to have deciduous trees to the south of the house. The leaves of these trees shade houses from the heat but allow some light to penetrate indoors. In the wintertime, more solar heat and light can filter through their bare branches. The east and west façades are exposed to sun with lesser intensity, but should be about 10 to 15 percent fenestrated to allow for natural lighting. Maximizing the solar gain will lower energy consumption, which in turn lowers costs and reduces the amount of emitted pollution necessary to produce this energy to the environment.

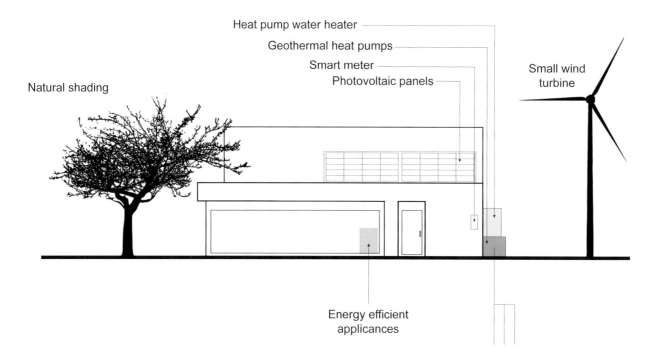

Heat pump water heater
Geothermal heat pumps
Smart meter
Photovoltaic panels

Small wind turbine

Natural shading

Energy efficient applicances

Figure 8.2:

Alternative means of energy production and savings in a net-zero home.

Net-zero energy is not merely about creating an efficient supply of energy but also ensuring it is not wasted; to limit heat loss, well-insulated structures are essential. A more traditional method by which to minimize heat loss is to combine different insulators. For instance, one can mix open-cell spray foam and cellulose insulation in the walls, floors, and roof of a house with rigid insulation on the exterior (Macht 2010). A more innovative technique involves thick walls, wrap-and-strap, double walls, and truss walls. Whichever of these strategies is implemented, it is important that every net-zero dwelling is carefully sealed with a membrane to prevent airflow through the walls—this is sustainable practice, and further, in fact, a commonplace requirement among current housing standards.

The selection of windows and doors is another important part of reducing energy consumption in a dwelling; the smart management of these openings is critical to reducing heat loss. Krypton gas-filled low-emissivity glass is often used in double- or triple-pane windows and doors, which are up to four times more efficient than traditional double-pane windows (Macht 2010). Another more innovative glass—*electrochromic* or *thermochromic* glass—contains glazing that changes from opaque to transparent instantly. This helps control sunlight penetration and glare (Gonchar 2010). The strategic placement of windows— ideally some near the ground of a room with others near the top—is vital to take advantage of the natural ventilation generated from airflow cycles of hot and cold air (Tanha 2010). Additionally, a structure with high ceilings encourages airflow through a dwelling, reducing the use of air conditioning in summer months and subsequently energy consumption (Haran 2009).

Fundamentally, both district heating systems and net-zero-energy buildings work much the same way. They harvest renewable energy in a centralized location, often a plant, and this heats or cools water that is then distributed to buildings within the neighborhood network. It is transported to the individual dwelling by underground pipes. This elaborate network can spread hot water, cold water, or even steam as illustrated in Figure 8.3. The pipes are installed in trenches within the neighborhood, or they are placed above ground (Harvey 2006). Various measures make this process efficient—the water may be returned to the main plant to be reheated, and the pipes that distribute the water are often pre-insulated to retain the heat.

There are many types of energy sources that can fuel a district heating system. Some district heating systems have centralized boilers. *Renewable energy sources* provide a self-sustaining resource to district heating systems. Geothermal heat, solar heat, wind turbines, and the combustion of biomass are all potential heat sources. Further, industrial heat pumps can extract heat from sea, river, or lake water, and heat can be founding the sewage or waste from industrial processes. The possibilities are many and exciting; we will explore some here in more detail.

Geothermal energy is harnessed from the heat stored beneath the earth's surface. The earth is comprised of various layers: core, outer core, mantle, and crust. In

Figure 8.3:
In district heating systems, underground pipes distribute hot or cold water and steam to each dwelling.

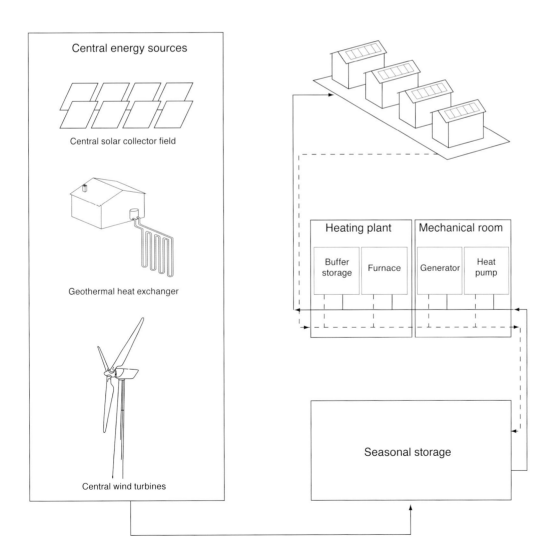

turn, this crust consists of separate tectonic plates of varying thicknesses. It is in the earth's core that geothermal heat is produced, generated by the slow decay of the radioactive chemical elements that make up the earth, like uranium and potassium (Mannvit Engineering 2013). As the tectonic plates slide, collide, or pull apart from each other, magma is brought to the surface of the ground. Therefore, in these places, the ground temperature is very high at a shallow depth. Geothermal power systems utilize that heat in different kinds of power plants: dry-steam plants, flash steam plants, and binary plants (Gevorkian 2008). Geothermal energy is a natural resource that can be found almost anywhere, especially in volcanic and granite-abundant regions, making it a particularly attractive source for district heating systems around the globe.

Solar energy heat is in principle available anywhere, although some neighborhoods in different regions of the world have more reliable access to sunlight than others. Solar collectors are mounted on a roof or on the ground and are connected to a circuit that transports the energy to households (CIT Energy Management AB 2010). As solar energy is less available during the winter than in the summer, the district heating system must be able to store the solar heat harvested during the summer. Collector arrays and storages are therefore built in close proximity to one another. Solar district heating plants require little maintenance and emit no greenhouse gases, offering neighborhoods a very sustainable option.

Wind turbines convert natural wind into usable energy. Some neighborhoods have higher wind speeds than others, so turbines must be carefully placed. Wind energy can be stored for many days, as there are wind lulls even in areas prone to high winds (Nordic Folkecenter for Renewable Energy 2010). First, turbines collect wind energy, and, as explained earlier, water is heated at the central district heating plant by harvesting that energy. The turbines are directly

connected to heat pumps, and the hot water is thereafter distributed to household via the pipes connected to the central heating system (Environmental Protection Agency 2011). Wind energy, like both geothermal and solar power, is a natural and local energy source, offering neighborhoods an alternative source to fossil fuel combustion.

District heating systems can also take advantage of nearby large bodies of water by way of industrial heat pumps. This incredible technology can extract heat from sea, river, or lake water. The surface of a lake cools to 4°C (39°F) in the winter, and that cool surface water sinks to the bottom of the lake during the summer, as cold water is denser than warm water (Enwave Energy Corporation 2011). Conversely, surface water in the summer remains at the surface of the lake because the warmer water is less dense than the cool water. The bottom of a lake, like any deep body of water, will therefore remain cold, even during the summer season. A lake is a natural reservoir of cold water, a renewable resource in itself. District heating systems can harness energy from the coldness of the water, rather than the water itself (Enwave Energy Corporation 2011). Heat pumps, also used to harness geothermal energy and sewage or waste heat, force heat flow from a lower to a higher heat (the reverse of the natural flow), using a small amount of power, like electricity. The pumps can also cool by transferring heat in the opposite direction (Heat Pump Center 2014).

Biomass energy, produced from low-carbon waste and plant materials, is a renewable resource, though it does not inherently qualify for use in a net-zero energy neighborhood. Nevertheless, the greenhouse gases that are emitted, released from burning biomass, are significantly reduced when compared to the combustion of fossil fuels. However, if the biomass is unsustainably harvested, its renewability is outweighed by the pollution produced and water consumed in the process. Coal plants can be retrofitted to run entirely on biomass and natural gas production can be replaced by biogas, a gas produced from the careful conversion of biomass. District heating systems that already rely on fossil fuel combustion can be converted to biomass energy, reducing emissions and increasing sustainability (Union of Concerned Scientists 2010).

This all goes to illustrate the advantages of various district heating systems beyond that of lowering greenhouse gas emissions. District heating systems are low-maintenance, have a long life span, and, of course, eliminate the need for individual household maintenance of heating systems. Space is freed in houses by removing the need for boilers, and noise is reduced, subsequently increasing home property values (Enwave Energy Corporation 2011). There are also cost savings in using natural resources, be it after a large initial investment, although prices will depend on location and availability of the energy source, obviously. Energy security is improved with district heating as it uses local resources (Euroheat and Power 2011). Its local nature also decreases importation and transportation of energy.

These are all advantages atop an incredible environmental benefit. Using renewable resources instead of fossil fuels reduces the demand and dependency on primary energy sources. Further, district heating is up to three times more efficient in furnishing energy to individual homes than an isolated heating system (Austin 2010).

Despite the many advantages of district heating, like any energy system, it is not without fault. It requires large initial investment on the part of the neighborhood to install a plant. If the neighborhood had previously relied on another form of energy or individual boilers, households must be willing to change their heating systems to district heating. Residents also must be willing to improve insulation. There are therefore individual costs in addition to a larger-scale community investment. Moreover, though breaks are rare, any break in a district heating system will result in service interruption for the entire neighborhood. Another cost is represented by the fact that a neighborhood must have a formal establishment to run the district heating system. It is essential that its policy be committed to long-term gain, and infrastructure must be well planned out to maximize these gains (Burke 2012).

Iceland is an excellent example of the successful implementation of geothermal district heating. Over 90 percent of all homes in Iceland receive energy from three plants that provide both heat and power by way of geothermal technology (Mannvit Engineering 2013). Despite the nation's abundance of geothermal energy, the switch from fossil fuels only occurred after the first oil shock in the 1970s (Mims 2008).

Net-zero neighborhoods and the district heating systems that support them will no doubt be an essential part of sustainable construction practices in future. That said, creating a net-zero-energy community requires long-term planning and forethought, as its district heating requires a large initial investment on behalf of the neighborhood and individuals. Municipal planners must implement guidelines regarding home orientation to encourage passive solar gain. Households need to contribute by updating their insulation, windows, and doors. Despite the price of initial investment, a district heating system is well worth it. It offers residents a relatively cost-effective method by which to reduce their carbon footprint given that the system relies on renewable resources like geothermal energy, solar energy, wind power, bodies of water, and biomass. It is also worth considering that net-zero living does not require individuals to change their consumption habits but rather to simply update the system by which their habits are supplied, making it a realistic way for everyone to achieve sustainable living.

8A

Project:
Hammarby Sjöstad

Location:
Stockholm, Sweden

Design Firm:
White

Hammarby Sjöstad is recognized as one of the most sustainable communities in the world. The project was initially planned as part of Stockholm's Olympic bid to host the most "environmentally conscious" games. Even after the city's rejection by the Olympic committee, officials recognized the importance of sustainable community design and so went forward with the 20,000-unit project. This was evidently a sound decision: Hammarby is now a community revered by environmentalists and planners worldwide—a true success in experimental sustainable development.

Hammarby is a refreshing approach to sustainable design. It is in fact an embodiment of many principles outlined in this book: transit-oriented development, mixed-use design, cyclist/pedestrian priority, carbon neutrality, and, of course, net-zero energy consumption. It was planned as an extension of the city, rather than a suburb; despite its distance from the city center, the neighborhood has a distinctly urban feel.

Several alternatives to car travel were created with the community in the hopes of reaching a goal of 0.5 cars per residential unit. Two new bus routes serve the development and operate using biofuel. A tramline runs through the center of the community, offering service to a nearby metro station. This station offers residents easy connection to the city center. As Stockholm is comprised of several islands, a free ferry service also connects Hammarby to the rest of the city.

An ENVAC waste collection system is used to dispose of the community's garbage and recycling. Pressurized air transports the waste to central collection points. This eliminates the need for pick-up services and thus heavily reduces the carbon produced in the process of waste collection. Only one-third of the waste plant is actually devoted to incineration. The remaining two-thirds are for emission management—that is, these sectors are responsible for the fact that 94 percent of emissions are released as vapor water. Liquid sewage is converted into heat and biogas, in turn used to power municipal buses. Solid sewage is used as compost for forested areas.

8.4

Figure 8.4:
Site plan.

Figure 8.5:
A view of the community from
the bridge linking Hammarby and
Stockholm.

Figure 8.6:
Tram corridor in Hammarby.

8.5

8.6

Figure 8.7:

Many of the buildings have residences built on top of commerce.

Figure 8.8:

Entrance to one of the apartment buildings.

8.7

8.8

The involvement of forty private contracting companies drove up competition, as each one wanted their contribution to be the most "green" building on-site. As a result, contractors went to spectacular lengths. In fact, this competitive spirit gave rise to some of Hammarby's greatest achievements, especially in the realm of photovoltaic panels and shells. Early on, contractors recognized the advantages conferred by installing solar panels on their structures. As a result, in the summer months, 50 percent of all energy used in Hammarby is sourced through photovoltaic panels. The solar energy harnessed, coupled with the energy produced by organic waste, compose the vast majority of the district's supply—meaning that the community is run almost entirely on renewable energy. As if this weren't enough, various techniques have been used to ensure maximum sun shading to keep apartments cool in the summer months.

The success of the Hammarby project lies not only in its incredible infrastructure, but also in the commitment of its citizens to the sustainable ethos. In the first place, Swedes, as a people, have widely embraced the green lifestyle. For instance, 79 percent of all Stockholmers walk, bike, or use public transport for their daily commute; in the past ten years, bike usage has spiked by 70 percent in the city. Seeking to improve on these already impressive commitments to environmental living, Hammarby's developer set up an education center to encourage pro-environmental behavior on a micro level. These initiatives have been highly successful in encouraging a variety of green practices. For example, daily water usage has been lowered to 150 liters (40 gallons) compared to a citywide average of 200 liters (53 gallons).

Figure 8.9.

These tubes are part of the waste collection system that is used for energy production.

Figure 8.10:

A boat dock area in the heart of the community, which also serves as a natural amphitheater.

Figure 8.11:

Pedestrian path.

Figure 8.12:

A section showing the waste collection system for energy production.

Figure 8.13:

Hammarby is served by an extensive network of bike paths.

Figure 8.14:

Balconies on an apartment building.

Housing costs in Hammarby compare favorably to apartments in the city center. This serves as further proof that sustainability can be achieved on a budget. The lure of affordability, alongside the district's pedestrian-friendly design and abundance of schools and daycare centers, has made the development very popular among young families—another part of why the district is such a vibrant place.

Hammarby has established Stockholm as a world capital in sustainable design. Indeed, the district is a first-rate model for environmentally conscious change, especially with regards to energy production and conservation methods. One can only hope more communities follow their lead.

8.13

8.9

8.11

8.14

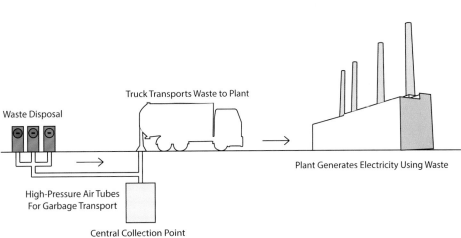

Waste Disposal

Truck Transports Waste to Plant

Plant Generates Electricity Using Waste

High-Pressure Air Tubes For Garbage Transport

Central Collection Point

8.12

8.10

8B

Project:
Paisano Green

Location:
El Paso, Texas, USA

Design Firm:
Workshop8

Figure 8.15:
Overview of site plan.

Figure 8.16:
Section of community flats showing cross-ventilation.

Paisano Green is the first senior living community in the US to allow net-zero, fossil fuel-free living in a LEED platinum environment. The development houses ninety-three low-income occupants over the age of sixty-five. These residents were selected for their interest in the community's sustainable goals; even to be considered, applicants were required to express commitment to the lifestyle choices associated with net-zero status.

The community is comprised of four three-story apartment blocks in the west and a long one-story building for single-occupancy residences in the east. There is a community center to the north of the site. All of these buildings together surround a large garden, and in addition to this substantial outdoor space, several courtyards have been placed between the flats.

Solar panels have been incorporated into most flat, rooftop surfaces. These are extremely effective in El Paso's climate, taking advantage of the 302 days of continuously bright sun each year. The 640 solar panels provide a 165-kilowatt energy source, accounting for the majority of electricity use in the development. Two Xzeres 4425 wind turbines are also located on-site and provide an additional 10 kilowatts, totaling 175 kilowatts of renewable power generated locally. A large canopy wall connects the three-story flats, upon which one can find even more solar panels. This connection also protects residences against wind and hot afternoon sun, while blocking out noise from the street. The local energy provider does not support a net meter rate, but an exception has been made for Paisano Green. Energy is purchased by the grid at the same rate the community is charged for use. This arrangement provides residents exceptional savings on their utility bills; further, it is more evidence that sustainable living and affordable housing go hand-in-hand.

Orientation was extremely important to the development to both maximize the energy collected from the sun and minimize the solar heat entering the residences. Windows rarely face east or west, and have been placed on the north and south façades. Sun is strongest to the east and west, and since El Paso has a hot climate, natural heating is undesirable.

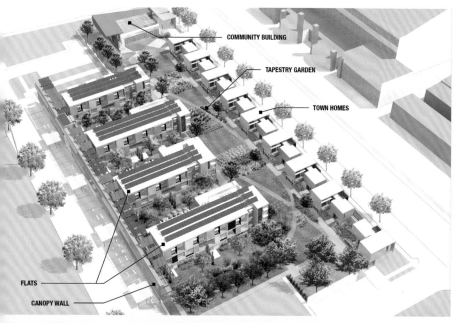

COMMUNITY BUILDING

TAPESTRY GARDEN

TOWN HOMES

FLATS

CANOPY WALL

8.15

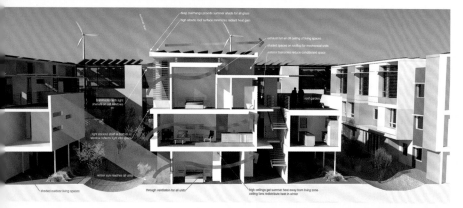

8.16

Figure 8.17:

Community flats along open corridor.

Figure 8.18:

Public space between community flats.

Figure 8.19:

View of a row of community flats.

Figure 8.20:

The landscaping takes into consideration the arid environment.

Proper insulation and sun-deflective technology ensure that minimal air conditioning is needed. Walls contain R-26 hybridized insulation and minimal thermal bridging. Roofing has been chosen to reflect the sun's energy rather than absorb it. The use of mini-split heat pumps and energy-recovery ventilators, in addition to a high-efficiency heating and cooling system, together make for highly sustainable air conditioning when needed. All connection spaces are open to the exterior environment, and therefore do not require heating, cooling, or ventilation. All apartments have been equipped with efficient fixtures and appliances including LED lighting, a heat pump instead of an electric water heater, and low-flow plumbing fixtures, which utilize air to create pressure rather than the water itself.

Resident participation is of key importance in the project. The developer offers a variety of training programs and incentives for its residents to keep participation levels high. The initial number of solar panels installed is not enough to sustain net-zero energy use for a community living a typical American lifestyle. Rather than spend extra money and install more panels than needed, the developer decided to first observe the lifestyle choices of residents and install the panels as required in order to reach net-zero. Ample rooftop space has been left for additional panels.

Paisano Green is a landmark achievement in American housing practice. Not only is it a model of environmental conservation—in serving low-income seniors, but the project also offers comfort and opportunity to a demographic in need. Further, and especially in its provision of low-cost utilities, the community readily demonstrates the affordability of sustainable living.

8.17

8.18

8.19

8.20

Figure 8.21:
Dusk view of community flats.

Figure 8.22:
Community flats canopy wall turbine.

Figure 8.23:
Community townhouses.

Figure 8.24:
A gazebo in the public area.

8.22 (above)   8.23 (below)

8.21

8.24

8C

Project:
UC Davis West Village

Location:
Davis, California, USA

Architect of Record:
SVA Architects, Inc.

The University of California at Davis has realized an excellent opportunity for net zero energy community design in their dearth of local housing for students, faculty, and staff. A new sustainable community to house the university's patrons and staff is being built, and the plan is comprised exclusively of buildings that can sustain their own energy usage. The development currently houses 800 university-affiliated residents in 350 apartments, and will consist of 662 apartments and 343 single-family homes when finished.

Federal and state governments have supported the community with US $7.5 million in grants. The money is used to fund research projects in waste-to-renewable energy, technology, business strategies for photovoltaic solar energy systems, and various other efforts of harnessing sustainable energy. One such experimental energy source is *bio-digester* technology, a system that converts organic matter and waste into energy. This is currently being developed with the aid of UC Davis professor of biological and agricultural studies Ruihong Zhang. The community doubles as a research facility for the university and has provided a unique environment for education and experimentation.

If a community of comparable size had been built in adherence to California energy-efficiency requirements, 22 million kilowatts of energy would be consumed annually. Incredibly, the community uses only half this standard, running on only 11 million kilowatts per year. Sustainable energy is harnessed on-site using a four-megawatt solar photovoltaic system. This is crucial to meet the community's net-zero goal. Moreover, as aforementioned, several other forms of sustainable energy are currently under research for use on-site.

Residences were designed to meet maximum energy efficiency and have been fitted with energy- and water-efficient appliances. In each dwelling, patio doors and oversized windows allow ventilation and cooling throughout the entire living area. Blinds and sophisticated sunshades are utilized to minimize natural heating in the apartments during California's hot summers. Heat-reflective roofing, heat-blocking roof sheathing, and roof overhangs also help to keep heat out of the apartments, while cold air is kept in using extra insulation in exterior walls.

Sensors have been installed to turn off lights when residents are out. All lighting in the community is highly efficient and uses LED technology. Outdoor lighting uses the same technology and dims or turns off altogether when not needed. Water fixtures also run at a high efficiency: Low-flow fixtures use significantly less water and create pressure using air. Toilets and shower faucets are water-saving, with toilets using only 4.8 liters (1.28 gallons) per flush (22 percent more efficient than standard), and showers using 5.6 liters (1.5 gallons) per minute (40 percent more efficient than standard). Living area floors have been constructed using 50 percent recycled materials, and countertops are made of recycled granite.

Figure 8.25:
Site plan.

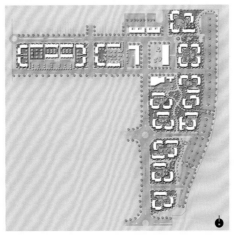

8.25

The energy-conscious lifestyles of residents are of pinnacle importance to the success of the community. The university has recognized this and taken several steps to encourage limited consumption. A cap has been placed on utilities; all residents that exceed their usage will be charged extra. Energy usage can be monitored online. Similarly, a smartphone app is being developed for the same purpose and, further, to enable residents to turn off their lighting and appliances when out.

UC Davis has shown a commitment to sustainable living that is true of few educational institutions. The community has provided students and staff a fully equipped working environment in which to research and, moreover, to observe the results of the very technologies and practices they develop. Thus, this project represents an innovative integration of livability and function.

Figure 8.26:
Overview of public space.

Figure 8.27:
Pathway and bicycle storage area.

Figure 8.28:
Shared pedestrian path between units.

Figure 8.29:
Outdoor area near residence.

Figure 8.30:
Bike path.

Figure 8.31:
Sun-breakers on facades of residences A.

Figure 8.32:
Front elevation of one of the buildings.

8.26

8.27

8.28 (above)　　　8.29 (below)

8.30

8.31

8.32

Figure 8.33:
One of the units' interiors

Figure 8.34:
Sun-breakers on facades of
residences B.

Figure 8.35:
Green space between buildings.

8.33

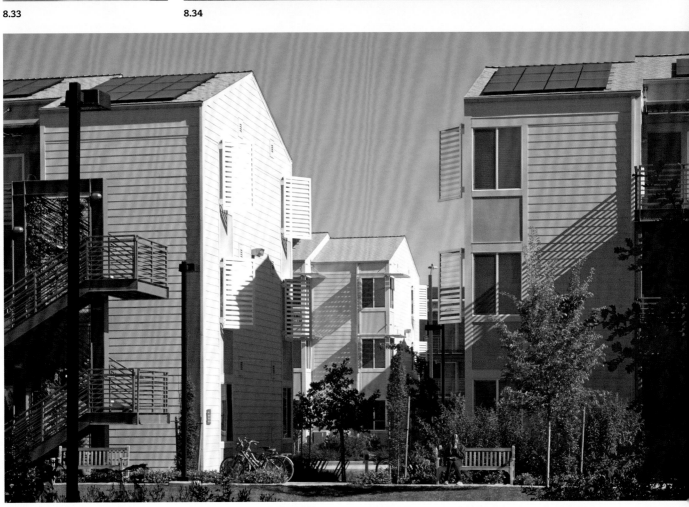

8.34

8.35

8D

Project:
zHome

Location:
Issaquah Highlands,
Washington, USA

Design Firm:
David Vandervort Architects

zHome is the first net-zero, carbon-neutral development in the US. Its 16,000 square meters (172,000 square feet) site, located in the Issaquah Highlands, accommodates ten housing units. Every aspect of zHome, including the building process (which used 78 percent FSC-certified lumber), has been designed to minimize energy consumption and carbon emission.

The most noticeable feature of zHome is a series of roof-mounted photovoltaic panels. These add considerably to the aesthetic quality of the townhomes. After careful investigation, the roofing size was calculated to house the exact number of photovoltaic panels needed for net-zero energy consumption. The houses are tied into the local electric grid. During the summer months, the panels produce more energy than is needed by the community. All excess energy is put into the local grid to be used by the wider community. In the winter, the panels produce less energy than is needed to support the homes, and so the grid assists in supplying the development with energy. This relationship benefits both parties and allows zHome to have net-zero energy usage without the need for extensive facilities to store excess energy.

High-quality insulation procedures were put into place to prevent excessive heating or air conditioning. Walls and ceilings are highly heat retaining. Windows are tightly sealed and their panes of extremely high quality. Fresh air is pumped into the house using heat-recovery ventilation, and, on top of all this, heating and air conditioning use a ground-source heat pump system.

Rainwater is harvested and stored for communal use. During storms, water is collected in areas around the community to avoid flooding. This drainage of storm water further decreases the development's impact on the existing site, allowing excess water to travel through the same path it would have followed in the original forested area. Heat and hot water are shared by the dwellings through ground-source wells. The units use 70 percent less water than average through the use of efficient fixtures and the rainwater recycling system.

The community's pre-existing transit system helps to limit car usage. The ample transit connections allow residents to travel locally with ease and to commute west to Seattle. Car parking is located at the periphery of the development. For those who own a motor vehicle, electric cars are encouraged; exclusive electric-car parking and charging stations have been installed.

Figure 8.36:
Site plan.

Figure 8.37:
A sun and wind diagram through the project.

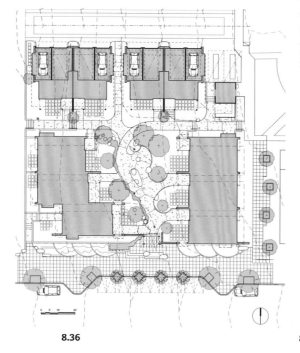

8.36

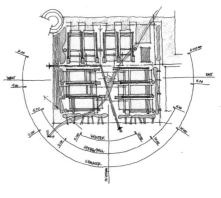

8.37

Figure 8.38:
Main entrance to the community.

Figure 8.39:
Public charging station for electric vehicle.

Figure 8.40:
Entry passageway.

Figure 8.41:
Public space in the heart of the cluster.

8.38

8.39

8.40

8.41

A primary concern of the architect was that a focus on technologically advanced features, while necessary to ensure sustainability, would take away the community feel of the development. In order to counter this effect, several features encouraging neighborly interaction were installed. The houses surround a public courtyard, and windows have been strategically placed to look out onto the street, all in an effort to familiarize residents with their neighbors and surrounding area.

As the first net-zero, carbon-neutral development in the US, zHome has set an exceptional precedent. Following its construction, many environmentally sustainable developments borrowing ideas and principles from the project have been built across the country. The community has in effect introduced a new standard for environmentalism in the American housing market.

Figure 8.42:
Kitchen/Dining area.

Figure 8.43:
Living space.

Figure 8.44:
View of the living and dining areas.

Figure 8.45:
View of the living room and a balcony.

8.42

8.43

8.44

8.45 (below)

8E

Project:
BedZED

Location:
London, UK

Design Firm:
ZED Factory

BedZED is the largest carbon-neutral mixed-use development in the UK. The London development houses eighty-two affordable residential units and accommodates 2,500 square meters (27,000 square feet) of office and workspace. Pedestrians and cyclists have been given priority in the community, and car parking has been placed on the periphery. The development prioritized carbon neutrality first and foremost but also took considerable measures to create a livable community. Thus the community boasts ample outdoor space and opportunity for social interaction.

Developers made conscious decisions to minimize carbon emissions during construction in both their material sourcing and building techniques. Much of the community's structural steelwork and softwood wailing studs were recycled from local demolition sites. This both saved money for the developer and ensured that useful components would not end up in a landfill. The majority of bulk materials were made within 80 kilometers (50 miles) of the site, eliminating the need for wasteful long-haul shipping. As a result, the carbon emission due to travel is close to industry standard, even with the use of thicker walls and a much larger thermal mass.

A combined heat and energy biomass plant was installed on-site. Unfortunately, the plant was too small to run, from both a technical and financial perspective, and had to be shut down. There are plans to install a wood-fire boiler as a replacement, and photovoltaics currently account for a considerable portion of the development's electricity. That said, the plant is still an interesting design that bears investigation.

The energy biomass plant was unique in that it produced the same amount of carbon as a typical heat-only boiler but also met the electrical demands of the community for some time. It was designed ingeniously to run off wood chips. In fact, it was so efficient and productive that when it ran consistently—only shutting down for scheduled maintenance—it created power in excess of BedZED's needs. All of this extra energy was then pumped back into the grid for the use of the broader community. Planners estimated that if this system achieved a surplus of 5 to 15 percent of the annual demand, the generator could compensate for all carbon produced during its construction.

A water treatment plant on-site allows the community to recycle its water supply. Water-conserving appliances have been installed in all residences. Using these techniques, coupled with the diligence of its residents, households use only 72 liters (19 gallons) of fresh water each day, with an additional 15 liters (4 gallons) of recycled water.

A passive ventilation system utilizing wind-driven cowls has been installed on the roof. This system—combined with the triple glazing applied to all windows, super insulation, and south-facing conservatories—eliminates a need for intensive air conditioning. In the winter, these features, along with a passive solar heating system, serve to keep the interior warm. Heating in the development has been lowered by 80 percent compared to the typical British home.

Figure 8.46:
Site plan.

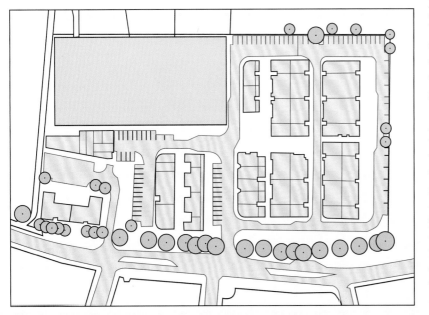

Figure 8.47:
Aerial view.

Figure 8.48:
Street entrance to the project.

Figure 8.49:
Pedestrian walkway along the building's side.

Figure 8.50:
Roofscape and balconies.

Figure 8.51:
View of the vehicle mews from above.

Using a diverse mix of energy-conscious features, BedZED has cut household energy usage to 2579 kilowatt hours per year, 45 percent lower than the surrounding area. For heating, its average annual usage is 3526 kilowatt hours, 81 percent lower than average. The carbon emissions attributed to this energy use are 72 percent that of similar houses built in the same period. In sum, BedZED utilized sustainable housing practice, including the installation of resource-efficient amenities, to spectacular result: Residents have cut their overall carbon emissions by 50 percent.

8.49

8.47

8.48

8.50

8.51

8.52

8.53

8.54

8.55

8.56

8.57

Figure 8.52:
Vehicle mews.

Figure 8.53:
Top of air ventilation.

Figure 8.54:
Plenty of glass lets in natural light into the units.

Figure 8.55:
Solar panels generate alternative energy.

Figure 8.56:
Ground floor gardens.

Figure 8.57:
The project's Living Machine.

8F

Project:
Almere Sun Island

Location:
Almere, the Netherlands

Design Firm:
Nuon Energy and OMA

Figure 8.58:
Site plan.

Figure 8.59:
Solar-powered home facing a canal.

Figure 8.60:
A section of the community with solar-powered homes A.

Almere Sun Island is a fast-growing solar-energy development designed to showcase the advantages of renewable energy. Its master plan is the work of architect Rem Koolhaas. One of two recent sustainable developments in Almere city.

The "Sun Island" is a collection of solar panels in the Noorderplassen district of Almere. The massive solar farm is comprised of 520 panels, spanning an area of 7,000 square meters (64,600 square feet)—the equivalent of 1.5 football fields. It is the world's third-largest solar energy center. The island supplies some of the development's electricity and runs the district's central heating system. The system is extremely easy to clean and maintain, as there are no rotating parts. There are, in fact, far fewer maintenance-related hiatuses at the solar farm than with typical power plants, as turbines tend to be the source of most technical malfunctions.

The process of utilizing solar energy for district heating is relatively simple. Water is heated using the energy gathered by the panels and then pumped into the district heating system. This provides 2,700 homes with hot water and central heating. Ten percent of all energy required by Almere residents is produced through the solar plant. Annually, the plant provides residents of Almere with 9,750 gigajoules of sustainable energy, enough to provide one-third of all electricity needed by the district.

Through the use of the district heating system and solar energy, carbon dioxide emissions by residents has been lowered by 50 percent. This reduction is the equivalent of every household driving 12,000 kilometers (7,456 miles) less by car each year. Private residences and public buildings have also installed solar panels on their roofs and façades, further minimizing the use of nonrenewable energy.

8.59

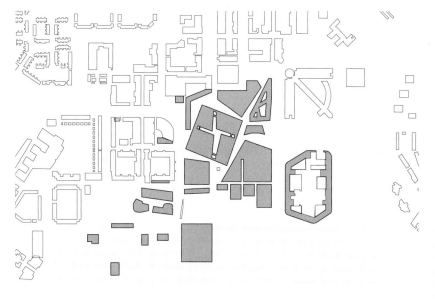

8.58

8.60

The community's success plan lies in the design of its individual dwellings. There are 550 solar homes and 600 low-energy homes in the Noorderplassen-West area of Almere. More solar homes are planned for the newer district of Columbuskwartier, all of which will have a minimum of 10 square meters (108 square feet) of solar panels installed on each roof or façade. Typical housing in Almere is built to be 10 percent more efficient than standard.

The master plan developed for Almere's city center promises a bright future and will incorporate its much-anticipated growth. Focus for redevelopment has been placed on only two central sites that are both easily accessible to residents and commuters alike. These new centers are easily reached by the commuter train and the city's comprehensive bicycle lane network. Most of Almere's office spaces and new commercial buildings will be constructed in this area, eliminating the need for many residents to commute into Amsterdam.

The City of Almere has shown a major commitment to renewable energy as it continues to grow from town to city. It is an example for all newly developed metropolitan centers that aim to achieve sustainability. Though it will of course take time to observe its true success, it is clear that the city has set a trajectory for healthy growth.

Figure 8.61:
Apartment houses with commercial functions on lower level.

Figure 8.62:
Townhouses that get their power from a central solar source.

8.61

8.62

8.63

8.64

8.65

Figure 8.63:
A section of the community with
solar-powered homes B.

Figure 8.64:
A section of the community with
solar-powered homes C.

Figure 8.65:
Apartments that get their power
from a central solar source.

Summary and Key Considerations

- Energy demand has risen sharply with population growth, average size of residence, and household appliance usage in developed nations.

- The use of alternative power sources is emerging as a key strategy by which to decrease energy demand, but individual heating and cooling systems are inefficient and unsustainable systems to provide renewable power.

- Net-zero energy neighborhoods, powered by a central alternative source in district heating and cooling systems, offer cost savings, energy efficiency, and a lower carbon footprint to each household.

- Within the neighborhood, net-zero dwellings decrease energy consumption. The energy conservation of such a house is achieved by limiting the structure's size and orienting it to take advantage of passive solar gain, natural daylight, and indoor airflow.

- Homes in net-zero neighborhoods must also be built to limit heat loss and therefore must be well insulated.

- Windows and doors are other essential considerations in the reduction of a dwelling's energy consumption. They must be carefully chosen to reduce heat loss.

- There are many types of energy sources that can fuel a district heating system. Renewable energy sources are self-sustaining and sustainable options.

- These are some such possible heat sources: geothermal heat, solar heat, wind turbines, industrial heat pumps that extract heat from sea, river, or lake water, sewage or waste heat from industrial processes and combustion of biomass.

- The use of sustainable resources lowers greenhouse gas emissions and offers users other less-obvious advantages. For one, district heating systems require little maintenance and have a long life span; they additionally eliminate the need for individual household maintenance of heating systems.

- There are further advantages to district heating systems. Space is freed in houses by removing the need for boilers, and noise is reduced, subsequently increasing home property value. Also, these systems are approximately three times more efficient in furnishing energy to individual homes than isolated heating systems.

- District heating requires a large initial investment on the part of the neighborhood in order to install a plant. Furthermore, if the community had previously relied on another form of energy or individual boilers, households must be willing to change.

- Despite the investment required, net-zero neighborhoods are an immensely attractive practice given that they do not require individuals to change their consumption habits, but rather, to simply update the system by which their habits are supplied.

Exercises

1. List the characteristics of net-zero communities. What do you think can be done to improve their performance?

2. List the characteristics of net-zero residences. What do you think can be done to improve their performance?

3. Identify alternative renewable-energy sources, and investigate which of them offers the fastest payback period.

4. Study the communities described in the case studies that introduced district heating, and list the advantages and disadvantages of having such a system.

5. List the challenges faced by existing communities that wish to introduce district heating. How, in your view, can these challenges be overcome?

Chapter 9
Planning for Healthy Living

Rates of obesity and other noncommunicable, lifestyle-related diseases are steadily increasing at the global level; this despite ongoing efforts to curb the phenomenon. In both the public and private sector, well-intentioned organizations have attempted to limit the size of soda drinks, promote healthier school lunches, and expose calorie content in chain restaurant menus. Though these are important first steps, the said initiatives are simply not enough—far more change is required.

For one, our current built environments offer little opportunity to be physically active. Indeed, over the past century, our communities and homes have been tailored around the aim of performing reduced physical labor; we are thus burning fewer and fewer calories, building less and less muscular strength, and neglecting our aerobic capacities. This chapter will illustrate how better planning can offer opportunities for physical activity—after all, given that designers have so effectively achieved the goal of physical labor reduction, perhaps this suggests we have the power to do the opposite.

Places and Well-Being

Preventable diseases stemming in good part from poor diet and a lack of exercise are the great epidemics of the twenty-first century, this according to the World Health Organization (WHO) (Beaubien 2015). You read correctly—in today's world, lifestyle factors claim larger death tolls worldwide than those of communicable viruses and other highly publicized global health crises. In the words of WHO representative Dr. Shanthi Mendis: "It's a slow-motion public health disaster, seemingly invisible and rapidly gathering speed … The important thing to remember is it's not just killing a couple of thousands of people. It's killing millions, and it's going to kill millions for decades" (cited in Beaubien 2015).

The global prevalence of overweight and obese populations among all ages, and in particular, children, has become of special concern to public health officials in recent years. For example, two-thirds of American adults twenty years and older are obese or overweight (Flegal, Carrol, and Ogden 2010). This population is at an increased risk of certain cancers, heart disease, stroke, high blood pressure, joint and bone disease, and depression. Further, chronic disease rates have grown even as medical spending increases and more medical resources are used.

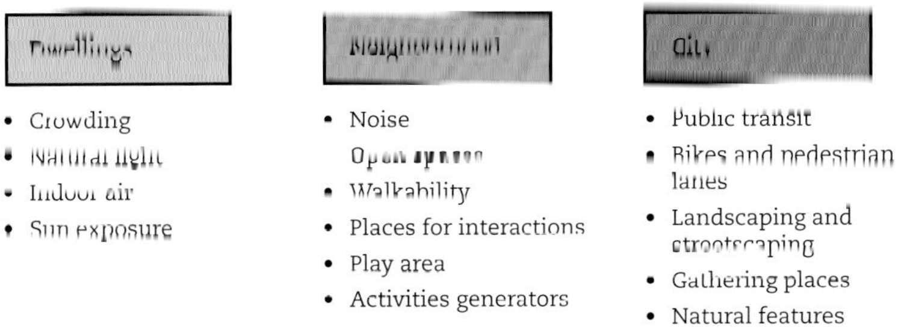

Dwellings	Neighborhood	City
• Crowding	• Noise	• Public transit
• Natural light	• Open space	• Bikes and pedestrian lanes
• Indoor air	• Walkability	• Landscaping and streetscaping
• Sun exposure	• Places for interactions	• Gathering places
	• Play area	• Natural features
	• Activities generators	

Figure 9.1:
Direct and indirect factors affecting a community's active lifestyle.

spontaneity, unfortunately, has been taken out of the equation. It is no wonder that TV watching and computer games have replaced outdoor play. Studies suggest that TV viewing is North American youth's primary activity, with 1.5 to 2.5 hours on average per day. It is notable that this opens children up to a variety of health issues—for instance, some of this time almost inevitably includes watching advertisements for high-caloric foods (Larson 2001).

Contemporary low-density planning's detrimental health effects can additionally be traced to the role of the sidewalk in contemporary design. In some communities they have been left out altogether, forcing seniors, parents pushing strollers, and children of all ages to share the road with motorists. Where the sidewalk has vanished, very often benches have followed, and so too trees to stand underneath on a sunny day.

Joens-Matre et al. (2008) found that the rates of obesity were higher among rural children at 25 percent compared to those from urban areas at 19 percent and small cities at 17 percent. Indeed, low-density residential developments support automobile dependency, and therefore unhealthy lifestyles. Similarly, the disappearance of the sidewalk, back lane, and small play yard in these settings leave today's children with fewer opportunities to take part in unorganized play. This is particularly distressing given the many benefits conferred particularly to children through exercise—consider, for instance, that participation in physical activity in natural settings is an effective method of reducing symptoms of childhood attention deficit disorder (Kuo and Taylor 2004).

In addition, in the name of efficiency, schools have been relocated from their traditional spots in the hearts of neighborhoods to the outskirts where they can easily be accessed from major roads by car. That has meant that a pupil's short walk or easy bike ride to class is a thing of the past. Small play areas near residential developments represent yet another feature that has by and large found its way into the municipal planner's wastebasket, having been replaced by the huge play field, an often faraway area to which children have to be driven. The play itself has in turn been morphed by way of regimented leagues and strict schedules;

Retooling Neighborhoods for Health

Here we attempt to answer a question so often asked by public health officials: How should active lifestyle be reintroduced in neighborhoods? Recasting the features of the built environment that have been subtracted over the past half-century picture would be a good place to start. Those features include direct and indirect aspects as illustrated in Figure 9.1. In effect, homes and neighborhoods must be regarded as "exercise machines," offering recreation and active lifestyle opportunity for people of all ages (Figure 9.2). Additionally, along with the extensive reintroduction of healthy physical features, the need to warn citizens about the grim consequences of inactive lifestyles has become abundantly clear.

Interestingly, communities can be retooled for physical health by utilizing strategies designed to address other sustainability issues. Thus, some of the planning approaches articulated in earlier chapters readily apply to this discussion: Building higher-density, mixed-use areas with efficient public transit systems, walkable neighborhoods, and engaging parks together represent an effective paradigm for health planning. Again, these initiatives will not only inherently make people more physically active but also serve to make a city more environmentally friendly. The sustainability of a healthy and active neighborhood derives not only from the reduction of car usage and increase in green space but also, less obviously, from the reduction in resources needed to treat preventable diseases. In short, the introduction of accessible exercise opportunities is less costly and more effective than spending more on medical treatments (Dannenberg, Frumkin, and Jackson 2011). In addition, to improve public health, attention should be paid to water quality and having access to heathy nutrition, which will be discussed in Chapter 10.

Neighborhoods should encourage physical activity through both transportation- and recreation-focused measures. *Walkable communities* have distinct characteristics related to their built environments that make them supportive of active mobility. Firstly, walkable communities are compact, and generally, mixed-land developments. As amenities are located within walking distance, residents are more likely to take advantage of the proximity and walk instead of drive to work and to shop. Secondly, *street connectivity* is another important aspect of walkable neighborhoods. Greater connectivity offers shorter routes to walkers, increasing the appeal of this transportation mode. Finally, residential density is another factor related to physical activity. Higher-density neighborhoods support local retail and public transit systems (Dannenberg, Frumkin, and Jackson 2011). According to MacDonald et al. (2010) daily public transportation users are healthier and weigh less. While examining walking to public transit, Besser and Dannenberg (2005) concluded that walking to and from public transportation can help physically inactive populations, especially low-income groups, attain the recommended level of daily physical exercise.

Figure 9.2:

Homes and neighborhoods need to offer recreation and active lifestyle opportunities for people of all ages.

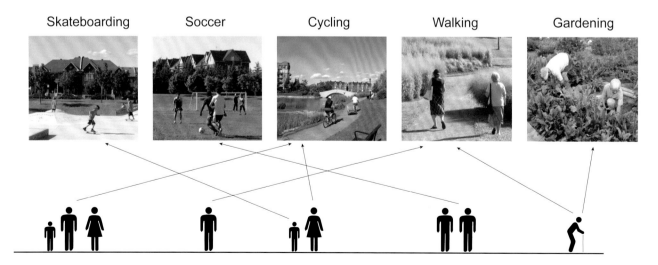

Both street connectivity and residential density are components that determine a neighborhood's rating on the walkability index. This recently developed tool should be a key consideration for planners today. In comparison to low-walkability neighborhoods, adults in high-walkability areas are more physically active by forty-one minutes every week (Saelens et al. 2003).

However, areas with high street connectivity do not necessarily support more physical activity in youth. Girls are more active in areas with low street connectivity (Norman et al. 2006). Boys are more active living in a cul-de-sac by five to twenty-two minutes daily compared to boys in high-connectivity environments (Carver, Timperio, and Crawford 2008). In sum, physical activity levels for children are not only dependent on the accessibility of *active transportation*—they need areas to play near their home with less traffic, for example, back lanes and small parks.

Participation in active transportation, like walking or biking, is also dependent on the quality of the transportation facilities and pedestrian infrastructure (Dannenberg, Frumkin, and Jackson 2011). Children are more likely to engage in physical activity where pedestrian infrastructure offers safe crossings and traffic-calming features such as speed humps and traffic lights (Carver, Timperio, and Crawford 2008). However, these features are not necessarily prevalent in mixed-use and walkable communities, and so do not reliably relate to increased physical activity levels for adults (Saelens and Handy 2008).

Active recreation, like active transportation, is dependent on access to and the quality of recreational facilities. People who live in proximity to a park or a play area will be the most likely users of that place (Kaczynski and Henderson 2007; Saelens and Handy 2008). In one study of park users, those who lived within 0.4 kilometers (0.25 miles) of the park used it most frequently at 43 percent, while living 1.6 kilometers (1 mile) away lowered use to 13 percent (Cohen et al. 2007). Similarly, a person's outdoor trail use decreases by 42 percent for every 0.4 kilometer (0.25 mile) distance from their home (Troped et al. 2001). Living near areas that foster active recreation in a natural context leads to more physical activity. Indeed, in areas near lakes, beaches, or the ocean, residents engage in increased levels of recreational physical activity when compared to their inland counterparts (Owen et al. 2004).

Both active transportation and recreation are dependent on the social environment just as they are on the built environment. Youth are positively influenced by the sight of others participating in physical activity. Also, areas with an absence of crime were also positively correlated with youth being more active (Evenson et al. 2007). Similarly, the quality of recreational facilities can affect a social environment and in turn the likelihood for both adults and youth to engage in physical activity. Park trails should be clean and safe; otherwise poor lighting, litter, and graffiti may discourage their use (Lovasi et al. 2009). The aesthetics of a facility or infrastructure are as conducive to physical activity as is access to those spaces.

Factors that relate the built and social environments to physical activity can be explained in a way other than how it has been laid out above. Instead of grouping the factors by motivation, like active transportation and active recreation, the characteristics of a healthy community can be categorized into *the 5 Ds of Development* (Cervero and Kockelman 1997, Ewing and Cervero 2001, Ewing and Cervero 2010). *Density*, *diversity*, *design*, *destination accessibility*, and *distance* have been touched upon in the previous paragraphs—they were simply organized differently.

To summarize, higher density ensures the walkability of an area. Diversity guarantees a range of people and amenities within one community. The careful design of a pedestrian-oriented environment ensures that residents feel inclined to take advantage of what their neighborhood offers. Destination accessibility ensures that residents and nonresidents have access to parks and facilities. Distance covers the accessibility of public transit systems to support the healthy pedestrian-oriented initiatives of the neighborhood.

Design considerations and initiatives can go beyond the link between physical activity and health. Just as social and built environments are related to health, a neighborhood's food environment affects a resident's well-being. Community planning can determine where food is obtained—for instance, in allocating space for a farmer's market and determining accessibility to grocery and convenience stores (Dannenberg, Frumkin, and Jackson 2011). Lovasi et al. (2009) characterized twenty-two studies regarding the relationship between food environments and obesity risk in lower socio-economic status populations. Many studies found a positive link between neighborhoods in proximity to supermarkets and favorable health outcomes, as supermarkets have a variety of fresh foods. Higher rates of obesity, hypertension, and diabetes were linked to neighborhoods with residents dependent on smaller grocery or convenience stores, hubs stocked with more limited food options.

The access and availability of fresh food are important considerations in the pursuit of health. However, food from full-service restaurants and fast-food chains is not a contributor to a healthy food environment: Fast is not fresh. For instance, the Bronx has New York City's highest hunger rates at 37 percent, and the borough is also characterized by the abundance of fast-food chains and lack of grocery stores (McMillan 2014).

This discussion revolves around an often-obscured relationship between hunger and weight. Certainly, the number of food-insecure households in the US has risen dramatically in the last fifty years, including an increase of 57 percent since the 1990s. However, many of America's hungry are also overweight. Melissa Boteach, vice president of the Poverty and Prosperity Program of the Center for American Progress, explains that hunger and obesity are two sides of the same coin, and that people are making trade-offs between food that's filling but not nutritious and may actually contribute to obesity. Suburbs have higher growing rates of hunger than urban environments, as there are often fewer choices regarding food and more money spent to pay for transportation (McMillan 2014).

Urban planning has further effects on human health in regards to poor air quality and pollution. These phenomena are often so omnipresent as to be visible in urban areas and can be found at levels that threaten physical well-being across the world, including developed nations. Indeed, they certainly pose a real health risk: Improving air quality is linked to an increase in life expectancy (Pope et al. 2002; Pope, Ezzati, and Dockery 2009). A stark truth: People living with higher levels of pollution at concentrations common in the US have an increased risk of death (Environmental Protection Agency 2009).

More to the point, the built environment can augment this exposure to pollution. Marshall, Brauer, and Frank (2009) found a link between lower-income areas, pollution, and low walkability. Measures taken to increase levels of physical activity, such as creating more walkable communities, can simultaneously reduce greenhouse gas emissions and pollution.

The methods touched upon in this chapter to achieve healthier communities have also been described in other chapters. Walkable neighborhoods are associated with mixed use developments, which were elaborated on in Chapter 4. Similarly, green spaces, which can be used for recreational activity, were covered in Chapter 5, while healthy food choices can be supported by edible landscape initiatives to be discussed in Chapter 10.

The advantages of enabling residents to make smart, healthy choices are boundless. To enable residents to such, planners may introduce, along with their master plans, design guidelines similar to the ones that have been illustrated in Figure 9.3. It bears repeating healthier communities are more sustainable, less expensive, and more engaging. Influencing a neighborhood's built, social, and food environments can help combat sedentary living patterns, activating positive change in every sphere of life.

Figure 9.3:
Public health guidelines that were developed by the author for a community in Middlesex Center, Ontario, Canada.

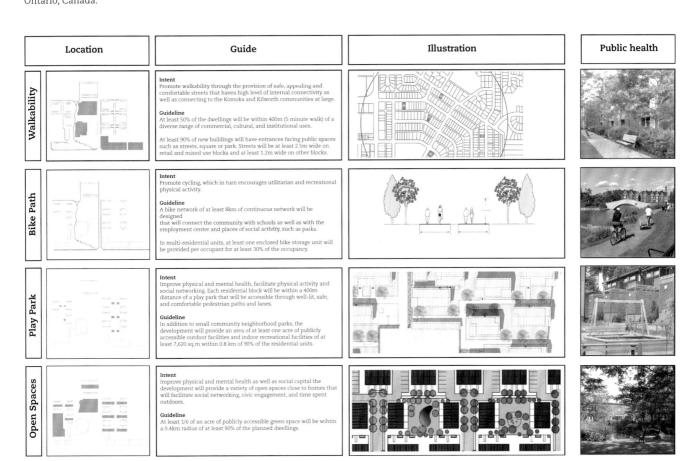

Location	Guide	Illustration	Public health
Walkability	**Intent** Promote walkability through the provision of safe, appealing and comfortable streets that have a high level of internal connectivity as well as connecting to the Komoka and Kilworth communities at large. **Guideline** At least 50% of the dwellings will be within 400m (5 minute walk) of a diverse range of commercial, cultural, and institutional uses. At least 90% of new buildings will have entrances facing public spaces such as streets, square or park. Streets will be at least 2.5m wide on retail and mixed use blocks and at least 1.2m wide on other blocks.		
Bike Path	**Intent** Promote cycling, which in turn encourages utilitarian and recreational physical activity. **Guideline** A bike network of at least 8km of continuous network will be designed that will connect the community with schools as well as with the employment center and places of social activity, such as parks. In multi-residential units, at least one enclosed bike storage unit will be provided per occupant for at least 30% of the occupancy.		
Play Park	**Intent** Improve physical and mental health, facilitate physical activity and social networking. Each residential block will be within a 400m distance of a play park that will be accessible through well-lit, safe, and comfortable pedestrian paths and lanes. **Guideline** In addition to small community neighborhood parks, the development will provide an area of at least one acre of publicly accessible outdoor facilities and indoor recreational facilities of at least 7,620 sq.m within 0.8 km of 90% of the residential units.		
Open Spaces	**Intent** Improve physical and mental health as well as social capital the development will provide a variety of open spaces close to homes that will facilitate social networking, civic engagement, and time spent outdoors. **Guideline** At least 1/6 of an acre of publicly accessible green space will be within a 0.4km radius of at least 90% of the planned dwellings.		

9A

Project:
High Point Community

Location:
Seattle, Washington, USA

Design Firm:
Mithun

Figure 9.4:
Community plan.

Figure 9.5:
Vernacular colors have been selected
for the homes' façades.

Figure 9.6:
View of cluster of homes.

The High Point Community in West
Seattle sits on the former site of a
military worker neighborhood that
was originally developed after the
Second World War. The former housing
complex was in a state of disrepair, its
veteran-oriented services forgotten and
infrastructure failing. In High Point, the
developer saw a special opportunity to
restore a neighborhood while applying
sustainable practices that encourage
healthy living.

Unfortunately, the majority of pre-
existing buildings had to be demolished;
their structure had been left unattended
and was unsafe to refurbish. However,
many of the area's mature trees
were salvaged. These trees help to
provide the community with a sense
of establishment, despite its recent
development. They also offer generous
sun shading to pedestrians, cyclists, and
children playing outside.

Redevelopment projects, though
increasing the apparent quality of the
neighborhood, can drive out former
tenants in a process often described
as gentrification. As the popularity
and infrastructure of a neighborhood
improve, rent and ownership prices can
increase dramatically. In High Point,
many efforts were made to retain the
neighborhood's existing tenants. A mix
of private-ownership and low-cost,
affordable rental units has therefore
been included.

Pedestrians have been given priority and
car use has been discouraged through
street design. Individual blocks are small,
thereby limiting the speed of motor
vehicles and decreasing convenience
for the driver. The roads themselves are
quite narrow. This allows more room for
pedestrian walkways and other roadside
amenities. Additionally, walkways have
been purposefully widened. This allows
more room for pedestrians and creates
a laneway inclusive to cyclists. Between
the roads and pathways are strips for
community gardens, which ameliorate
the appearance of the street and provide
a safe buffer zone between cars and
pedestrians.

1 Community Center
2 Sports / Recreation Park
3 Elementary School
4 Neighborhood Center
5 Senior Village - '36' DUA
6 Central Park
7 Neighborhood Shopping / Mixed Use
    Low Rise Condominiums '28' DUA
    Townhouse / Duplex '14' DUA
8 Community Health Center
9 Branch Library
10 Longfellow Creek Watershed
11 Pond Park (Stormwater)

9.4

9.5

9.6

9.7

9.8

9.9

9.10

Figure 9.7:
The shared common space has many pedestrian paths to encourage walkability.

Figure 9.8:
Pedestrian path in the public space.

Figure 9.9:
The community garden.

Figure 9.10:
Façade close-up of one of the homes.

Many parks are scattered throughout the community. These range from smaller pocket parks to large central community spaces, all connected by pathways for walking or cycling. Together, these places encourage a healthy lifestyle and provide spaces for children to play and exercise. Connecting the parks provides residents with an easily accessible variety of outdoor environments and further encourages physical activity as a means of reaching them.

Sixty "Breathe Easy" homes have been built in the neighborhood. These provide allergen–free environments to families with asthmatic children. Such homes are very effective—in helping to decrease incidences of asthma attack, they have brought emergency room visits down by 67 percent. Catering to this demographic is important given that children living with asthma can easily fall victim to a lack of physical activity; the risk of asthma attacks limits the strain they can place on their bodies. Measures to limit the attacks encourage healthier, lower-risk lifestyles to affected children.

The development has helped to preserve the Longfellow Creek basin through sustainable building practice. Had another developer built on the land without using sustainable practices, the consequences for the creek would have been catastrophic. The developer's conscientiousness is especially important given the vibrant ecosystem in need of conservation found in Longfellow Creek's waters—this habitat supports one of Seattle's most abundant salmon populations, as well as a variety of other aquatic species.

The High Point Community has turned a desolate military housing unit into a sustainable community that fosters active living. A variety of urban planning techniques encourage a healthy lifestyle and alternative modes of transportation. These measures, along with the community's environmental preservation characteristics, contribute to Seattle's reputation for sustainability.

Figure 9.11:

A view of homes from the community garden.

Figure 9.12:

Vegetation has been planted next to a pedestrian path to encourage walkability.

Figure 9.13:

Cycling path near the stormwater Pond Park.

Figure 9.14:

A resident watering the community garden.

9.11

9.12

9.13

9.14

9B

Project:
Skaftkärr

Location:
Porvoo, Finland

Design Firm:
Sitra

Figure 9.15:
Site plan of Skaftkärr.

Figure 9.16:
The Skaftkärr housing project is situated in the town of Porvoo, Finland.

The community of Skaftkärr, in the Finnish city Porvoo, boasts impressive low carbon emission and healthy lifestyle features. Various planning techniques have also been put into place in an effort to minimize energy consumption of its 6,000 residents. Since its first buildings were constructed, the community has inspired the design of similar neighborhoods across Europe.

Planners of Skaftkärr recognized a direct correlation between the activity levels of its residents and their carbon emissions; residents with healthier, more active lifestyles on average generated less carbon. This is because these individuals walk or cycle to complete their daily routines. This is as opposed to using a car for this purpose—and, of course, car use makes up a large portion of the world's carbon emissions; the fewer cars are needed within a community, the more sustainable it is.

Skaftkärr has been designed to promote walking and cycling over driving. A large, high-speed bike lane has been installed in the area and connects residents to the city center. This lane offers cyclists a hassle-free commute or leisure ride with minimal interruptions. It also connects with several bordering services, making it the most efficient and oftentimes quickest means of travel. These optimal bike lanes serve as strong encouragement for residents to bike rather than drive, as cyclists experience fewer disturbances in traffic flow. There are plans to cover the high-speed lanes with solar panels. This would serve as a barrier against harsh sun and wind conditions while providing the community with an easy source of renewable energy.

The same principles behind the high-speed bike lanes drove the design of pedestrian pathways in Skaftkärr. Efforts were made to minimize interference in each path's flow, therefore maximizing pedestrian convenience. For example, the system has been planned to avoid the need for pedestrians to walk across busy streets in front of the high-speed bike lanes or any other barrier that would cause a gap in the path. As a result, these routes are extremely safe and decrease the overall commute time of those traveling by foot. There are abundant paths throughout the community. As with bike lanes, pedestrians can reach the city center and many services on Skaftkärr's periphery exclusively by way of walking path.

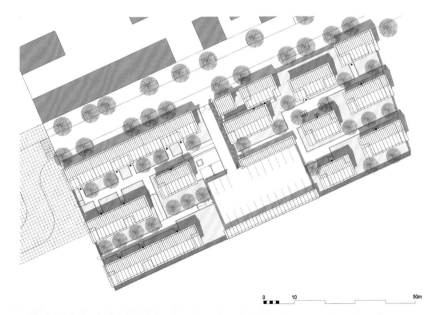

9.16

9.15

Green space also plays an important role in the active lifestyles of Skaftkärr's residents. Large parks surround the community and small play areas are designated within, offering an inviting environment for children to play and adults to socialize. The provision of green space encourages residents to leave the home—and further, to walk, play sports, and partake in leisurely activities in a comfortable environment. The green space of one park cuts through the middle of the community, connecting with another park on the opposite end of the neighborhood. This maximizes the accessibility of green space, Residents are always close to a park, whether they are on the edge or in the center of the community.

The planners of Skaftkärr have proven the relationship between active lifestyles and carbon emissions. As a result, they have encouraged modes of transport that minimize car usage while keeping residents healthy and energetic. The sustainability of the community relies on the healthy lifestyles of its inhabitants as much as it does its meticulously planned infrastructure.

9.17

9.18 (above)   9.19 (below)

Figure 9.17:
A row of homes on the perimeter of the project.

Figure 9.18:
Pedestrian paths link the community edges.

Figure 9.19:
One of the play areas near a cluster of homes.

Figure 9.20:
Façades of homes in Skaftkärr.

Figure 9.21:
A path connecting clusters of homes.

Figure 9.22:
A dwelling near a common open area.

Figure 9.23:
The dotted line marks separation between pedestrians and cyclists.

Figure 9.24:
Play area near a cluster of homes.

Figure 9.25:
Communal parking.

9.20

9.21

9.22

9.23

9.24

9.25

9C

Project:
Bois-Franc

Location:
Saint Laurent, Quebec,
Canada

Design Firm:
Daniel Arbour et associés,
Urban Planners

The community of Bois-Franc was designed to promote an active lifestyle and utilize outdoor space. Through stringent urban planning techniques, the developers have managed an incredible feat in preserving the existing natural environment while creating a dynamic, livable space home to 2,883 residential units. Several man-made features interact extensively with the pre-existing environment, maximizing opportunities for residents to enjoy the outdoors.

An abundance of green space provides residents the facilities needed to enjoy sporting activities and relax outside. Parks foster an active social environment within the community while encouraging energetic living. These parks are used for outdoor picnics and other social gatherings in addition to being large enough to incorporate a variety of ball sports.

The presence of waterways throughout the neighborhood improves upon its aesthetic appeal while protecting the pre-existing natural landscape. These waterways are habitat to many species of birds and further foster rich aquatic vegetation. Moreover, during construction, thousands of mature trees were planted, creating the comforting impression that the neighborhood is well established. They also serve as sun and rain canopy for pedestrians and cyclists. In fact, the incorporation of trees and water create beautiful scenery that works wonders to encourage residents to walk and bike.

On that note, the community is lined with an extensive network of sidewalks and bike paths. This increases safety for pedestrians and bicyclists on the streets and demonstrates the developer's commitment to active modes of transportation. The cycling paths, running through streets and natural settings alike, serve well for both commuting and leisure purposes.

Figure 9.26:

A model showing the plan of Bois-Franc.

9.27

9.28

9.30

Figure 9.27:
An overview of Bois-Franc.

Figure 9.28:
A play area surrounded by homes.

Figure 9.29:
A row of terrace homes face a shared yard.

Figure 9.30:
A network of bike paths crosses the community.

Figure 9.31:
Terrace homes face a man-made lake.

9.31

Figure 9.32:
A public square framed by dwellings.

Figure 9.33:
The community's main commercial square.

Figure 9.34:
The plan of Bois-Franc includes opportunities for outdoor active lifestyle.

9.32

There is very little need for car ownership, as most amenities are within walking and biking distance. La Grande Place is the area's main commercial center; most side streets, bike lanes, and pedestrian pathways lead to this feature. This street offers most goods and services required for suburban living. Though parking is offered, it is placed to the side, out of view, and thus symbolically separate from the community. The community is traffic calmed through the strategic placement of signs and intelligent street design. This decreases convenience for drivers while creating a safer, more inclusive environment for pedestrians and cyclists.

Any amenities located far away can be conveniently reached through a comprehensive public transportation network. Montreal's metro system and commuter trains can be reached within a five-minute bus ride. This supports those who work in downtown Montreal and reduces car ownership. The Montreal metro service provides easy access to most areas of the city and many neighboring suburbs.

9.33

9.34

Summary and Key Considerations

- Over the past century, communities, homes, and lifestyles have been tailored around burning fewer calories.

- Planning communities that encourage physical activity—ironically, a process of undoing measures installed to minimize exertion—can combat sedentary living patterns. Communities can affect their residents' well-being by developing built, social, and food environments that support healthy lifestyles.

- Communities can be transformed into "exercise machines" by planning higher-density, mixed-use areas with efficient public transit systems, walkable streets, and engaging parks.

- Chronic disease rates have grown even as medical spending increases and more medical resources are used. The introduction of accessible exercise opportunities is less costly and more effective than spending more on medical treatments.

- Neighborhoods can encourage physical activity in various spheres, most obviously transportation and recreation.

- Active recreation, like active transportation, is dependent on access to and quality of recreational facilities.

- The characteristics of a healthy community can be organized into the 5 Ds of development: density, diversity, design, destination accessibility, and distance.

- Just as social and built environments are related to health, a neighborhood's food environment affects residents' well-being. Community planning can determine where food is obtained—for instance, in allocating space for a farmer's market and determining accessibility to grocery and convenience stores.

- Higher rates of obesity, being overweight, hypertension, and diabetes were linked to neighborhoods with residents dependent on smaller grocery or convenience stores—hubs stocked with limited food options.

- Measures taken to increase levels of physical activity, including the creation of walkable communities, can simultaneously reduce greenhouse gas emissions and pollution.

Exercises

1. List the social and economic toll of having a sedentary lifestyle on both individuals and society.

2. Select a low-density community in your region and demonstrate how you would retool it to promote active lifestyles.

3. Select a community in your region and demonstrate how you would improve street connectivity to foster walkability.

4. Study communities that have introduced innovative play areas for active recreation.

5. What is the contribution of each "D" in the 5 Ds of development principles in creating active lifestyle environments?

Chapter 10
Edible Landscapes

The reality of contemporary food security is characterized by stark contrast. On one hand, an increase in global trade and highly mechanized agriculture permit fresh produce to be readily available in grocery stores all year long. On the other, more than 12 percent of the world's population is undernourished, this according to the Food and Agriculture Organization of the United Nations (2014). Even in wealthy nations like Canada there are sizable disparities: Almost 850,000 people per month receive assistance from food banks (Food Banks Canada 2013).

Cities are simultaneously growing and moving people away from rural and agricultural environments. Produce travels farther to reach hungry mouths, thus increasing demand for gasoline. We rely on nitrogen fertilizers to grow our produce and excessive plastic packaging to make it appealing in-store. This chapter explores a promising challenge to this wholly unsustainable system: the practice and implementation of urban agriculture within a neighborhood setting.

Agricultural Urbanism

A push to grow food domestically—paired with the desire to create aesthetically pleasing yards—has led to the proliferation of edible landscaping. *Urban agriculture* is the use of food-producing plants in communities by combining fruit and nut trees, berry bushes, vegetables, herbs, edible flowers, and other ornamental plants into aesthetically pleasing designs (Oregon State University 2011). While such things bring to mind, first and foremost, domains like horticulture and agriculture, these considerations also form an essential part of sustainable residential development.

Agricultural urbanism (AU) is a planning principle that integrates a sustainable food and agriculture system into urban environments (de la Salle and Holland 2010). Although issues concerning food security and sustainability have become more visible, the most prominent efforts to combat these problems have been focused on making produce organic and genetically modified organism (GMO) free. AU covers a broader spectrum of concerns related to growing food, including food processing, packaging, distribution, wholesaling, retailing, restaurants, education systems, a local culture of food, and finally, food security (de la Salle and Holland 2010). Under the guidance of this principle, an entire community food system can be reimagined to support an edible landscape, from personal gardens to plots lining the street.

Local food consumption reduces *food miles*—a measure of the distance products must travel from cultivation to point of purchase. Imports by plane generate more greenhouse gas (GHG) emissions than imports by ship (Figure 10.1). For example, in 2005, the import of fruits, nuts, and vegetables into California by airplane released more than 70,000 tons of CO_2, which is equivalent to more than 12,000 cars on the road (Natural Resources Defense Council 2007). However, food miles are an imperfect form of measurement, as they only consider GHG emissions, while ignoring the energy needed to produce the food itself. Even if a meat product were to travel a smaller distance than a vegetable, it cannot be taken for granted as the more ecological choice. A meat-based diet takes five times more land than a vegetarian-based diet, which is especially concerning given that meat consumption has tripled over the last hundred years (de la Salle and Holland 2010). The human diet has become reliant on primarily four crop species and twelve animal species; this limits diversity and nutritional content by way of large-scale production.

AU aims to shorten the transition from individual consumers to autonomous producers, encouraging people to put more thought into what they eat, and mainly, to eat locally (To 2014).

Localized production and distribution bring food closer to the consumer as illustrated in Figure 10.2. It attempts to restore the decline of food production and distribution that was central to the economy of many cities. Best expressed by Lim in *Food City* (2014), food can be a driver in the restructuring of employment, education, transport, tax, health, culture, communities, and the justice system, as well as re-evaluating how the city functions as a spatial and political entity. Thus, this is a geographically specific practice, since certain types of produce are more suited to certain climates and environments. According to Smit (2001) the resultant process produces higher correspondence between supply and demand, and greater awareness of the role of agriculture. With this method, answers to the problems of food transport and storage abound: Fewer fruit, vegetables, and meat products will spoil on their long journeys due to improper storage, thus reducing waste; less nutritional value is lost in the time elapsed between harvest and table; demand for the genetic modifications applied to produce in order to help them to survive such trips is decreased (Smit 2001).

It is hard to know where to begin in discussing the micro-level benefits of AU. First, there is most obviously the nutritional content of food and the availability of fresh produce. Then there is its affordability—an especially important consideration for low-income households. Moreover, edible landscapes create opportunities for physical activity.

Figure 10.1:

Energy input, measured in BTUs, invested in growing, processing, transporting, and consuming grocery store-bought food.

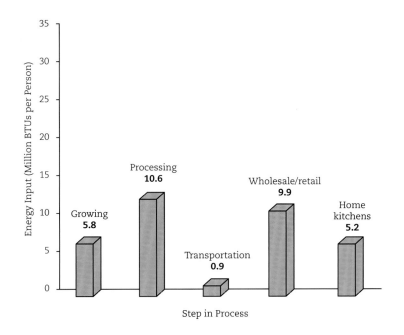

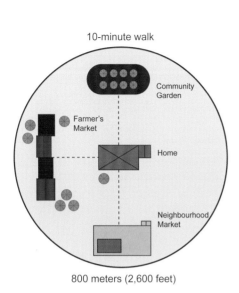

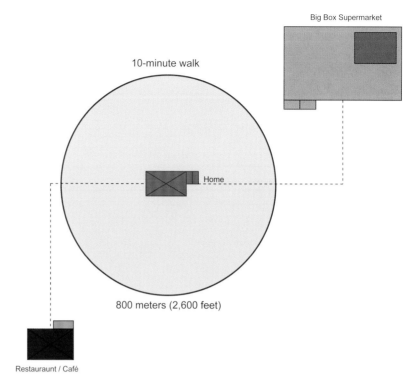

This facilitation of physical activity is no small feat given that preventable diseases related to diet and lifestyle are the great epidemics of the twenty-first century according to the World Health Organization (WHO) (Beaubien 2015). You read correctly—in today's world, lifestyle factors claim larger death tolls worldwide than those of communicable viruses and other such highly publicized global health crises. This creates a considerable drain on medical systems and resources. For example, in Canada, the treatment of obesity, Type 2 diabetes, heart disease, and some cancers cost two billion dollars to treat annually (de la Salle and Holland 2010).

Edible landscapes also support mental health. Participation in planting and agricultural activities has been found to confer considerable therapeutic benefits. Therapeutic horticulture is used to promote cognitive, physical, social, emotional, and spiritual well-being (Canadian Horticultural Therapy Association 2014).

Furthermore, urban agriculture can have a favorable social effect on a neighborhood as a whole. Urban farming is often undertaken through community organizations. A sense of solidarity within the community will develop from shared concerns about the success of the project (Smit 2001). Communities that participate in urban farming also have higher levels of social interaction and better security, as activities take place outdoors. Further, engaging in urban agriculture provides lower-income households with opportunities to earn additional income (this, and fresh, nutritious, cheap food).

Figure 10.2:

Localized production and distribution bring food closer to the consumer (left) where neighborhoods void of such establishments will force long-distance driving (right) (After De la Salle and Holland 2010).

Figure 10.3: (right)

Several avenues of food production that can be integrated into community design or a resident's home.

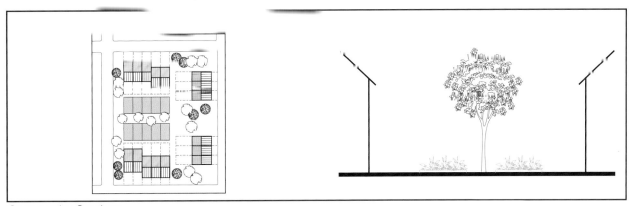

Community Gardens

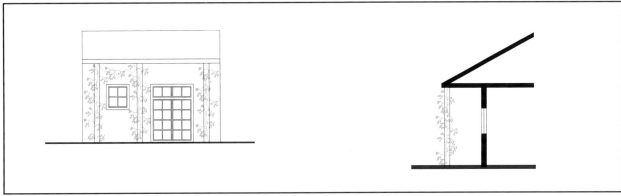

Vertical Planting

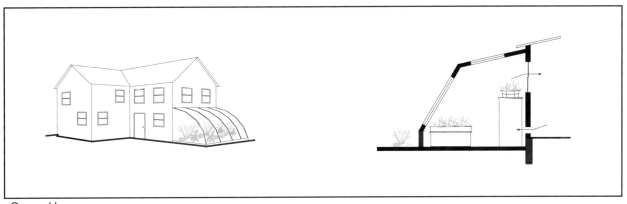

Green House

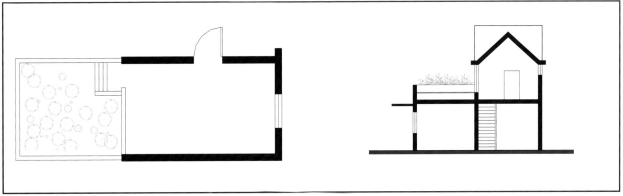

Roof Top Cultivation

AU also confers neighborhood-level economic benefits. Economic activities related to the food industries, such as those that supply agricultural by-products, as well as storage, transportation, canning, marketing, and food processing will create more jobs with fewer costs related to transportation. By producing food locally, families may reduce the amount of money spent per month on food. Idle resources such as wastewater and rooftops or plots of land are put to use and exploited thanks to urban agriculture such as wastewater and rooftops. On top of all this, a study in Philadelphia found that turning ten 0.2 to 0.4 hectare (0.5 to 1 acre) city-owned lawns into farms would save the city US $50,000 per year. The financial risks associated with urban-agriculture ventures are small given that food is a basic need with a stable demand—even during economic recession (Smit 2001).

Conversely, small-scale rural farmers face an uncertain future. Competition with large-scale production offers little economic incentive—especially in that it requires huge investment in expensive land and equipment. The key to urban agriculture is operation on a much smaller scale. The land used in cities for micro-scale agriculture is often, in fact, free. This is because such a small area requires far less maintenance than farmland and further can serve a decorative function for the landowner. Indeed, the urban farmer has innumerable advantages over a comparably sized small-scale rural operation: A city is warmer (shielded from high winds because of large buildings), has fewer pests, and more easily accessed markets.

In sum: localized food production can greatly benefit a community. It can motivate residents to have active lifestyles—even unite a community with a common sense of identity. Further, such operations are more sustainable than their rural counterparts. To emphasize food production as a mainstay of everyday life may seem like a timeworn pastime, but urban farms are progressive and forward-looking initiatives, here to stay and grow.

Initiating Local Food Production

Several types of urban agriculture can be integrated into community design or a private residence, as illustrated in Figure 10.3. Private residential efforts vary in scale and location, from a basil plant on a kitchen counter to a plot in a centrally located community garden. For those without access to a lot of land, *vertical farming* offers the opportunity to grow vine-like plants supported by strings on walls or fences. Another alternative is to grow crops layered by level. The plants requiring the largest amount of watering should be placed on the lowest layer. Other types of private residential farming include greenhouses, small yards, and rooftop gardens. Greenhouses can be operated to extend the growing season of a vegetable or fruit beyond its natural cycle. Rooftops are ideal for garden spaces as they are generally unused and leftover; however, the roof must be able to support the weight of a garden—its soil, plants, and maintenance equipment.

Fundamentally a thriving patch of edible landscape depends on its organization. A well-planned garden can benefit from natural features like sunlight and waterflow to create a low-maintenance and high-yield place. On the other hand, a poorly planned garden can fail in part from the lack—or excess—of the same factors. Therefore, each yard requires careful planning, layouts, and consideration of existing structures, lawn size, orientation, topography, climate, and chosen plants. For example, owners of a house with a small lot might opt for vertical farming while those with a larger lot might plan in consideration of the fact that maintenance will be time-consuming.

Another aspect of edible landscapes is water- and soil-systems design. It is important that the needs of each plant be verified and catered to. Furthermore, the absorption, depth, and richness of the soil are also critical to the success of a garden for their water retention. With a proper design, rainwater can be collected and dispersed according to need while draining away excess. Another consideration: Planting vegetation can treat lead-laced soils until levels of the substance are low enough for vegetables to be grown (de la Salle and Holland 2010).

A proper garden layout should respect a few simple principles: It should have adequate water and sunlight exposure while allowing easy access to each plant (Kourik 2004). It is first important to know the sun's path since it will define areas that will receive light and those that will not, designations upon which the rest of the design depends. This will also influence the placement of fruit trees and vegetables patches (Haeg 2010). Next, it is important to select a planting plot within a yard. The recommended size for a single-family edible garden varies from 55.7 square meters to 111 square meters (600 square feet to 1200 square feet) depending on how active the homeowners plan to be (Kourik 2004).

If the home has a small plot or none at all, vertical farming should be considered. It is most advantageous in smaller spaces due to its higher yield per unit of area. There are two commonly used types of vertical farming. The first is a simple method in which vine-like plants grow upward using strings, walls, or fences (Haeg 2010). The second consists of a layered garden in which crops are planted in two or three levels (Berezan 2007). This benefits water distribution as the plants that need more water are placed in the lowest layer, where water permeates slowly. Urban agriculture does not need to be limited to trees and vegetables; other possible products include poultry, rabbits, goats, sheep, and cattle (Resource Centre on Urban Agriculture & Food Security 2013). Fish can be raised using aquaponics in an urban setting. *Aquaponics* is a food-production system that raises small aquatic animals—such as snails, fish, crayfish, or prawns—in tanks, and is thus a combination of aquaculture with hydroponics (Urban Fish Farmer 2013). Units of varying size are available and can be placed on rooftops. A multitude of types of fish can be raised in an aquaponic farm, from trout and tilapia to salmon. In these systems, the fish's water feeds the plants, and the plants cleanse the water for the fish.

At the community scale, agricultural urbanism must operate within a food and agriculture system to be truly efficient and sustainable. The system is dependent on a series of specialized infrastructures, including organic waste management, irrigation, and energy systems. The systems integrate these infrastructures to imitate a natural ecosystem that can exist independently from fossil fuels—unlike many urban agriculture operations today. Composting is one of the most important of these systems. Food waste from nearby residents and residuals from the urban farm's own operations can be composted, enhancing soil quality, preventing certain plant diseases, and even increasing production. Residuals that are composted become a useful soil amendment within months without a large need for input energy and can be done at many scales, from worm bins to large enclosed systems (de la Salle and Holland 2010).

Reclaimed water from residential and commercial buildings can be used for irrigation. The wastewater must go through treatment before use. To this end, smaller localized treatment centers offer fewer health risks than industrial-sized treatment centers.

Growing Power, an organization in Milwaukee, Wisconsin, successfully integrates many of the eco-friendly innovations discussed here. Their Community Food Center is a 0.8-hectare (2-acre) farm, the last of its kind in operation in the City of Milwaukee in the US. In a space the size of a supermarket, more than 20,000 plants and vegetables, thousands of fish, chickens, ducks, rabbits, and bees are farmed and distributed. The Center has aquaponic houses that use fish waste to supply nutrients to plants. The operation has more than thirty pallets of compost systems that produce "compost tea" for

plant application and soil amendment. Two of the greenhouses are heated from warmth generated by these compost systems. Finally, the Center also benefits from a rainwater-catchment system (Growing Power 2014). The produce and animal products generated from the farm are sold in a small store.

Lufa Farms of Montreal, Canada, similarly operates using an integration of systems. The farm is a greenhouse located on a metropolitan area rooftop. It captures rainwater and recirculates irrigation water. The system is run using hydroponics, and is between 50 and 90 percent more efficient than a system that does not use recirculation. The 2,880 square meter (31,000 square foot) farm feeds 2,000 people by offering weekly baskets on subscription filled with fresh fruit and vegetables. Although the greenhouse is heated with natural gas on Montreal's coldest winter nights, the company mitigates this usage by never refrigerating produce. Further, the plants themselves help alleviate the urban heat island effect (Lufa Farm 2014). In judging these matters, it is important to consider that the urban greenhouse must deal with warmer temperatures than would a comparably productive rural counterpart.

Lufa Farms and Growing Power are examples of community-wide urban-agriculture systems. Smaller-scale productions can also reproduce the sustainable systems of these two organizations. For instance, personal or community gardens can take advantage of composting and rainwater. Urban agriculture can also take the form of revitalizing the streetscape, a cost-effective method that replaces small grass plots with edible plants, a practice that in fact minimizes maintenance fees. Here, we explore some of these exciting possibilities in a series of case studies.

10A

Project:
Lafayette Greens

Location:
Detroit, Michigan, USA

Design Firm:
Kenneth Weikal Landscape
Architecture

Lafayette Greens, situated in downtown Detroit, has been a vibrant addition to its neighborhood. The project has been a joint effort between private and public sectors and was completed in 2010. In its design, Weikal Landscape Architecture emphasized the relationships between the local food system, built environment, and landscape—connections often overlooked yet highly significant. The project was designed to be site-specific. It was built on an empty lot formerly occupied by the historic Lafayette building. At its front, the site directly faces a parking lot and an alley. It is enclosed by two parking-deck garages and two busy streets on either side. The raised vegetable beds have been oriented so as to receive as much sun as possible—light being a limited resource in this instance, as it is in good part blocked by surrounding buildings. Walking paths run diagonally across the site, designed to allow pedestrians to move efficiently through the space, and so find benches on which to rest or to enter the garden to explore the place. Clear and distinct geometric shapes are utilized to echo the structural order of the urban environment, making for a striking visual impact when viewed from surrounding parking decks and buildings.

Hundreds of pounds of fresh and organic produce and flowers are grown each year and all of these harvests are returned to the community. They are either given to volunteers or charitable food distributors like food banks. In addition to producing food, Lafayette Greens offers community members the opportunity to participate in educational programs, workshops, and farmers' markets—allowing residents to learn skills like gardening or tasting and to interact with their neighbors.

Lafayette Greens addresses many sustainability concerns on-site: storm water management, water usage, material reuse, urban bio-diversity, and of course, efficient and organic growing methods. The project became a very multi-functional space. It integrated agriculture into urban life in a way that is both aesthetically exciting and participatory—it is simply exemplary work.

Figure 10.4:
Site plan.

Figure 10.5:
Aerial photo.

Figure 10.6:
View of the flower beds.

10.5

10.6

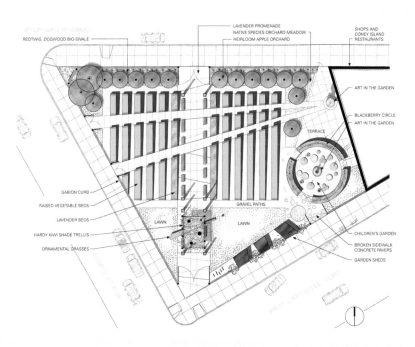

10.4

Figure 10.7:
Flower beds.

Figure 10.8:
A family visits the garden.

Figure 10.9:
Harvesting produce.

Figure 10.10:
Environmental sculpture, part of the garden.

Figure 10.11:
Stormwater management and materials.

Figure 10.12:
Children's garden.

10.7

10.9

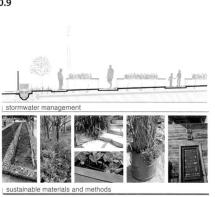

10.11

10.8

10.10

10.12

10.13

10.14

10.15

Figure 10.13:
Seating arrangement.

Figure 10.14:
Flower pots.

Figure 10.15:
Tool structure.

Figure 10.16:
Flower pot.

Figure 10.17:
Notice board.

10.16

10.17

10B

Project:
Gary Comer Youth Center

Location:
Chicago, Illinois, USA

Design Firm:
Hoerr Schaudt Landscape
Architects

Located in the Grand Crossing neighborhood of Chicago's South Side, the Gary Comer Youth Center was designed as an after-school haven for inner-city youth and home to the South Shore Drill team. It is built on an infill site close to a main road and railway. The center includes a gym, stage, art center, recording and dance studio, classrooms, library, kitchen, and a beautiful 760 square meter (8,180 square foot) rooftop garden.

The garden is a part of Chicago's Green Roof Grant Program, a project that encompasses 200 green roofs throughout the city, covering 23 hectares (57 acres) of green space. It is accessible by light-weight pathways made of recycled milk containers. Its plant beds are approximately half a meter deep, long, and strip-shaped. These beds house a variety of organic food crops. Every year the harvest amounts to approximately 450 kilograms (992 pounds) of fresh produce, most of which is utilized by the

youth center's own culinary arts classes. The vegetation includes both flowers (for instance, daisies, tulips) and vegetables (like carrots, okra, and broccoli). It is planned and designed in such a way that different produce may be harvested every season; it is a year-round plant palette. The roof garden also collects and recycles rainwater in order to water the plants. The space also acts as an outdoor classroom where the young are taught horticulture and environmental awareness. This is to say nothing of its value as a beautiful respite.

The center is designed as a place for youths to spend their after-school hours in safety, and further, a space in which to have fun and socialize, even learn. To this end, there is a wealth of recreational and educational programming available. The roof garden is the crowning achievement of an award-winning building, and demonstrates the possibility of finding great value in underutilized space.

Figure 10.18:
The garden is surrounded by walls on four sides and protected from the street.

Figure 10.19:
The second-story garden helped children grow 1,000 pounds of vegetables per year.

Figure 10.20:
Linear strips of recycled tire pavers are the framework for the garden and delineate the geometry of the corridor's viewing windows.

Figure 10.21 (right):
View of the garden strips from the roof.

10.18

10.19

10.20

10.22

Figure 10.22:
Students and administrators benefit from views of the garden from within the center as they move from class to class.

Figure 10.23:
Vegetables and fruits cultivated in the garden are nurtured using tools designed specially for the roof's 18" soil depth.

Figure 10.24:
Plan diagram of the planting rows.

Figure 10.25:
North–South section.

10.23

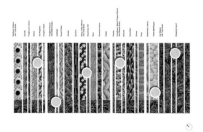

10.24

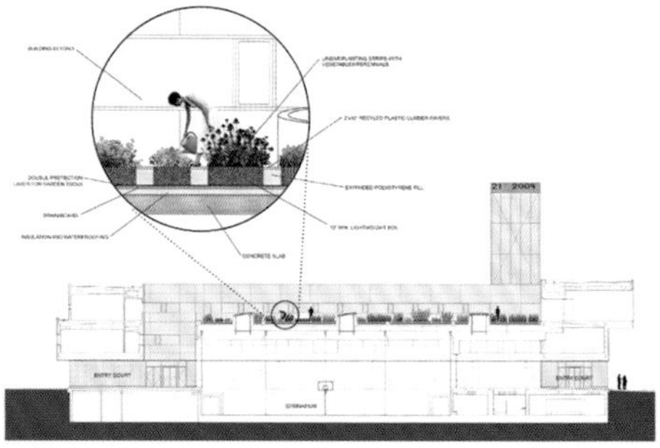

10.25

10C

Project:
Pasona O2

Location:
Tokyo, Japan

Design Firm:
Kono Designs

In the heart of Tokyo's commercial district, under Otemachi's headquarters, lies the city's first underground community farm. Pasona O2 was completed in 2005 and has attracted much attention since. It was drawn up by Kono Designs with the goal of expanding agriculture to uninhabited and innovative spaces. It is not only an experiment in urban farming but also an attempt to provide education for the neighboring urban population and to increase employment opportunities in the area. It was also intended simply as respite from the urban lifestyle.

The space for the project was originally used as a bank vault. It is now transformed into six different rooms with each being home to a specific field, including flowers, herbs, rice shelves, fruits, vegetables, and seedlings. The

rice paddies introduce the lobby of the building and are thus visible from the streets outside, demonstrating to passersby that agriculture can be integrated into the urban environment to both aesthetic and practical benefit.

The system is entirely controlled by computers and sensors, regulating variables from temperature to light. This optimizes crop yields. Light comes from LED, metal halide, high-fluorescent and high-pressure sodium lamps. Critics may argue that using artificial lighting is inefficient, but in view of the fossil fuel consumed during alternate transportation, harvest, and packaging processes, using artificial lighting may be the better method. Farming in a controlled environment also ensures that the produce is 100 percent organic, with no need for pesticides. With the rising concern for food safety and contamination, O2 represents a safer and faster alternative to the traditional farming method.

Most work done in the O2 is by unemployed citizens, people seeking a second career, or those who are simply interested in receiving agricultural training and experience. Seminars and lectures are even provided within the complex to educate the workers who wish to become future farmers.

Figure 10.26:
Floor plans.

Figure 10.27:
Sections.

Figure 10.28:
A Pasona O2 employee inspects the crop in the rice field room.

10.26

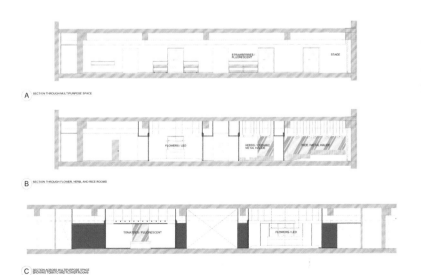

10.27

10.28

O2 is valued not only because it is able to supply the company cafeteria with fresh, organic produce and good air, nor only because it provides employees escape from their everyday working environment. It is also an experiment using the latest advances in urban horticulture. Further, it is an attempt to teach the public of the importance of farming—an effort to try and bring the agricultural world closer to urban citizens, initiating a dialogue about how to integrate food production into the urban environment.

10.29

10.30

10.31

Figure 10.29:
The tomato room, showing fluorescent light arrays and plants in various stages of bloom.

Figure 10.30:
The lettuce room uses fluorescent lights to regulate the environment. Plants in a variety of stages can be seen here, some ready to be picked, others just starting to bud.

Figure 10.31:
A wide variety of herbs are grown in the herb room, where ceramic metal halide lights are used.

Figure 10.32:
The flower room, showing different color LED arrays for specific plants.

10.32

Figure 10.33:

Plants are able to grow continuously in the root vegetable room; the lettuce room and multipurpose room are visible beyond.

Figure 10.34:

A close-up of one of the tomato vines with the fruits ripe and ready to be picked.

Figure 10.35:

Different growing conditions can be seen side by side yet separate, with the strawberries grown in the midst of the multipurpose space and the root vegetables in the room beyond.

Figure 10.36:

Ripe strawberries ready to be picked.

10.33 (above)   10.34 (below)

10.35

10.36

Summary and Key Considerations

- Produce travels further and further to reach hungry mouths, thus increasing demand for gasoline. We rely on nitrogen fertilizers to grow our produce and excessive plastic packaging to make it appealing in-store.

- More sustainable methods of food production and sourcing need to be established within an urban context to fix our currently wasteful food system.

- Agricultural urbanism (AU) is a planning principle that integrates sustainable food and agriculture systems into urban environments like neighborhoods or cities.

- Localized food production brings food closer to the consumer. It is area-specific, since certain types of produce are more suited to the climates and environments of various regions of the world.

- Neighborhoods are also more physically active if they partake in edible landscaping activities. This betters physical and mental health.

- The urban farmer has many advantages over a comparably sized, small-scale, rural operation. Idle resources (like rainwater) or plots of land (think rooftops) are put to use and exploited thanks to urban agriculture.

- A study in Philadelphia found that turning ten 0.2 to 0.4 hectare (0.5 to 1 acre) city-owned lawns into farms would save the city US $50,000 per year (de la Salle and Holland 2010).

- Urban agriculture does not need to be limited to trees and vegetables; other possible products include "poultry, rabbits, goats, sheep, cattle, pigs, guinea pigs, etc." (RUAF 2013). Fish can be raised using aquaponics in an urban setting. Aquaponics is a food production system that raises small aquatic animals, like snails, fish, crayfish, or prawns, in tanks, combining aquaculture with hydroponics (UFF 2013).

- At the community scale, agricultural urbanism operates within a food and agriculture system to be truly efficient and sustainable. This system is dependent on a series of specialized infrastructures, including organic waste management, irrigation, and energy systems.

Exercises

1. Investigate the environmental toll of food import practices and find the food miles that some produce in your community's supermarket travels.

2. Find a community garden in your region and interview its participants about their growing practices (e.g., time it takes, type of produce, etc.).

3. Select a community in your region and demonstrate how some open spaces can become places for urban agriculture initiative.

4. List practices that a homeowner can introduce outdoors to create food production for personal consumption.

5. List practices that a homeowner can introduce indoors to create food production for personal consumption.

Conclusion:
Connecting the Dots

Each of the preceding chapters focuses on a subject vital to the building of sustainable communities. Ideally, planners will include all of them in their designs. Yet, developments in many countries are initiated by profit-motivated companies whose priorities lists may be in conflict with sustainable ideals; thus, compromises are often made. Simply put, proposed solutions that ignore the priorities of the initiating party are destined to fail. In this concluding chapter, practical aspects of building communities are reviewed. It describes basic steps that planners can follow at the outset of their design, offers an outlook on home building and buying, and outlines common environmental certification methods.

Basic Initial Steps

One challenge planners of new sustainable communities face at the outset of a design process is how to integrate the various elements that are outlined in this book's chapters. The process commonly begins by conceiving of a proper form and paying particular attention to three key aspects: mobility and connectivity networks, a system of open spaces, and the selection of dwellings types (e.g., single-family homes, townhouses) on their built density.

The urban form will be determined by the type of existing or new road system. A community may be built around an arterial road, located a short distance from a major highway, or have a public transit line at its heart. These features are likely to dictate key aspects of the local road network and consider a range of uses and users including motorists, cyclists, and pedestrians. As a rule, the plan should give motorists a lower priority by providing pedestrians and cyclists with generous sidewalks and bike paths and improving accessibility to those with limited mobility.

Determining areas and types of the public and private open space systems is another initial stage in conceiving a sustainable neighborhood. Environmentally, development patterns need to work around natural systems and features, which in turn allow residents to be active and enjoy the outdoors. Large-scale parks located outside neighborhoods often constitute the majority of public green spaces. Enclosed outdoor areas adjacent to homes, on the other hand, are private ones. Within these two poles are neighborhood parks and communal areas for clusters of homes. As density increases, the importance of open space rises due to the declining area allocated to each home. Open spaces accommodate the recreational needs of people of all ages. While architects and planners cannot solve political problems, they can certainly design open spaces for neighbors to congregate and have friendly civic engagement.

Choosing the type of home and how it should relate to another is another initial phase. To increase density, the traditional single-family dwelling on a large lot can be replaced with apartments or stacked dwellings.

In addition, clustering structures of various densities will lead to a variety of dwelling types and mixed households. A combination of various land uses will also foster a vibrant neighborhood feel and will reduce the use of private vehicles and therefore should be considered initially. Given the dynamic nature of our lives, communities need to include homes with easily modifiable layouts, as well as a range of services and support required by different age groups, family types, and occupants.

Ensuring Viable Solutions

Implementing sustainability in communities presents several challenges and often involves compromises. Some strategies that aim to improve the design's environmental quality may be either too costly or require changes that the project's initiator might resist implementing. Therefore, an important requirement to keep in mind is the existing building industry's efficiency, which has evolved into a concise, unique operation. Any innovation that severely delays this process runs a high risk of being rejected or will prolong the process substantially.

Designers should therefore study at the outset the effect that their proposal will have on common practices if they wish to change them.

From the homebuyers' perspective, the purchase of a home represents the largest investment they are likely to make in their lifetime. Since the decision to buy a home is subject to personal aspirations, culture, and location, among other factors, a designer must keep these aspects in mind. The end user might reject innovative concepts if their needs are not considered.

Economic considerations often take precedence in any development process. It is not certain how much more the buyer would be willing to pay for an environmentally sound alternative.
First-time homeowners would most likely prefer to invest in functional amenities, such as bigger kitchens, rather than net-zero technologies. Even if the added investment would decrease their energy costs, the expected occupancy period may not justify ideas with long payback periods. No matter what the estimated annual savings are, a substantially higher buying price might put the home out of consumers' reach altogether. On the other hand, some can demonstrate that such investments may increase property value.

The development of a sustainable community involves a process that includes site planning, design, and construction. As noted in Chapter 1, when examining the environmental impact and comparing alternatives, the project's entire life cycle should be accounted for. The efficiency with which natural resources, including energy, are utilized in the dwellings and the community macro and micro levels will determine the overall environmental impact of the project. For obvious reasons, not all the environmental challenges can be solved in an absolute sense. What may appear to be a suitable alternative in one respect, such as having solar power, may exhibit compromising qualities in another, such as using nonrenewable natural resources. In the absence of reliable, quantitative data, many decisions are often based on qualitative assessment, some of which are objective. Although life cycle analyses are complex, it can be useful in choosing alternatives.

Finally, early public consultation, primarily in projects initiated by the not-for-profit sector, is another important step in ensuring success. When future occupants let their voice be heard during the design, it is less likely they will feel alienated, and the chosen solution will better meet their needs. Welcoming and making future occupants an integral part of the decision-making process by providing ongoing updates will foster a strong public engagement. Meetings of various levels of governments—be they local or national—should preferably include members of the public or, at the very least, be open to them.

Certifications of Sustainable Practices

In recent decades, governments, construction associations, and nongovernmental organizations around the world have set standards for sustainable building practices. Green building movements are thriving in many countries and are having significant effects on education and construction practices. Innovative approaches to residential design, such as passive and net-zero homes and neighborhoods, are recasting the way design is conceived, with the goal of minimizing the environmental footprint of communities. In addition to national building codes, which established minimum requirements for energy performance, the new standards address other criteria for a higher level of efficiency.

Agencies and rating systems have been established to foster greater environmental awareness and streamline evaluation criteria. BREEAM in the UK, the High Quality Environmental standard or HQE in France, and Green Star by the Green Building Council in Australia are some examples. Other notable institutions include the Passivhaus Institut in Germany and the World Green Building Council, which is a union of national councils.

The United States Green Building Council (USGBC) is the nation's leader in the promotion of environmental responsibility. The agency established the Leadership in Energy and Environmental Design (LEED) Green Building Rating System, which became a nationally accepted benchmark for the design, construction, and operation of high-performance green buildings. The method has also been extended to Canada. It includes rating of new construction, existing buildings, interiors, schools, as well as homes and neighborhoods as outlined below. The LEED standard is divided into several categories with prerequisites and additional credits. Points are accumulated for each satisfied requirement and certification is given once a minimum specified number of points are acquired. Depending on how many points the building is awarded, it can be considered as LEED Platinum, Gold, Silver, or Certified.

LEED for Neighborhood Development (LEED-ND) seeks to create environmentally responsible communities that protect and enhance overall health, natural environment, and quality of life. LEED-ND seeks to aid in the design of neighborhoods that promote efficient use of energy and water. Some of its components are listed below.

The "Location Efficiency" category examines the relationship between a site and its surroundings. The first prerequisite requires access to efficient modes of transportation that promote pedestrian activity and use of public transit. Neighborhoods should be well connected to reduce reliance on cars. The second prerequisite is proximity to existing water and stormwater sources necessary to conserve resources and minimize new infrastructure. Additional points are allotted for projects that plan to remediate contaminated land and/or infill projects.

Several prerequisites stipulate that public parkland and farmland must be preserved. The siting of a project may not be such that it poses a threat to animals on the endangered species list or threaten the presence of existing bodies of water or wetlands. Finally, an erosion and sedimentation control plan to protect existing soil, bodies of water, and air needs to be carried out. The main goal of this category is to minimize disturbance to the site.

The "Complete, Compact, and Connected Neighborhoods" category borrows from the principles of New Urbanism. Established in the 1980s, the movement seeks to create denser communities based on traditional town design and advocates narrow streets, mixed-land uses, walkability, and public transit. Projects therefore must foster a sense of place, conserve land, be transportation efficient, and attract diverse uses.

Projects that incorporate LEED-certified "green" structures or other eco-friendly buildings providing energy and/or water efficiency can also accumulate points. Plans

should include designs that provide shade over paved surfaces, use of light-colored materials to diminish the urban heat island effect, underground parking, and/or green roofs. Infrastructure, such as street and traffic lights, should be energy efficient and additional points can be allotted where on-site power generation or renewable energy sources are installed.

The LEED for Homes (LEED-H) standard initially focused on the construction of new single-family homes but eventually expanded to include low-rise, multi-family housing. Categories and credits were adapted to the residential sphere and are similar to LEED for new construction. They concern construction, design, and site aspects specific to the house.

The "Location and Linkages" category recommends that the home be sited in a community that fulfills requirements similar to those of a LEED neighborhood. The location should be served by existing or adjacent infrastructure, developments should be compact and efficient, and the community equipped with services such as banks, convenience stores, post offices, pharmacies, and schools to encourage walking.

The goal of the "Sustainable Sites" category is to encourage responsible site development, which minimizes ecological impacts as well as the effects on the environment as a whole. Landscape features that reduce the need for irrigation and synthetic chemicals are encouraged, and paved areas—such as sidewalks, driveways, and patios—can be shaded with trees and shrubs. To reduce unnecessary consumption of potable water, rainwater collection and greywater reuse are recommended. Where the need for irrigation is necessary, highly efficient

systems are a must. In terms of indoor water use, low-flow faucets and showerheads are recommended, as are dual-flush toilets.

The "Materials and Resources" section of LEED-H recommends the use of recycled and local materials and environmentally friendly products. It goes one step further by providing guidelines for appropriate sizing of homes. Based on the number of bedrooms—usually a good indicator of the number of residents in a home—square footage recommendations are provided for the home's floor area.

In the "Energy and Atmosphere" section, once again, the "energy star package" is recommended. The house should be well insulated, with efficient windows, minimal air leakage from ducts, highly efficient space heating and cooling, and an efficient water heating and distribution system. Outdoor lighting fixtures should have motion sensors to minimize use, and indoor lighting, as well as appliances, should be highly efficient. Installing renewable energy sources, such as wind generators and photovoltaic panels, is encouraged, and points are allocated for each 10 percent of annual electrical load met by the system. Finally, homeowners should receive a user manual and a sixty-minute walk-through of their new home to provide them with the necessary information for proper operation. For the design of a green home to be effective, its features must be used correctly and efficiently.

In urban planning, it is often a challenge to make a leap from general theories to specific site plans. Yet, by knowing what the different stakeholders will consider and by having standards such as BREEAM and LEED, designers of sustainable communities may stand a better chance of making their ideas a reality.

Bibliography

AIA (American Institute of Architects) (2012). Economics, http://www.aia.org/practicing/economics/AIAS076588. Accessed November 25, 2014.

Al-Kodmany, K. (2011). "Placemaking With Tall Buildings," *Urban Design International*, September, 252–269.

Andrews, C. L. and M. Townsend, (2000). "Perspectives on Housing and Neighbourhoods of the Future," Abingdon: Northcourt Press.

Austin, I. M. (2010). "Potential for District Heating as a Solution to Fuel Poverty in the U.K." Reykjavik Energy Graduate School of Sustainable Systems. http://en.ru.is/media/reyst/Ingrid_Austin.pdf. Accessed November 25, 2014.

Badland, H. M. and G. M. Schofield (2006). "Understanding the Relationship Between Town Size and Physical Activity Levels: A Population Study." *Health and Place*, 12, 538–546.

Badland, H. M. and G. M. Schofield, & N. Garrett (2008). "Travel Behaviour and Objectively Measured Urban Design Variables: Associations for Adults Traveling to Work." *Health & Place*, 14, 85–95.

Beaubien, J. (2015). "What's Most Likely To Kill You? Hint: Probably Not an Epidemic." *National Public Radio.* http://www.npr.org/blogs/goatsandsoda/2015/01/19/377760851/whats-most-likely-to-kill-you-hint-probably-not-an-epidemic. Accessed February 2, 2015.

Ben-Joseph, E. and D. Gordon (2000). "Hexagonal Planning in Theory and Practice," *Journal of Urban Design*, 5(3), 237–265.

Berezan, R. (2007). "The Edible Landscape: An Urban Farming Renaissance?" *The Canadian Organic Grower*, Fall 2007. http://www.cog.ca/documents/TCOG/07Fall-EdibleLandscapeFall07.pdf. Accessed November 25, 2014.

Besser, L. M. and A. L. Dannenberg (2005). "Walking to Public Transit: Steps to Help Meet Physical Activity Recommendations." *American Journal of Preventive Medicine, 29*(4), 273–280.

Bollerud, E. (2013). "Heat Island Effect." *Environmental Protection Agency.* http://www.epa.gov/hiri/. Accessed November 25, 2014.

Brueckner, J. K. (2000). "Urban Sprawl: Diagnosis and Remedies," *International Regional Science Review*, Volume 23, Issue 2, April, 160–171.

Burke, D. (2012). "Is District Heating the Way Forward for Renewable Energy?" Renewable Energy World. http://www.renewableenergyworld.com/rea/blog/post/2012/12/district-heating-can-be-seen-as-the-way-forward-for-renewable-energy. Accessed November 25, 2014.

Calthorpe, P. (1993). *The Next American Metropolis*. New York: Princeton Architectural Press.

Canada Mortgage and Housing Corporation (CMHC) (2000). *Practice for Sustainable Communities*. Ottawa.

Canada Mortgage and Housing Corporation (CMHC) (2009). "Transit-Oriented Development (TOD): Canadian Case Studies." *Canada Mortgage and Housing Corporation*. Last modified November 12, 2009. http://www.cmhc-schl.gc.ca/en/inpr/su/sucopl/sucopl_007.cfm. Accessed November 25, 2014.

Canadian Heart and Stroke Foundation (2005). *Heart and Stroke Foundation 2005 Report Card on Canadian's Health: Has the Suburban Dream Gone Sour?* Montreal: Canadian Heart and Stroke Foundation.

Canadian Horticultural Therapy Association (CHTA). (2014) "About Horticultural Therapy and Therapeutic Horticulture." http://www.chta.ca/about_ht.htm. Accessed November 25, 2014.

Cao, X., Mokhtarian, P. L., & Handy, S. L. (2007). "Do Changes in Neighbourhood Characteristics Lead to Changes in Travel Behaviour? A Structural Equations Modeling Approach." *Transportation, 34*, 535–556.

Carver, A., A. F. Timperio, and D. A. Crawford. (2008). "Neighborhood Road Environments and Physical Activity among Youth: The Clan Study." *Journal of Urban Health: Bulletin of the New York Academy of Medicine* 85: 532–44.

Center for Transit-Oriented Design (2010). *TOD: 203 Transit Corridors and TOD.* http://reconnectingamerica.org/assets/Uploads/HSR-in-America-Complete.pdf. Accessed November 25, 2014.

Center for Transit-Oriented Design (2011). *Metro TOD Development Strategic Plan.* http://reconnectingamerica.org/assets/Uploads/2011-portland-tod-final-web.pdf. Accessed November 25, 2014.

Cervero, R. (2008). Public Transport and Sustainable Urbanism: Global Lessons. In Curtis, C., J. Renne, and L. Bertolini (Eds), *Transit Oriented Development: Making It Happen*. England: Ashgate.

Cervero, R., and K. Kockelman. (1997). "Travel Demand and the 3Ds: Density, Diversity, and Design." *Transportation Research D* 2: 199–219.

CIT Energy Management AB. (2010). "Success Factors in Solar District Heating." Intelligent Energy Europe. Last modified December 2010. http://www.solar-district-heating.eu/Portals/0/SDH-WP2-D2-1-SuccessFactors-Jan2011.pdf. Accessed November 25, 2014.

City of Bloomington. (2013). "Community Gardening." https://bloomington.in.gov/communitygardening. Accessed November 25, 2014.

City of Vancouver (2005). *RM-1 and RM-1N Courtyard Rowhouse Guidelines*, Vancouver, B.C.: City of Vancouver Land Use and Development Policies and Guidelines.

Cohen, D. A., T. L. Mckenzie, A. Sehgal, S. Williamson, D. Golinelli, and N. Lurie. (2007). "Contribution of Public Parks to Physical Activity." *American Journal of Public Health* 37: 475–80.

Corbett, J. and M. Corbett (2000). *Designing Sustainable Communities: Learning from Village Homes*. New York: Princeton Architectural Press.

Crowhurst Lennard, S. H. and H. L. Lennard. (2002) *The Wisdom of Cities*. Carmel, California: International Making Cities Livable.

Danneberg, A. L., H. Frumkin, and R. J. Jackson (2011). *Making Healthy Places*. Washington: Island Press.

David Suzuki Foundation (2014). "Discourage Urban Sprawl," http://www.davidsuzuki.org/what-you-can-do/reduce-your-carbon-footprint/discourage-urban-sprawl/. Accessed November 25, 2014.

De la Salle, J., M. Holland, R. Barrs, S. Clarke, P. Condon, K. Cramer, D. Crockett, B. Fraser, J. Karakas, P. Ladner, K.Mullinix, F. Porter, B. Ransford (2010). *Agricultural Urbanism: Handbook for Building Sustainable Food and Agriculture Systems in 21st Century Cities*. Winnipeg: Green Frigate Books.

Deng, T. and J. D. Nelson (2011). "Recent Developments in Bus Rapid Transit: A Review of the Literature." *Transport Reviews*, 31(1). 69–96.

Diamond, J. (1976). Residential Density and Housing Form, *Journal of Architectural Education*, Vol. 3, February.

Docherty, I., J. Shaw, R. Knowles, and D. Mackinnon (2009). "Connecting for Competitiveness: Future Transport in UK City Regions." *Public Money and Management* 29 no. 5, 321–328.

Downsview Park Inc. (2007). "Sustainable Community Development Guidelines." N.P., Dec 2007. http://www.trca.on.ca/web-assets/meetings-and-agendas/AuthorityAgenda02-07-March30_2007-AddedItems.pdf . Accessed August 24, 2016.

Dumbaugh, E. and W. Li, (2011). Designing for the Safety of Pedestrians, Cyclists, and Motorists in Urban Environments. *Journal of the American Planning Association,* 77, No. 1, 69–88.

Environmental Protection Agency (EPA) (2009). *Integrated Science Assessment for Particulate Matter*. Final Report. EPA/600/R-08/139F. Washington: US Environmental Protection Agency.

Environmental Protection Agency (EPA) (2011). "WaterSense: Outdoor Water Use in the United States." Last modified July 7, 2011. http://www.epa.gov/WaterSense/docs/ws_outdoor508.pdf. Accessed November 25, 2014.

Environmental Protection Agency (EPA) (2012). "Parking Spaces / Community Places." http://www.epa.gov/smartgrowth/pdf/EPAParkingSpaces06.pdf. Accessed November 25, 2014.

Enwave Energy Corporation. "Deep Lake Water Cooling." (2011) http://www.enwave.com/district_cooling_system.html. Accessed November 25, 2014.

Euroheat and Power. "District Heating in Buildings" (2011). http://www.buildup.eu/sites/default/files/content/District%20Heating%20in%20buildings_final.pdf Accessed August 24, 2016.

Evans, G. W. (2003). "The Built Environment and Mental Health," *Journal of Urban Health*, 80(4). 536–555.

Evenson, K. R., M. M. Scott, D. A. Cohen, and C. C. Voorhees (2007). "Girls' Perception of Neighborhood Factors on Physical Activity: Sedentary Behavior, and BMI." *Obesity* 15: 430–45.

Ewing, R. and R. Cervero (2001). "Travel and the Built Environment." *Transportation Research Record*, no. 1780: 87–114.

Ewing, R. and R. Cervero (2010). "Travel and the Built Environment: A Meta-Analysis." *Journal of the American Planning Association* 70 no. 3: 265–94.

Farr, D. (2008). *Sustainable Urbanism: Urban Design with Nature*, John Wiley & Son, Inc., Hoboken, New Jersey.

Feehan, D., and M. D. Feit (2006). *Making Business Districts Work: Leadership and Management of Downtown, Main Street, Business District, and Community Development of Organizations*, New York: Haworth Press.

Flegal, K. M., M. D. Carroll and C. L. Ogden. (2010) "Prevalence and Trends in Obesity among US Adults, 1998–2000." JAMA 3003, no. 3: 235–41.

Food and Agriculture Organization of the United Nations (FAO) (2014). "Hunger Portal." http://www.fao.org/hunger/en/. Accessed November 25, 2014.

Food Banks Canada (2013). "About Hunger in Canada." http://www.foodbankscanada.ca/Learn-About-Hunger/About-Hunger-in-Canada.aspx. Accessed November 25, 2014.

Friedman, A. (2001). *The Grow Home*. Montreal: McGill-Queen's University Press.

Friedman, A. (2002). *The Adaptable House*. New York: McGraw-Hill Professional.

Friedman, A. (2005). *Homes Within Reach*. Hoboken: John Wiley & Sons.

Friedman, A. (2007). "The Use of Architectural Flexibility for Achieving Affordability in Housing," in *Chasing the American Dream: New Perspective on Affordable Homeownership*, William Rohe and Harry Watson, Editors, Cornell University Press, Ithaca & London, pp. 146–167.

Friedman, A. (2012). *Fundamentals of Sustainable Dwellings*. Island Press, Washington, DC.

Friedman, A. (2013). *Innovative Houses: Concepts for Sustainable Living*, Laurence King Publishing, London, UK.

Friedman, A., D. Krawitz, M. Senbel, D. Raphael, J. Steffel, J. Frechette, J. Watt (2002a). *Planning the New Suburbia*. Vancouver: UBC Press.

Garmendia, M., J. M. Urena, C. Riablaygua, J. Leal, & J. M. Coronado (2008). "Urban Residential Development in Isolated Small Cities that Are Partially Integrated in Metropolitan Areas by High Speed Train." *European Urban and Regional Studies*, 15, 249–264.Gehl, J. (2010) *Cities for People*. Washington: Island Press.

Gevorkian, P. (2008). *Alternative Energy Systems in Building Design*. New York: McGraw Hill.

Gleick, P. (2010). "Turf Wars: Circle of Blue: Water News." *Reporting the Global Water Crisis*. http://www.circleofblue.org/waternews/2010/world/peter-gleick-turf-wars/. Accessed November 25, 2014.

Gonchar, J. (2010). "Zeroing in on Net-Zero Energy." *Architectural Record*, Vol. 198, Issue 12, December. https://continuing education.bnpmedia.com/course.php?L=5&C=728&P=4.

Grant, J. (2004). "Encouraging Mixed Use in Practice," Paper prepared for: *International Planning Symposium on Incentives, Regulations, and Plans—The Role of States and Nation-States in Smart Growth Planning*. National Center for Smart Growth Research and Education, University of Maryland, 57–70. https://books.google.ca/books?hl=en&lr=&id=OxmkuP7nHG4C&oi=fnd&pg=PA57&dq=Grant,+J.+(2004).+%E2%80%9CEncouraging+Mixed+Use+in+Practice,%E2%80%9D&ots=TFZ-Qtbr8E&sig=JGkuCD2e61I3gnAa5j5027m8fcc#v=onepage&q=Grant%2C%20J.%20(2004).%20%E2%80%9CEncouraging%20Mixed%20Use%20in%20Practice%2C%E2%80%9D&f=false, Accessed December 9, 2016.

Green Parking Lot Resource Guide (2008). *Stream Tea Mok*. Environmental Protection Agency. http://www.streamteamok.net/Doc_link/Green%20Parking%20Lot%20Guide%20%28final%29.PDF. Accessed May 9, 2013.

Growing Power (2014). "Our Community Food Center." https://web.archive.org/web/20140403194934/http://

growingpower.org/headquarters.htm. Accessed November 25, 2014.

Haeg, F. (2010). *Edible Estates: Attack on the Front Lawn*. New York: Bellerophon Publications, Inc.

Hall, P. (2008). Urban Renaissance, Urban Villages, Smart Growth: Find the Differences. In Haas, T. (Ed.), *New Urbanism and Beyond: Designing Cities for the Future*. New York: Rizzoli.

Haran, S. (2009). "Green Space: Lighting Less to Achieve Net-Zero." *Consult-Specific Eng Magazine*. http://www.controleng.com/oldarchive/327275. Accessed on November 25, 2014.

Harvey, L. and D. Danny (2006). *A Handbook on Low-Energy Buildings and District-Energy Systems: Fundamentals, Techniques and Examples*. Earthscan. London: Sterling.

Health Canada. (2011). *Communicating the Health Risks of Extreme Heat Events: Toolkit for Public Health and Emergency Management Officials*. Water, Air and Climate Change Bureau, Healthy Environments, and Consumer Safety Branch, Health Canada.

Heat Pump Center (2014). "How Does a Heat Pump Work?" http://www.heatpumpcentre.org/en/aboutheatpumps/howHPworks/Sidor/default.aspx. Accessed on November 25, 2014.

Hinshaw, M., A. Scrafone, J. Donnelly, Rich Kato (1998). *Model Code Provisions, Urban Streets and Subdivisions*. Prepared for Washington State Community Trade and Economic Development. Olympia, Washington.

Hodges, T. (2010). Public Transportations Role in Responding to Climate Change. *The Federal Transit Administration, U.S. Department of Transportation*. https://www.transit.dot.gov/sites/fta.dot.gov/files/docs/

Hood, Lyndon (2011). "Action against Tobacco, Pollution and Lack of Exercise." Scoop Independent News. 21 June. http://www.scoop.co.nz/stories/WO1106/S00460/action-against-tobacco-pollution-and-lack-of-exercise.htm. Accessed November 25, 2014.

Howard, E. (1902). *Garden Cities of Tomorrow* (original 1898 title: *Tomorrow: A Peaceful Path to Real Reform*). London: Swan Sonnenschein & Co.

International Energy Agency (ITA) (2008). *Worldwide Trends in Energy Use and Efficiency—Key Insights from IEA Indicator*

Analysis. Paris: International Energy Agency.

Jacobs, J. (1969). *The Economy of Cities*. New York: Random House.

Jacobsen, P.L., F. Racioppi, & H.Rutter (2009). "Who Owns the Roads? How Motorised Traffic Discourges Walking and Bicycling." *Injury Prevention*, 15, 369–373.

Joens-Matre, R. R., G. J. Welk, M. A. Calabro, D. W. Russell, E. Nicklay and L. D. Hensley (2008). *National Rural Health Association*, Winter.

Kaczynski, A. T., and K. A. Henderson (2007). "Environmental Correlates of Physical Activity: A Review of Evidence about Parks and Recreation." *Leisure Sciences* 29, 315–354.

Kim, Y. K., L. Jolly, A. Fairhurst, and K. Atkins (2005). "Mixed-Use Development: Creating a Model of Key Success Factors," *Journal of Shopping Center Research*, Volume 12, Issue 1.

Knowles, R. D. (2012). "Transit Oriented Development in Copenhagen, Denmark: From the Finger Plan to Ørestad." *Journal of Transport Geography* 22, 251–261.

Kostof, S. (1991). *The City Shaped*. New York, NY: Bulfinch Press.

Kourik, R. (2004). *Designing and Maintaining your Edible Landscape Naturally*. Hampshire, U.K.: Permanent Publications.

Kuby, M., A. Barranda, & C. Upchurch (2004). "Factors Influencing Light-Rail Station Boardings in the United States." *Transportation Research Part A*, 38, 223–247.

Kuo, F. E., and A.F. Taylor (2004). "A Potential Natural Treatment for Attention-Deficit/Hyperactivity Disorder: Evidence from a National Study." *American Journal of Public Health* 94 no. 9: 1580–1586. http://www.ncbi.nlm.nih.gov/pmc/articles/PMC1448497/. Accessed November 25, 2014.

Kwok, A. G., W. T. Gronkzik (2007). *The Green Studio Handbook: Environmental Strategies For Schematic Design*. Amsterdam: Elsevier Architectural Press.

Larson, R. W. (2001). "How U.S. Children and Adolescents Spend Time: What It Does (and Doesn't) Tell Us About Their Development," Current Directions in Psychological Science, 10(5), October.

Lim, J. C. (2014), Food City, Routledge, London, UK.

Lindsay, M., K. Williams, and C. Dair (2010). Is There Room for Privacy in the Compact City? Built Environment 36 (1)

Litman, T. (2004). Evaluating Public Transit Benefits and Costs. Last modified 2004. www.vtpi.org. Accessed November 25, 2014.

Litman, T. (2009). "Parking Requirement Impacts on Housing Affordability." Victoria Transport Policy Institute, November.

Llewelyn, D. (2000). Urban Design Compendium. England: English Partnerships.

Logan, T. (1976). "The Americanization of German Zoning." Journal of the American Institute of Planners. 42.4: 377–385.

Lovasi, G.S., M. A. Hutson, M. Guerra, and K.M. Neckerman (2009). "Built Environments and Obesity in Disadvantaged Populations." Epidemiologie Reviews 31: 7–20.

Lufa Farms (2014). "About the Farm." https://montreal.lufa.com/en/about-the-farm. Accessed November 25, 2014.

MacDonald, J. M., R. J. Stokes, D. A. Cohen, A. Kofner, and G.K. Ridgeway (2010). "The Effect of Light Rail Transit on Body Mass Index and Physical Activity." American Journal of Preventative Medicine 39 no. 2: 105–112.

Macfadyen, D. (1933). Sir Ebenezer Howard and the Town Planning Movement. Manchester, UK: Manchester University Press.

Macht, W. P. (2010). "Modular Net-Zero-Energy Townhouses." Urban Land, July/August.

Malin, N. (2010). "The Problem with Net-Zero Buildings (and the Case for Net-Zero Neighborhoods)." Environmental Building News. July 30. https://www.buildinggreen.com/feature/problem-net-zero-buildings-and-case-net-zero-neighborhoods. Accessed August 24, 2016.

Mannvit Engineering (2013). "What is Geothermal?" http://www.mannvit.com/GeothermalEnergy/WhatisGeothermal/. Accessed on November 25, 2014.

Marcus, C. C. (2003). "Shared Open Space and Community Life," Place, vol. 15, no 2. Winter.

Marshall, J.D., M. Bauer, and L.D. Frank. (2009) "Healthy Neighborhoods: Walkability and Air Pollution." Environmental Health Perspectives 117 no.11: 1752 -1759.

McKenzie, B., M. Rapino.(2009) "Commuting in the United States: 2009 American Community Survey Reports", https://www.census.gov/prod/2011pubs/acs-15.pdf Accessed August 27, 2016.

McMillan, T. (2014). "The New Face of Hunger." National Geographic Magazine. July.

Miller, M. (1992). Raymond Unwin: Garden Cities and Town Planning. Leicester, UK: Leicester University Press.

Mims, Christopher (2008). "One Hot Island: Iceland's Renewable Geothermal Power." Scientific American. October 20. http://www.scientificamerican.com/article/iceland-geothermal-power/. Accessed on November 25, 2014.

Moughtin, C. (2003). Urban Design: Street and Square. Great Britain: Architectural Press.

National Association of Home Builders (NAHB) Research Center (2005). Higher Density Housing. Washington.

Natural Resources Defense Council (NRDC). (2007) "Food Miles: How Far Your Food Travels Has Serious Consequences for Your Health and the Climate." November. http://food-hub.org/files/resources/Food%20Miles.pdf. Accessed November 25, 2014.

Nebraska Energy Office.(2007) "Minimizing the Use of Lumber Products in Residential Construction." http://www.neo.ne.gov/home_const/factsheets/min_use_lumber.htm. Accessed November 25, 2014.

Nordic Folkecenter for Renewable Energy (2010). "District Heating Can Now Store Wind Energy." September. http://www.folkecenter.net/gb/rd/power-balancing/district-heating/. Accessed November 25, 2014.

Norman, G. J., S. K. Nutter, S. Ryan, J. F. Sallis, K. J. Calfas, and K. Patrick (2006). "Community Design and Access to Recreational Facilities as Correlates of Adolescent Physical Activity and Body-Mass Index." Journal of Physical Activity and Health 3: S118–128.

Oregon State University (2011) "Edible Landscaping," Oregon State University Master Gardner. http://extension.oregonstate.edu/mg/metro/sites/default/files/Edible_Landscaping.pdf. Accessed November 25, 2014.

Owen, N., N. Humpel, E. Leslie, A. Bauman, and J.F. Sallis (2004). "Understanding Environmental Influences on Walking: Review and Research Agenda." American Journal of Preventive Medicine 27: 67–76.

Palmer, J. and S. Ward. (2010). "The Adaptable House." https://web.archive.org/web/20130707154041/http://www.yourhome.gov.au/technical/fs32.html. Accessed November 25, 2014.

Peck, S., M. Kuhn (2008). Design Guidelines for Green Roofs. Published by Canada Mortgage and Housing Corporation (CMHC), Ottawa.

Piedmont-Palladino and Mennel (2009). Green Community. Chicago: American Planning Association.

Pope, C.A., 3rd., R. T. Burnett, M. J. Thun, E. E. Calle, D. Kewski, K. Ito, and G. D. Thurston (2002). "Lung Cancer, Cardiopulmonary Mortality, and Long-Term Exposure to Fine Particulate Air Pollution." JAMA 287: 1132–1141.

Pope, C. A., M. Ezzati, and D. W. Dockery (2009). "Fine Particulate Air Pollution and Life Expectancy in the United States." New England Journal of Medicine 360: 376–386.

Poticha, S. and J. Wood (2009). Transit Oriented for All: Delivering Mixed-Income Housing. In Curtis, C., Renne, J., Bertolini, L (Eds.), Transit Oriented Development: Making it Happen. England: Ashgate.

Pucher, J. and R. Buehler (2008). "Making Cycling Irresistible: Lessons from the Netherlands, Denmark and Germany." Transportation Reviews, 28(4), 495–528.

Pucher, J., R. Buehler, & M. Seinen (2011). Bicycling Renaissance in North America? An Update and Reappraisal of Cycling Transit and Policies. Transportation Research Part A, 45, 451–475.

Resource Centre on Urban Agriculture and Food Security (RUAF) (2013). "Urban Agriculture: What and Why?" http://www.ruaf.org/urban-agriculture-what-and-why. Accessed November 25, 2014.

Robertson, K. (2006). "Rural Downtown Development: Guiding Principles for Small Cities." *Rural Research Report*, Vol. 17, Issue 3, Spring.

Rohrer, J., J. R. Pierce Jr, & A. Denison (2004). Walkability and Self-Rated Health in Primary Care Patients. *BMC Family Practice*, 5, 29–35.

Russ, T. H. (ed.) (2002). *Planning and Design Handbook*. New York: McGraw-Hill.

Saelens, B.E., and S.L. Handy (2008). "Built Environment Correlates of Walking: A Review." *Medicine & Science in Sports & Exercise* 40: S550–566.

Saelens, B.E., J. F. Sallis, J. B. Black, & D. Chen (2003). Neighbourhood-Based Differences in Physical Activity: An Environment Scale Evaluation. *American Journal of Public Health*, 93(9), 1552–1558.

Schneider, T. and J. Till (2005). Flexible Housing: Opportunities and Limits, *Architectural Research Quarterly*, Vol.9, No.2 pp.157–66, Cambridge UP Cambridge, Great Britain.

Schoenauer, N. (2000). *6,000 Years of Housing*. New York: W.W. Norton.

Schwanke, Dean (2003). *Mixed-Use Development Handbook*. Washington, D. C.: Urban Land Institute.

Schwela, D. and O. Zali (1999). *Urban Traffic Pollution*. E & FN Spon, London.

Smit, Jac, Nasr, J., Ratta, A. (2001). *Urban Agriculture: Food, Jobs, and Sustainable Cities*. The Urban Agriculture Network, Inc. Unitied Nations Development Programme (UNDP). http://jacsmit.com/book/Chap07.pdf. Accessed November 25, 2014.

Stamm-Teske, W. and L. C. Uhlig (2006). "From villa to terraced house: typological observations on semi detached and terraced homes," in C. Schittich (ed.) In

Detail: Semi-Detached and Terraced Houses. Munchen, Germany: Birkhauser.

Stokes, R. J., J. MacDonald and G. Ridgeway (2008). "Estimating the Effects Of Light Rail Transit on Health Care Costs," *Health & Place*, Volume 14, Issue 1, March, 45 -58.

Tanha, A. (2010). "Net-Zero Apartment Buildings." Unpublished Master's Report. McGill University, School of Architecture.

Tasker-Brown, J. and S. Pogharian (2000). *Learning from Suburbia: Residential Street Pattern Design*. Ottawa: CMHC.

Thibert, J. (2007). "Inclusion and Social Housing Practice in Canadian Cities: Following the Path from Good Intentions to Sustainable Projects," *Canadian Policy Research Networks*, August.

To, Y. (2014). "Food Security: Transplanting Rural to Urban." Huffington Post. Last modified March 24, 2014. http://www.huffingtonpost.com/yen-to/food-security-transplanti_b_4645792.html. Accessed November 25, 2014.

Tombari, A. E., (2005). Smart Growth Smart Choices Series: Mixed Use Development, National Association of Home Builders, Land Development Services.

Torres, J. (2009). Children and Cities: Planning to Grow Together. Vanier Institute for the Family. http://reconnectingamerica.org/assets/Uploads/childrencities2009.pdf. Accessed November 25, 2014.

Town and Country Planning Act 1997 (1997)http://www.legislation.gov.uk/ukpga/1997/8 Accessed August 24,2016.

Troped, P. J., R. P. Saunders, R. R. Pate, B. Reininger, J. R. Ureda, and S. J. Thomson (2001). "As a Community Rail-Trail." *Preventative Medicine* 32: 191–200.

Tumlin, J. (2012). *Sustainable Transportation Planning: Tools for Creating Vibrant, Healthy, and Resilient Communities*. Dundas: John Wiley & Sons.

Union of Concerned Scientists (2010). "How Biomass Energy Works." Last modified October 29, 2010. http://www.ucsusa.org/clean_energy/our-energy-choices/renewable-energy/how-biomass-energy-works.html. Accessed November 25, 2014.

Unwin, R. (1909). *Town Planning in Practice: An Introduction to the Art of Designing Cities and Suburbs*. London: Adelphi Terrace.

Urban Design Tools (2012). "Introduction to LID," http://www.lid-stormwater.net/background.htm. Accessed November 25, 2014.

Urban Fish Farmer (UFF) (2013). "Urban Fish Farmer." http://urbanfishfarmer.com. Accessed November 25, 2014.

U.S. Department of Transportation (2010). Transportation's Role in Reducing U.S. Greenhouse Gas Emissions: Volume 1, Washington, DC,http://www.reconnectingamerica.org/assets/Uploads/DOTClimateChangeReport-April2010-Volume1and2.pdf. Accessed August 24, 2016.

Van Der Ryn, S. and P. Calthorpe (1986). *Sustainable Communities: A New Design Synthesis for Cities, Suburbs and Towns*. San Francisco: Sierra Club Books.

Winters, M., M. Brauer, E. M.Setton, & K. Teschke (2010). "Built Environment Influences On Healthy Transportation Choices: Bicycling Versus Driving." Journal of Urban Health, 87(6), 969–993.

World Commission on Environment and Development (WCED) (1987). *Our Common Future*. Oxford, NY: Oxford University Press.

Glossary of Terms

Above-Grade Open Space—spaces such as balconies and roof terraces that permit a greater level of privacy.

Active Recreation—recreation that offers opportunity for and access to range of activities such as play or walkability.

Active Transportation—mode of commuting that relies on a person's activity such as walking or cycling.

Adaptability—built macro- or micro-environments that let occupants modify them to meet evolving demands. It is also referred to as *Flexibility*.

Add-In Building Method—leaving interior spaces, like attics and basements, unfinished to allow conversion into livable spaces at a later date.

Add-On Building Method—design for the addition of rooms to an original structure at a later date.

Affordability of Housing—when a household spends more than 32 percent of its income on mortgage principal, interest, taxes, and utilities costs, it is said to have housing *affordability challenge*.

Agricultural Urbanism (AU)—a planning principle that integrates sustainable food and agriculture systems into urban environments.

Angled Lots—lots arranged in an angle to reduce the amount of land consumed.

Aquaponics—a food-production system, a combination of aquaculture with hydroponics, that raises small aquatic animals, like snails, fish, crayfish, or prawns, in tanks.

Biomass Energy—energy produced from low-carbon waste and plant materials.

Carbon Footprint—the total amount of greenhouse gases produced to directly and indirectly support human activities, usually expressed in equivalent tons of carbon dioxide (CO_2).

Car-Free Neighborhoods—are places where vehicular traffic is reduced and citizens rely instead on active mobility.

Cluster Combination—a method related to horizontal separation of spaces and their grouping in districts.

Complete Communities—communities where people live, work, and are entertained.

Conservation Design—design that maintains the original landscape by designing buildings around nature as opposed to leveling an entire site.

Convenience Centers—are developments that generate more pedestrian traffic than public transit or car activity.

Corridor of Greenery—green natural or man-made areas where various species can survive and circulate much as they do in wilder spaces. The corridor is also known as a Green Belt.

Diagram Pattern Planning—communities with layout based on formal geometry.

Ecological Footprint—a place's ecological footprint is its productive area divided by the number of those who use it. The footprint of a community, for example, will include the entire crop and grazing land necessary to produce food and other resources that the place consumes, and the area needed to absorb the waste produced and the pollution emitted.

Euclidean Zoning—zoning regulations that separate large swaths of uniquely residential areas from all other occupancies.

Five (5) Ds of Development—planning principles that include density, diversity, design, destination accessibility, and distance, which make a place walkable.

Food Miles—a measure of the distance products travel from cultivation to point of purchase.

Grand Manner—buildings, streets, and public spaces are arranged to convey visual effect of grandeur and coherence. Such patterns are typical of the Renaissance.

Grid Layout Planning—communities with a layout based on geometrical or orthogonal principles that are thought to have been developed by the Greeks and spread far afield by the Romans. Named after the town of Miletus for its form of town planning, neighborhoods of this form are divided into relatively autonomous areas.

Life Cycle Approach—a planning process that envisions the long-term effect of present decisions.

Microclimate—is a design consideration that shelters an area from wind and snow as well as to balance sun and shade to extend seasonal use.

Mixed Developments—developments with a mix of land uses and wide range of dwelling types.

Narrow-Front Row House—dwelling unit 4.3 to 6 meters (14 to 20 feet) wide built on narrow plots that share sidewalls with neighboring structures.

Neighborhood Unit—a concept developed by Clarence Arthur Perry in 1907 and included five aspects: clear boundaries, an internal street system of superior design, a variety of well-chosen land uses, the provision of open spaces, and vitally the presence of a central area.

Net-Zero Energy Neighborhood—a community where all the dwellings rely on combined heat and power systems from one shared, centralized source; this method is also known as *District Heating*.

Net-Zero Homes—energy-efficient dwellings that produce and return as much energy to the grid as they use. Consumption of energy is decreased by limiting size and orienting the structure to take advantage of passive solar gain, natural daylight, and indoor airflow.

Offset Angled Lots—lot for high-density planning where homes sit in a tooth-saw pattern to maximize solar exposure and ensure that neighbors to do not block one another's side-window views.

On-Grade Open Space—spaces such as front, back, and side yards, courtyards, and patios used by residents.

Organic Growth—communities with a layout that developed by way of uncontrolled growth.

Path of Least Negative Impact—an approach that minimizes any negative impact on social, cultural, economic, or governmental practices, and on the environment.

Planned Cities—cities whose form follows a charted plan much like post–Second World War suburban towns. They are also known as *Created Cities*.

Renewable Energy Sources—self-sustaining energy resource to include geothermal, solar, and wind.

Resiliency—the capacity of a system from individual people to a whole community to hold together and function in the face of outside change and pressure.

Road Bumps—elevated strips on the road that are meant to reduce driving speeds. The bumps can be placed at the entrance to a street to indicate an increase in residential density.

Self-Sustaining Systems—(also known as *self-sufficient*) a community planned for self-sufficiency in resource consumption.

Setback Regulations—measures introduced to control the distance between the lot line and the home.

Spatial Organization—developments that focus on horizontal *and* vertical separation of spaces.

Spontaneous Settlements—communities that grow by a non-regulated process.

Street Connectivity—an aspect of walkable neighborhoods where streets and paths are well planned to permit reaching various local destinations with ease.

Supporting Relationships—a principle where the key sustainable aspects (i.e., economic, environment, social, and cultural) in a community are acting in support of each other.

Sustainable Development—development that meets present needs without compromising the ability of future generations to meet their own needs (WCED 1987).

The Next Home—an adaptable narrow three-story structure with adaptable interiors that can be designed to house one, two, and three households.

Transit Corridor—roads intensively used for public transit. There are commonly three types of corridors: destination connector, commuter, and district circulator.

Transition Nodes—concentration of large-scale retail centers, like shopping malls or big-box retailers.

Transit-Oriented Development (TOD)—an approach to regional planning that integrates public transit and urban concepts. These developments lie on the main trunk line of a transit system and residents have direct access to it.

Transit-Oriented Neighborhoods (TON)—neighborhoods that are located along transit corridors.

Urban Agriculture—the practice of integrating food-producing plants in communities by combining fruit and nut trees, berry bushes, vegetables, herbs, edible flowers, and other ornamental plants into aesthetically pleasing designs.

Urban Heat Island—a phenomenon that occurs because urban lands are warmer than surrounding rural areas due to the distribution of absorbing heat surfaces, like concrete and asphalt.

Urban Sprawl—growth of a city's perimeter areas that often result in low-density suburban development and long commute.

Vertical Farming—a growing food method of vine-like plants supported by strings on walls or fences.

Walkable Communities—are places with distinct characteristics related to their built environments, such as wider sidewalks, that make them amenable to walkability.

Woonerf ("streets for living" in Dutch)—streets that are shared between pedestrians, bicycles, transit vehicles, and automobiles with no distinction between sidewalks and car lanes.

Zero Lot Line—placing the home on the front or side lot lines in order to save land.

Project References

In addition to the information that was provided by design firms of the projects that have been featured in this book, the following sources have been consulted.

Chapter 2: Transit-Oriented Development

Ørestad
Richard D. Knowles (2012). "Transit Oriented Development in Copenhagen, Denmark: From the Finger Plan to Ørestad," *Journal of Transport Technology*, 22, May 2012, 251-261.

Contra Costa Transit Village
Congress for the New Urbanism (2014). "Contra Costa Centre Transit Village" http://www.ite.org/css/ContraCosta.pdf. Accessed November 25, 2014.

Greenwich Millenium Village
Nicole Foletta and Simon Field (2014). "Europe's New Low Car(bon) Communities." http://www.gwl-terrein.nl/files/artikelen/low%20carbon%20communities.pdf. Accessed November 25, 2014.

Vauban
Richard Cervero and Cathleen Sullivan (2010). "Toward Green TODs" (Working paper, University of California, Berkeley, 2010). http://www.its.berkeley.edu/sites/default/files/publications/UCB/2010/VWP/UCB-ITS-VWP-2010-7.pdf. Accessed August 24, 2016.

Nicole Foletta and Simon Field (2014). "Europe's New Low Car(bon) Communities" http://www.gwl-terrein.nl/files/artikelen/low%20carbon%20communities.pdf. Accessed November 25, 2014.

Chapter 3: Mixing Dwellings and Amenities

Dockside Green
Dockside Green. "Sustainability." www.docksidegreen.com. Accessed November 25, 2014.

Terrain.org. "Dockside Green." www.terrain.org. Accessed November 25, 2014.

The Atlantic (2011). "Is This the World's Greenest Neighborhood?" Last updated August 25, 2011. www.theatlantic.com/health/archive/2011/08/is-this-the-worlds-greenest-neighborhood/244121/#.TlfeIYgBaMU.twitter. Accessed November 25, 2014.

The American Institute of Architects (2009). "Synergy at Dockside Green." Last updated April 15, 2009. http://www.aiatopten.org/node/123. Accessed November 25, 2014.

87 Chapel Street
MGS Architects (2013) *MGS Company Profile*. Melbourne, 4.

Statutory Planning Committee of Port Philip (2008). "87 Chapel Street, St. Kilda." Last updated August 11, 2008. http://www.portphillip.vic.gov.au/default/meeting_agenda_archive/87_Chapel_Street_St_Kilda.pdf. Accessed August 24, 2016.

Archi Channel. (2014). "87 Chapel Street, Melbourne, Australia." http://www.archichannel.com/project/87-chappel-street-st-kilda/. Accessed November 25, 2014.

Stadstuinen Rotterdam
KCAP Architects & Planners (2014). "Stadstuinen." http://www.kcap.eu/en/projects/v/stadstuinen/details. Accessed November 25, 2014.

DKV Architecten (2014). "Stadstuinen, Kop van Zuid te Rotterdam." https://web.archive.org/web/20120823030117/http://www.dkv.nl/projecten/woningbouw/9606-Stadstuinen/9606-Stadstuinen_nl.html. Accessed November 25, 2014.

Rotterdam (2014). "Stadstuinen." http://www.stadstuinen.com/. Accessed November 25, 2014.

1221 Broadway
Lake Flato Architects (2014). "1221 Broadway." http://www.lakeflato.com/projects/1221-broadway/. Accessed November 25, 2014.

Inhabit (2013). "San Antonio 'Ghost Buildings' Renovated into Beautiful Mixed-Use Project by Lake Flato Architects." Last updated March 8, 2013. Inhabitat.com/san-antonio-ghost-buildings-renovated-into-beautiful-mixed-use-project-by-lakeflato-architects/print/. Accessed November 25, 2014.

Chapter 4: Car-Free Neighborhoods

Västra Hamnen
Chris Hancock. (n.d.) "Towards a Sustainable City," in *Urban Ecology – City of Tomorrow, Bo01-area in Malmo, Sweden*. http://malmo.se/download/18.4a2cec6a10d0ba37c0b800012617/article_towards_sustainable_city.pdf Accessed August 24,2016.

Nicole Foletta and Simon Field (2014). "Europe's New Low Car(bon) Communities" http://www.gwl-terrein.nl/files/artikelen/low%20carbon%20communities.pdf. Accessed November 25, 2014.

Stellwerk 60
Nicole Foletta and Simon Field (2014). "Europe's New Low Car(bon) Communities " Accessed June 19, 2014. http://www.gwl-terrein.nl/files/artikelen/low%20carbon%20communities.pdf. Accessed November 25, 2014.

Grow Community
Kitsap Sun (2011). "Planned Solar-Powered Bainbridge Development Could Be Greenest Around." Last modified June 7, 2011. http://www.kitsapsun.com/news/local/planned-solar-powered-bainbridge-development-could-be-the-greenest-around-ep-418470436-357206. Accessed August 24, 2016.

Grow Community.(n.d.). *One Planet Action Plan for Grow Community*. 1–14. http://bioregional.ca/grow-community/ Accessed August 24, 2016.

"New Study Shows Multiple Cars Are King in American Households," (2008). Experian, Last modified February 12, 2008. http://press.experian.com/united-states/Press-Release/new-study-shows-multiple-cars-are-king-in-american-households.aspx. Accessed November 25, 2014.

Slateford Green
Edinburgh Architecture (2014). "Slateford Green Housing, Scotland: Architecture Information." Last modified March 6. http://www.edinburgharchitecture.co.uk/slateford-green-housing. Accessed November 25, 2014.

The Slateford Green Project (n.d.) https://ogilviej.wordpress.com/a-car-free-environment/. Accessed August 24, 2016.

Chapter 5: Creative Open Spaces

HafenCity
HafenCity Hamburg (2014). "Public Spaces West." http://www.hafencity.com/en/concepts/open-space-in-western-hafencity.html. Accessed November 25, 2014.

Architonic (2014). "HafenCity Public Space." http://www.architonic.com/aisht/hafencity-public-space-miralles-tagliabue/5100909. Accessed November 25, 2014.

Hamburg Magazine (2014). "Marco Polo Terraces." http://www.arhitext.com/english/andreea-livia-ivanovici-marco-polo-terraces/. Accessed August 24, 2016.

Jürgen Bruns-Berentelg (2013) Hafencity Hamburg – Identity, Sustainability and Urbanity, Published by Hauptkirche St. Katharinen ELBE&FLUT Edition/Junius-Verlag (2013)

http://hafencity.com/upload/files/files/DP_Identity__Sustainability_and_Urbanity_final.pdf Accessed August 27, 2016.

Superkilen

Arch Daily (2012). "Superkilen." Last updated October 25, 2012. http://www.archdaily.com/286223/superkilen-topotek-1-big-architects-superflex/. Accessed November 25, 2014.

Meinhold, B. (2012). http://inhabitat.com/arkadien-winnenden-is-a-family-earth-friendly-eco-village-near-stuttgart-germany/. Accessed November 25, 2014.

Pringle Creek Community

Metropolis (2011). "Lessons of Place – Pringle Creek Community" Last updated November 2011. http://www.metropolismag.com/November-2011/Lessons-of-Place/. Accessed November 25, 2014.

Terrain.org (2013). "One Green Thing Leads to Another: Sustainability at Pringle Creek Community." Last updated 2013. http://www.terrain.org/articles/23/fitzsimons.htm. Accessed November 25, 2014.

Earthsong Eco-Neighborhood
Earthsong Eco-Neighborhood. "Sustainability." http://www.earthsong.org.nz. Accessed November 25, 2014.

Chapter 6: Neighborhoods for Change and Growth

Benny Farm
Développements McGill (2009). "Projet Condo Square Benny." *Square Benny*. May 25, 2009. http://www.devmcgill.com/fr/nouvelle/16/projet-condo-square-benny-claude-cormier-architecte-paysagiste. Accessed November 25, 2014.

Canada Lands Company (2007). "Benny Farm." http://archive.is/Z31BC. Accessed August 27, 2016.

Bloembollenhof
Will Jones (2004). "Baby Boomers," *Housing Today*, May 28, 2004.

S333 (2014). "Bloembollenhof." http://www.s333.org/projects.43.html?no=true&projectFK=5&cameFrom=/projects.29.html. Accessed November 25, 2014.

Cité-Jardin Fonteneau
Pitre, Cherri (2004). *Self-Help Modifications of Affordable Single-Family Housing in Montreal,* Unpublished M.Arch., Report, McGill University, School of Architecture.

Friedman, A. (2005). *Homes Within Reach: A Guide to the Planning, Design and Construction of Affordable Homes and Communities*, John Wiley & Sons Inc., New Jersey.

Chapter 7: Affordable Neighborhoods

Floating Houses in IJBrug
ArchDaily (2011). "Floating Houses in IJburg / Architectenbureau Marlies Rohmer." Last updated March 20, 2011. http://www.archdaily.com/120238/floating-houses-in-ijburg-architectenbureau-marlies-rohmer/. November 25, 2014.

Carabanchel Housing Project
Morphosis Architects. "Carabanchel Social Housing Project in Madrid."

La Cité Manifeste
Lacaton and Vassal (2014). "Cité Manifeste, Mulhouse." http://www.lacatonvassal.com/?idp=19#. Accessed November 25, 2014.

Wohnmodelle (2014). "Social Housing in Mulhouse." http://www.wohnmodelle.at/index.php?id=80,71,0,0,1,0. Accessed November 25, 2014.

2 McIntyre Drive, Altona
Ray, E. (2014). "Living on Air," *The Age*, Friday September 13, 2014, p. 18.

Horrocks T. (2013). "Come Together," *Monument* 20th Anniversary Issue, pp. 58–63.

Chapter 8: Net-Zero Energy Neighborhoods

Hammarby Sjöstad
White (2014). "Hammarby Sjostad." http://www.white.se/en/project/15-hammarby-sjostad. Accessed November 25, 2014.

Future Communities (2014). "Building a 'Green' City Extension." http://www.futurecommunities.net/case-studies/hammarby-sjostad-stockholm-sweden-1995-2015. Accessed November 25, 2014.

Paisano Green
Architzer (2014). "Paisano Green Community Senior Housing."

http://architizer.com/projects/paisano-green-community-senior-housing/. Accessed November 25, 2014.

Meinhold, B., (n.d.). "Paisano Green Community Is the First Net-Zero Senior Housing Project in the US," inhabitat.com, http://inhabitat.com/paisano-green-community-is-the-first-net-zero-senior-housing-project-in-the-nation/. Accessed August 27, 2016.

ArchDaily (2012). "Paisano Green Community / Workshop8." Last updated September 20, 2012. http://www. archdaily.com/271384/paisano-green community-workshop8/. Accessed November 25, 2014.

University of California (UC) Davis West Village
Abi Kallushi, Jeffrey Harris, John Miller, Matt Johnston, and Ab Ream (2012). "Think Bigger: Net-Zero Communities." Last updated 2012. http://www.aceee. org/files/proceedings/2012/data/ papers/0193-000355.pdf. Accessed November 25, 2014.

UC Davis (2014). "UC Davis West Village." Last updated May 13, 2014. http:// westvillage.ucdavis.edu. Accessed November 25, 2014.

zHome
Tree Hugger (2013). "Zero Net Energy zHome Is 'A Model for Mainstream Housing in the Future.'" http://www. treehugger.com/sustainable-product-design/zero-net-energy-zhome-is-a-model-for-mainstream-housing-in-the-future.html. Accessed November 25, 2014.

ArchDaily (2013). "UPDATE: zHome / David Vandervort Architects." http:// www.archdaily.com/140346/zhome-david-vandervort-architects/. Accessed November 25, 2014.

BedZED
ZED Factory (2013). "BedZED." http:// www.zedfactory.com/zed/?q=node/102. Accessed November 25, 2014.

One Planet Communities (2013). "The Prototype: BedZED: One Planet Communities." http://www.bioregional. com/oneplanetliving/. Accessed November 25, 2014.

Almere Sun Island
Danish Architecture Centre (2012). "Almere: Sun Island." http://www.dac.dk/ en/dac-cities/sustainable-cities/all-cases/ energy/almere-sun-island/. Accessed November 25, 2014.

Concerto (2014). "Almere, The Netherlands." http://www.concerto. eu/concerto/concerto-sites-a-projects/ sites-con-sites/sites-con-sites-search-by-name/sites-crrescendo-almere.html. Accessed November 25, 2014.

Chapter 9: Planning for Healthy Living

High Point Community
Mithun (2014). "High Point." http:// mithun.com/projects/project_detail/ high_point/. Accessed November 25, 2014.

High Point Community (2014). "Welcome to the High Point Community in West Seattle." http://www.thehighpoint.com. Accessed November 25, 2014.

American Society of Landscape Architects. (2014) "High Point." http:// www.asla.org/sustainablelandscapes/ highpoint.html. Accessed November 25, 2014.

Skaftkarr
Nordic Energy Municipality (2014). "Skaftkärr – an Energy-efficient Residential Area." https:// www.norden.org/sv/nordiska-ministerraadet/ministerraad/nordiska-ministerraadet-foer-naeringsliv-energi-och-regionalpolitik-mr-ner/ nordiske-energikommuner/nominerade-kommuner/porvoo-factsheet. Accessed November 25, 2014.

Danish Architecture Centre (2014). "Porvoo: Energy Efficient Residential Area." Last updated January 21, 2014. http://m.dac.dk/en/dac-cities/ sustainable-cities/all-cases/energy/ porvoo-energy-efficient-residential-area/. Accessed November 25, 2014.

Norden Energy Municipality (2014). "Municipality of Porvoo." https:// www.norden.org/en/nordic-council-of-ministers/council-of-ministers/ nordic-council-of-ministers-for-business-energy-regional-policy-mr-ner/ nordiske-energikommuner/nominated-municipalities/porvoo factsheet. Accessed November 25, 2014.

Noponen, J. (2012)."Energy-Smart Town Planning Saves Millions", http://www. sitra.fi/en/news/construction/energy-smart-town-planning-saves-millions. Accessed August 27, 2016.

Bois-Franc
Racine, F. (2016), "From Disintegration to Reinterpretation: Urban Design Practice in Montreal, 1956–2015",Civil Engineering and Architecture 4(3): 120–132.

Chapter 10: Edible Landscapes

Lafayette Greens
"Lafayette Greens: Urban Agriculture, Urban Fabric, Urban Sustainability."General Design 2012 Professional Awards. N.p., n.d. Web. May 2, 2014.

"Lafayette Greens." Lafayette Greens. N.p., n.d. https://web.archive.org/ web/20140812232851/http://www. compuware.com/en_us/about/lafayette-greens-home.html. Accessed November 25, 2014.

Gary Comer Youth Center
"Chicago Rooftops." Carrot City. N.p., n.d. http://www.ryerson.ca/carrotcity/board_ pages/rooftops/chicago_rooftops.html. Accessed November 25, 2014.

"Gary Comer Youth Center Green Roof." Landscape Voice. N.p., October 27, 2012. http://landscapevoice.com/gary-comer-youth-center-green-roof. Accessed November 25, 2014.

"Rooftop Haven for Urban Agriculture Chicago USA." ASLA 2010 Professional Awards. N.p., n.d. http://www.asla. org/2010awards/377.html. Accessed November 25, 2014.

"The Gary Comer Youth Center / John Ronan Architects" (2011). ArchDaily. N.p., December 9. http://www.archdaily. com/189411/the-gary-comer-youth-center-john-ronan-architects/. Accessed November 25, 2014.

Pasona O2
Alter, Lloyd. "Pasona O2: Urban Underground Farming." TreeHugger. N.p., July 31, 2007.

http://www.treehugger.com/green-food/ pasona-o2-urban-underground-farming. html Accessed November 25, 2014.

Credits

Illustration Credits

Figures not listed here are in the public domain or have been conceived, drawn, or photographed by the author and members of his research and design teams. Their names are listed in the acknowledgments and the Project Teams list. Every effort has been made to list all contributors and sources. In case of omission, the author and the publisher will include appropriate acknowledgment or correction of any subsequent edition of this book. The full citations of the sources indicated below are noted in the Bibliography.

Chapter 1: Affixing a Lens

Figure 1.4: After Statistics Canada 2006

Chapter 2: Transit Oriented Development

Figure 2.1: After Hodges 2010

Chapter 7: Affordable Neighborhoods

Figure 7.3: After Diamond 1976

Chapter 10: Edible Landscapes

Figure 10.1: After Kourik 2004

Picture Credits

Every effort has been made to list all photographers and sources. In case of omission, the author and the publisher will include appropriate acknowledgment or correction in any subsequent edition of this book.

Chapter 2

Ørestad
Figures 2.5, 2.6, 2.7, 2.8, 2.9, 2.10, 2.11, 2.12, 2.13, 2.14:
APRT

Contra Costa Transit Village
Figures 2.15, 2.16, 2.17, 2.18, 2.19, 2.20, 2.21, 2.22, 2.23, 2.24:
MVE & Partners

Figure 2.25:
© 2010 Steve Whittaker—www.whittpho.com

Figure 2.26:
© 2011 Steve Whittaker—www.whittpho.com

Greenwich Millenium Village
Figures 2.27, 2.28, 2.29, 2.30, 2.31, 2.32, 2.33:
© EPR Architects

Chapter 3

Dockside Green
Figures 3.5, 3.6, 3.7, 3.8, 3.9, 3.10:
Courtesy Perkins+Will

Figures 3.11, 3.12, 3.13, 3.14, 3.15, 3.16, 3.17, 3.18:
Vince Klassen

87 Chapel Street
Figures 3.19, 3.20, 3.21:
MGS Architects

Figures 3.22, 3.23, 3.24, 3.25, 3.26, 3.27, 3.28:
John Gollings Photography

Stadstuinen
Figures 3.29, 3.30, 3.31, 3.32, 3.35, 3.36:
KCAP

Figures 3.33, 3.34, 3.37, 3.38, 3.39, 3.40, 3.41:
Avi Friedman

1221 Broadway
Figure 3.42:
Lake|Flato Architects

Figures 3.43, 3.44, 3.45, 3.46, 3.47, 3.48, 3.49, 3.50:
© Chris Cooper

Chapter 4

Vastra Hammen
Figures 4.5, 4.6, 4.7:
Klas Tham Architect & Planner SAR/MSA EF

Figures 4.8, 4.9, 4.10, 4.11, 4.12, 4.13, 4.14, 4.15, 4.16, 4.17, 4.18:
Avi Friedman

Stellwork 60
Figures 4.19, 4.20, 4.21, 4.22, 4.23, 4.24, 4.25, 4.26, 4.27:
BPD Immobilienentwicklung GmbH

Grow Community
Figure 4.28:
Davis Studio A+D

Figures 4.29, 4.30, 4.31, 4.32, 4.33, 4.34, 4.35, 4.36, 4.37, 4.38, 4.39, 4.40:
David W Cohen Photography

Slateford Green
Figures 4.41, 4.42, 4.43, 4.44, 4.45, 4.46, 4.47, 4.48, 4.49, 4.50, 4.51, 4.52:
© Hackland + Dore Architects Ltd

Chapter 5

HafenCity
Figures 5.5, 5.6, 5.10:
KCAP/ASTOC

Figures 5.7, 5.8, 5.9, 5.11, 5.12, 5.13, 5.14, 5.15:
Avi Friedman

Superkilen
Figures 5.16, 5.19, 5.20, 5.21, 5.23, 5.24:
BIG

Figures 5.17, 5.18, 5.22:
Iwan Baan

Pringle Creek Community
Figures 5.25, 5.26:
Opsis Architecture

Figures 5.27, 5.28, 5.29, 5.30, 5.31, 5.32, 5.33, 5.34, 5.35, 5.36:
Photos by Visko Hatfield, James Santana and James Meyer

Earthsong Eco-Neighborhood
Figures 5.37, 5.38, 5.39:
Algie Architects

Figures 5.40, 5.41, 5.42, 5.43, 5.44, 5.45:
Hellen Algie—Photographer

Chapter 6

Benny Farm
Figures 6.5, 6.6, 6.7, 6.8, 6.9, 6.10, 6.11, 6.12, 6.13, 6.14, 6.15:
Avi Friedman

Bloembollenhof
Figures 6.16, 6.17, 6.18, 6.19, 6.20, 6.21, 6.22, 6.23:
S333

Figures 6.24, 6.25, 6.27:
Jan Bitter

Figures 6.26, 6.28, 6.29:
Avi Friedman

Cité-Jardin Fonteneau
Figures 6.30, 6.31, 6.32, 6.33, 6.34, 6.35, 6.36, 6.37, 6.38:
Avi Friedman

Chapter 7

Floating Houses in IJBurg
Figures 7.5, 7.6, 7.7, 7.16, 7.18:
Marlies Rohmer Architecture +Urban Planning

Figures 7.8, 7.9:
John Gundlach

Figure 7.10:
Luuk Kramer

Figure 7.11:
Floris Lok

Figures 7.12, 7.13:
Avi Friedman

Figures 7.14, 7.17
Ton Van Namen

Figure 7.15:
Roos Aldershoff

Carabanchel Housing Project
Figures 7.19, 7.20, 7.21, 7.22, 7.23, 7.24:
Morphosis

Figures 7.25, 7.26, 7.27, 7.28, 7.29, 7.30, 7.31, 7.32, 7.33, 7.34:
Roland Halbe

La Cité Manifeste
Figures 7.35, 7.36, 7.37, 7.38, 7.39, 7.40:
© Lacaton Vassal

2 McIntyre Drive, Altona
Figures 7.41, 7.42, 7.43:
MGS Architects

Figures 7.45, 7.46, 7.47, 7.48, 7.49, 7.50:
Trevor Mein Photography

Chapter 8

Hammarby Sjostad
Figure 8.4:
Avi Friedman

Figures 8.5, 8.6, 8.7, 8.8, 8.9, 8.10, 8.11, 8.12, 8.13, 8.14:
David Auerbach

Paisano Green
Figures 8.15, 8.16, 8.17, 8.18, 8.19, 8.20, 8.21, 8.22, 8.23, 8.24:
Workshop8

UC Davis West Village
Figure 8.25:
SVA Architects, Inc.

Figures 8.26, 8.27, 8.28, 8.29, 8.30, 8.31, 8.32, 8.33, 8.34, 8.35:
Photography by Dale Lang, www.nwphoto.net

zHome
Figures 8.36, 8.37:
David Vandervort Architects

Figures 8.38, 8.39, 8.40, 8.41, 8.42, 8.43, 8.44, 8.45:
Aaron Ostrowsky

BedZED
Figure 8.46:
Avi Friedman

Figures 8.47, 8.48, 8.49, 8.50, 8.51, 8.52, 8.53, 8.54, 8.55, 8.56, 8.57:
Zedfactory.com

Almere Sun Island
Figures 8.58, 8.59, 8.60, 8.61, 8.62, 8.63, 8.64, 8.65:
Avi Friedman

Chapter 9

High Point Community
Figure 9.4:
Mithun

Figures 9.5, 9.6, 9.7, 9.8, 9.9, 9.10, 9.11, 9.12, 9.13, 9.14:
Photos by Juan Hernandez Courtesy of Mithun

Skaftkarr
Figures 9.15, 9.16:
Drawn by Avi Friedman after Tuomo Siitonen

Figures 9.17, 9.18, 9.19, 9.20, 9.21, 9.22, 9.23, 9.24, 9.25:
Avi Friedman

Bois-Franc
Figures 9.26, 9.27, 9.28, 9.29, 9.30, 9.31, 9.32, 9.33, 9.34:
Avi Friedman

Chapter 10

Lafayette Greens
Figures 10.4, 10.5, 10.6, 10.7, 10.8, 10.9, 10.10, 10.11, 10.12, 10.13, 10.14, 10.15, 10.16, 10.17:
Ken Weikal Landscape Architecture

Gary Comer Youth Center
Figure 10.18:
Okrent Associates

Figures 10.19, 10.20, 10.21, 10.22, 10.23:
Scott Shigley

Figures 10.24, 10.25:
Hoerr Schaudt

Pasona O$_2$
Figures 10.26, 10.27:
Kono Designs

Figures 10.28, 10.29, 10.30, 10.31, 10.32, 10.33, 10.34, 10.35, 10.36:
Nacasa and Partners

Project/Case Study Details

02A Ørestad
APRT
Uudenmaankatu 2K
00120 Helsinki
Finland
Tel. +358 10 424 01 00
Web: aprt.fi
KHR Arkitekter
Kanonbadsvej 4
137 KBH K
Denmark
Tel. +45 4121 7000
Web: khr.dk

02B Contra Costa Transit Village
McLarand Vesquez Emsiek and Partners
1900 Main Street, Suite 800
Irvine, California, USA 92614-7318
Tel. 949.809.3388
Web: www.mve-architects.com
Sasaki Associates
64 Pleasant Street
Watertown, MA 02472
United States
Tel. +1.617.926.3300
Web: sasaki.com

02C Greenwich Millenium Village
Ralph Erskine and EPR Architects
30 Millbank
London
SW1P 4DU
Tel. +44 20 7932 7600
Web: epr.co.uk

03A Dockside Green
Perkins + Will Architects
1220 Homer Street
Vancouver, British Columbia
Canada V6B 2Y5
Web: http://perkinswill.com/

03B 87 Chapel Street
MGS Architects
10—22 Manton Lane
Melbourne VIC 3000
Australia
Tel. 03 9670 1800
Web: www.mgsarchitects.com.au

03C Stadstuinen
KCAP Architects & Planners
Piekstraat 27, 3071
EL Rotterdam
The Netherlands
Tel. +31 (0)10 7890 300/301/302
rotterdam@kcap.eu

03D 1221 Broadway
Lake|Flato Architects & OCO Architects
Lake|Flato Architects (in association with
OCO LPA Architects)
311 Third Street
San Antonio, Texas 78205
Tel. 210-227-3335
Web: lakeflato.com

04A Vastra Hammen
Klas Tham Architect & Planner
SAR/MSA EF
Karl Gerhards väg 21
SE13335 Saltsjöbaden
Sweden
Tel. +46 (0)70 3002005
Web: klas.tham@spray.se

04B Stellwork 60
Kontrola Treuhand/BPD
Immobilienentwicklung GmbH
BPD Immobilienentwicklung GmbH
Niederlassung Köln
Richard-Byrd-Straße 6a
50829 Köln
Tel. +49 (0) 221 9 98 00 - 12
Web: www.bpd-de.de

04C Grow Community
Davis Studio Architecture + Design
310 Madison Ave S, Suite A
Bainbridge Island, WA 98110
USA
Tel. 206-842-5543
Web: www.davisstudioAD.com

04D Slateford Green
Hackland + Dore Architects
16 Annandale Street, Edinburgh, UK
EH7 4AN
Tel. 0131 538 7707
Web: www.hackland-dore.com

05A HafenCity
KCAP/ASTOC
Piekstraat 27, 3071
EL Rotterdam
The Netherlands
Tel. +31 (0)10 7890 300/301/302
rotterdam@kcap.eu

05B Superkilen
BIG - Bjarke Ingels Group
Kløverbladsgade 56
2500 Valby, Copenhagen
Denmark
Tel. +1 646 541 1411
Web: big.pk

Topotek 1
Gesellschaft von Landschaftsarchitekten
mbH
Sophienstrasse 18
10178 Berlin
Germany
Tel. +49 (0)30 24 62 58 0
Web: www.topotek1.de

Superflex
Blågårdsgade 11B
DK-2200 Copenhagen
Denmark
Tel.: +45 3534 3462
Web: superflex.net

05C Pringle Creek Community
Opsis Architecture LLP
920 NW 17th Ave
Portland, Oregon 97209
USA
Tel. 503-525-9511
Web: www.opsisarch.com

05D Earthsong Eco-Neighborhood
Algie Architects Limited
19 Dublin Street, St. Mary's Bay
Auckland 1011
New Zealand
Tel. 64 9 3766829
Web: algiearchitects.co.nz

06A Benny Farm
Saia and Barbarese Architects
5605w Avenue de Gaspé, Suite 504
Montreal, Quebec H2T 2A4
Canada
Tel. (514) 866 2085
Web: www.sbt.qc.ca

06B Bloembollenhof
S333 Architecture + Urbanism
70 Cowcross Street
London, UK
EC1M 6EJ
Tel. +44 207 336 7026
Web: www.s333.org

06C Cité-Jardin Fonteneau
Cardinal, Hardy and Associates
Architects
100 Peel Street, 4th Floor
Montreal, Quebec H3C 0L8
Canada
Tel. (51) 316-1010
Web: www.cardinal-hardy.ca

07A Floating Houses in IJBurg
Marlies Rohmer Architecture +Urban
Planning
P.O. Box 2935
1000CX Amsterdam
Netherlands
Tel. 0031204190086
Web: www.rohmer.nl

07B Carabanchel Housing Project
Morphosis Architects
153 W 27th St. #1200
New York, NY 10001
USA
Tel. 424-258-6256
Web: morphosis.net

07C La Cité Manifeste
Lacaton and Vassal
206, rue La Fayette
75010 Paris
France
Tel. +33 (0)1 47 23 49 09
Web: lacatonvassal.com

07D 2 McIntyre Drive, Altona
MGS Architects
10-22 Manton Lane
Melbourne, VIC 3000
Australia
Tel. +61 3 9670 1800
Web: www.mgsarchitects.com.au

08A Hammarby Sjostad
White
Östgötagatan 100
Box 4700
11692 Stockholm
Tel. +46 8 402 25 00
Web: www.white.se

08B Paisano Green
Workshop8
1720 15th Street
Boulder, Colorado 80302
USA
Tel. 303 442 3700
Web: workshop8.us

08C UC Davis West Village
SVA Architects, Inc.
3 MacArthur Place, Suite 850
Santa Ana, California 92707
USA
Tel. 949-809-3380
Web: www.sva-architects.com

08D zHome
David Vandervort Architects
2000 Fairview Ave. E
Seattle, Washington 98102
USA
Tel. 206-784-1614
Web: www.vandervort.com

08E BedZED
ZED Factory
21 Sandmartin Way
Wallington, Surrey SM6 7DF
UK
Tel. 0208 404 1380
Web: www.zedfactory.com

08F Almere Sun Island
Nuon Energy and OMA
Postbus 41920
1009 DC Amsterdam, NL
The Netherlands
Tel. 0900 - 0808
Web: www.nuon.com

09A High Point Community
Mithun
Pier 56
1201 Alaskan Way, Suite 200
Seattle, Washington 98101
USA
Tel. 206-623-3344
Web: mithun.com

09B Skaftkarr
Sitra
Itämerenkatu 11-13
PO Box 160
00181 Helsinki
Tel. +358 294 618 991
Web: www.sitra.fi

09C Bois-Franc
Daniel Arbour et associés, Urban
Planners
100 Peel, 4th Floor
Montréal,Québec H3C 0L8
Canada
Tel. 514-316-1010
Web: www.arbour.ca

10A Lafayette Greens
Kenneth Weikal Landscape Architecture
33203 Biddestone Lane
Farmington Hills, Michigan 48334
USA
Tel. 248 477 3600
Web: www.kw-la.com

10B Gary Comer Youth Center
Hoerr Schaudt Landscape Architects
850 W. Jackson Blvd. Suite 800
Chicago, Illinois 60626
USA
Tel. 312-492-6501
Web: hoerrschaudt.com

10C Pasona O$_2$
Kono Designs
257 Park Ave. South 19th Floor
New York, NY 10010
UK
Tel. 212-674-8664
Web: konodesigns.com

Acknowledgments

The design and planning of sustainable homes and communities have been the focus of my work for many years. It included collaboration with colleagues and assistants who contributed to the ideas expressed here. I have attempted to remember and acknowledge them all. My apologies if I have mistakenly omitted the name of someone who contributed to the ideas, text, or illustrations that have been included in this book. I will do my best to correct an omission in future editions.

The book could not have been written without the contributions from a team of highly dedicated students. Patricia Johnsson, Lisa Chow, and Roxanne Turmel contributed to the research and writing of the chapters. David Auerbach, Charles Gregoire, Caroline Pfister, and Rose Deng were instrumental in finding the projects, describing them, and creating the illustrations.

The highly insightful editorial comments and clarification, as well as the meticulous proofreading of the text, by Nicole Stradiotto are much appreciated.

Special thanks to Nyd Garavito-Bruhn. Nyd was instrumental in writing to the firms, receiving and processing all the projects' illustrations and photos, and formatting the manuscript for submission. His attention to detail and quality is much appreciated.

Special thanks to all the design firms and the photographers whose work is included here for making the material available.

I would like to express my gratitude to Kate Duffy, Felicity Cummins, and Renee Last, Commissioning Editors (Architecture and Interior Design) at Bloomsbury Publishing Plc for ushering the book in and for their patience and guidance. Thanks to the McGill University's School of Architecture, where the background research for the book was carried out.

Finally, my heartfelt thanks and appreciation go to my wife, Sorel Friedman, Ph.D., and our children, Paloma and Ben, for their love and support.

Index